Critical Christianity

THE ANTHROPOLOGY OF CHRISTIANITY

Edited by Joel Robbins

Critical Christianity

Translation and Denominational Conflict in Papua New Guinea

Courtney Handman

UNIVERSITY OF CALIFORNIA PRESS

University of California Press, one of the most
distinguished university presses in the United States,
enriches lives around the world by advancing scholarship
in the humanities, social sciences, and natural sciences. Its
activities are supported by the UC Press Foundation and
by philanthropic contributions from individuals and
institutions. For more information, visit www.ucpress.edu.

University of California Press
Oakland, California

Library of Congress Cataloging-in-Publication Data

Handman, Courtney, author.
    Critical Christianity: translation and denominational
conflict in Papua New Guinea / Courtney Handman.
        p.   cm. — (The anthropology of christianity; 16)
    Includes bibliographical references and index.
    ISBN 978-0-520-28375-6 (cloth, alk. paper)
    ISBN 978-0-520-28376-3 (pbk., alk. paper)
    ISBN 978-0-520-95951-4 (electronic)
        1. Christian sects—Papua New Guinea—Social life and
customs.   2. Protestantism—Social aspects—Papua New
Guinea.   3. Lutheran Church—Papua New Guinea.
4. Bible—Translating—Papua New Guinea.
5. Guhu-Samane language—Papua New Guinea.
I. Title.   II. Title: Translation and denominational
conflict in Papua New Guinea.
BR1495.N5H36   2014
279.571—dc23   2014016336

24   23   22   21   20   19   18   17   16   15
10   9   8   7   6   5   4   3   2   1

For Addy and James

Contents

PART THREE. DENOMINATIONS

Illustrations

MAPS

Acknowledgments

When I started in the anthropology program at the University of Chicago, I knew it would be a long process, but I did not quite realize how many people would be involved in it or how much I would owe to them. I particularly want to thank the chair of my committee, Michael Silverstein, who has guided this project since my first year at Chicago. His insights and theoretical approach have been crucial throughout. Danilyn Rutherford and Amy Dahlstrom provided critical commentary and support over many years. Joel Robbins, who has stuck with this project longer than anyone, has been a constant source of questions, encouragement, and inspiration. Bambi Schieffelin has long been an important interlocutor and guide, and I thank her for her generosity and support.

Many friends and colleagues have heard far too much about Bible translation and Papua New Guinea, whether they wanted to or not. Luke Fleming, Robert Moore, and Rupert Stasch have probably suffered the most and yet have always offered so much in return in the form of generous commentary. Webb Keane, John Barker, Alejandro Paz, Shunsuke Nozawa, Thomas Strong, Jon Bialecki, Naomi Haynes, Ryan Schram, Jordan Haug, Gretchen Pfeil, Alan Rumsey, Francesca Merlan, Susan Gal, Matt Tomlinson, Debra McDougall, Matthew Engelke, Dan Jorgensen, Robert Blunt, Marsaura Shukla, and Amy Burce all provided important insights on specific chapters. At Reed College, Robert Brightman, Paul Silverstein, Charlene Makley, China Scherz, Gabriele Hayden, and, more recently, Sarah Wagner-McCoy have helped to create a rich intellectual environment as I finished this project. Rachel Apone read the final manuscript in full, provided very helpful feedback, and put together the index.

At the University of California Press, Eric Schmidt, Maeve Cornell-Taylor, and Cindy Fulton have been generous and extremely forgiving about missed deadlines. Jennifer Eastman was a superb copy editor.

Several chapters were presented at workshops and seminars in a number of places. I thank the organizers of the colloquium at the Australian National University's Research School of Pacific and Asian Studies, the anthropology department at Reed College, the Christian Politics in Oceania conference at Monash University, and the organizers of several graduate workshops at the University of Chicago: the Semiotics workshop, the Comparative Christianity workshop, and the Religion and Social Theory workshop.

Material in several of the chapters has been published previously. Some segments of chapter 2 appear in "Access to the Soul: Native Language and Authenticity in Papua New Guinea Bible Translation" from *Consequences of Contact: Language Ideologies and Sociocultural Transformations in Pacific Societies,* edited by Miki Makihara and Bambi B. Schieffelin. Chapter 6 incorporates "Events of Translation: Intertextuality and Christian Ethno-Theologies of Change among Guhu-Samane, Papua New Guinea," *American Anthropologist* 112 (4): 576–88, while chapter 7 incorporates "Mediating Denominational Disputes: Land Claims and the Sound of Christian Critique in the Waria Valley, Papua New Guinea" published in *Christianity and Politics in Oceania,* edited by Matt Tomlinson and Debra McDougall. Different parts of chapter 8 appeared in "Ideologies of Intimacy and Distance: Israelite Genealogies in Guhu-Samane Christian Commitment," *Anthropological Quarterly* 84 (3): 655–77 and in "The Future of Christian Critique" in *Future Selves in the Pacific,* edited by Will Rollason. Parts of chapter 1 and the introduction appear in *Current Anthropology* 55 (S10) as "Becoming the Body of Christ: Sacrificing the Speaking Subject in the Making of the Colonial Lutheran Church in New Guinea." I thank Oxford University Press, Wiley, Berghahn Books, the Institute for Ethnographic Research at George Washington University, and the Wenner-Gren Foundation for Anthropological Research for permission to use this material here.

My field research was supported by a Social Science Research Council International Dissertation Research Fellowship and a Fulbright-Hays Doctoral Dissertation Research Abroad Fellowship. I was supported by a Watkins Dissertation Year Fellowship and a Watkins Post-Field Fellowship, both from the anthropology department at the University of Chicago. I was also able to develop this material during my time as a junior fellow in the Martin Marty Center in the University of Chicago Divinity School and as a visiting scholar at the Research School of Pacific and Asian Studies at the Australian National University. A sabbatical award from Reed College made it possible to work extensively on a later version of the manuscript.

In Papua New Guinea, many people provided crucial assistance. Jim Robins at the National Research Institute was an invaluable help in obtaining visas and in generally negotiating Port Moresby. During my fieldwork, I was affiliated with the National Research Institute and the University of Papua New Guinea, and I thank both institutions for making this research possible. Archivists at the National Archives of Papua New Guinea in Port Moresby and at the Martin Luther Seminary in Lae generously provided me with access to documents from the colonial era of New Guinea. Everyone at the Salvation Army Motel in Lae, particularly Bernard and his family, made time away from rural Papua New Guinea a welcome break. I also thank the provincial administrator of Morobe Province for permission to conduct research in the Waria Valley.

Many people at SIL International, SIL Papua New Guinea, and the Bible Translation Association of Papua New Guinea very generously gave me their time, allowed me to stay at SIL PNG's Ukarumpa headquarters, and gave me access to archival documents. I am very grateful for their questions, criticisms, and openness to my project. Although we have not always agreed on everything, I have benefited greatly from their input. David Wakefield, Thomas Headland, Andrew Grosh, Brian Hodgkin, Thomas and Becky Feldpausch, David and Jackie Scorza, Duncan Kasokason, and Steven Thomas provided critical assistance, permissions, and wonderful meals.

I have spent about sixteen months in the Waria Valley, and I cannot adequately express my deep gratitude to everyone who made room for James and me in their lives. Rev. Mumure and Steven Ttopoqogo were instrumental to our entrance into the community and in setting up housing for us in Titio village. Both gave generously of their time throughout our stay. Kurubidza, Jehu, and Goso Ttopoqogo looked after us with incredible care and patience. Dansu and Dzaro Ahe Khara quickly became close and wonderful friends. Mary Gabeho went out of her way to talk with me and share her perspective. Hoopusu Gomai is an incredible man, without whom this book would not exist. I cannot hope to list everyone who helped us, but I must mention Pita ma kara, Heenoma ma kara, Isa ma kara, Tonori ma kara, Pauli ma kara, Piopo ma pai, Rev. Ububae ma kara, Rev. Pidgabi ma kara, Rev. Sopera ma kara, Ps. Benjamin ma kara, Ps. Roy ma kara, Ps. Joe ma kara, Kokoi ma kara, the late Bariama ma kara, Hadzata ma kara, Boseba ma Ipita-mina ma kara, Oneipa ma kara, Simeon ma kara, Saru ma kara, Dzap-anena ma kara, Khameto Heme ma kara, Kito ma kara, Arubidza ma kara, Timani ma kara, Kusuquba ma Marihuba ma kara, Norobe ma kara, Obera ma kara, Goitibi ma kara. Dzoobe mina. All Guhu-Samane names in the rest of this book are pseudonymous.

I have an embarrassment of riches when it comes to supportive family. Judy Smith, Drew Smith, Ken Handman, and Alana Handman have kindly supported me personally and financially and have generally tried not to ask what I have been working on this whole time. For all of this, I thank them deeply. Karen and Peter Slotta have been generous, welcoming, and supportive. I wish I could share this accomplishment with Peter Slotta. Older brothers don't come any better than Chris Handman. For the record, I am slightly taller than he is.

Two people remain. If all of the acknowledgments and thanks to my colleagues, friends, and family so far have seemed inadequate, the thanks printed here can't even begin to commemorate and celebrate the deep joy that I have in sharing my life with James Slotta and, more recently, Addy Slotta. We work best when we are side by side by side. I treasure every conversation that James and I have had, about our projects and (thankfully, occasionally) about other things, mostly Addy-related things. Addy is just starting in on conversations, and I look forward with all my heart to a lifetime of them to come. This book is for them.

Introduction

Like many communities across the world, Guhu-Samane Christians in the Waria River valley were excited to celebrate the start of a new millennium on New Year's Eve, 2000. As usual for local celebrations, Christians gathered in separate denominational groups, ringing in the new year with church services, prayer sessions, and as much noise as they could muster at midnight. New Year's Day brought more church services, especially for the large group of Reformed Gospel Church members celebrating at Garasa, the site of the local airstrip and an abandoned mission station.

That morning, people had just started to congregate in the *biiri,* a large structure that takes its name from the Guhu-Samane translation of the biblical Hebrew word for "temple." Suddenly, from the foothills of the Chapman Mountain Range that rises steeply from the grassy valley floor, a group of armed, masked men descended upon the gathered Christians. People ran in every direction as the gunmen fired their homemade shotguns. By the time the gunmen were chased away, several Reformed Gospel members had been shot. One of the leaders of the church, Mark Timothy, had a two-way radio that connected him to the Papua New Guinea headquarters of the Summer Institute of Linguistics (SIL), the Bible translation group with which Mark is working to compose a Guhu-Samane translation of the Old Testament. Mark was able to get SIL helicopters to shuttle some of the wounded to regional hospitals, which were a three-day walk away. All of the wounded men survived (a sign of God's protection for Reformed Gospel members), none having received major injuries.

In the aftermath of this event, people up and down the valley speculated about the gunmen's identities and the causes for the attack. In one sense, the identity of the gunmen was no mystery at all—everyone agreed that they were members of the neighboring Goilala ethnic group who live at the top of the Chapman Range. Goilalans have long been alternately trading partners and enemies of Guhu-Samane people. But given that the attack took place on such an important holiday, they thought that there had to have been something else going on. Soon some members of Reformed Gospel Church started to claim that their rival Guhu-Samane church, New Life, must have had a hand in the attack. Did New Life leaders hire the gunmen, putting a hit on their rival church? Or did they simply let the Goilalans know that this major gathering was going to be held? The possibility of such intra-ethnic Christian violence was shocking, and the mystery was never adequately solved. Today Reformed Gospel leaders like Mark prefer not to talk about it. For him, it was merely one event—one particularly violent event—in what has become a long history of conflict between two churches that seemingly share so much in common.

Reformed Gospel and New Life are both Pentecostal churches that emerged out of a 1977 Holy Spirit revival among Guhu-Samane Christians. They both contrast their spiritually nourishing churches with the ineffectiveness of the colonial Lutheran mission. They both use the Guhu-Samane New Testament translation that SIL members produced in 1975 to create connections between local Christians and a global church, and they both hope for a singular Guhu-Samane church to one day emerge. Most importantly, they both concern themselves with the problems of making a moral life in rural Papua New Guinea. But that is where the similarities end, since members of these churches are deeply divided about how to achieve their many goals. If New Life embraces traditional culture, ancestral drums in church, and self-taught spiritual leaders, then Reformed Gospel distances itself from tradition, opting instead for guitars, tambourines, and an emerging Papua New Guinean Pentecostal norm constituted at regional Bible colleges. Members of these two churches work to construct as many dimensions of contrast between them as they can. Denominational life in the Waria Valley is thus a comparative project, an unending process of Christian critique that is fed as much by mundane critical talk as it is by the extraordinary violence of the New Year's attack.

Throughout the sixteen months that I spent in the Waria Valley between 2005 and 2007, Guhu-Samane Christians debated proper worship styles, the morality of traditional practices, and the appropriateness of the denominational divisions that have emerged from these long-standing debates. Much of this talk had as its touchstone the ongoing Bible translation projects that have been so central to the history of Christianization in the area. I began my research with a focus on this history of Bible translation, but I soon realized that translation was just one dimension of a larger project of critique, division, and communion that guided a variety of distinctly Christian religious practices.

Christians often present their own religious transformation as a product of turbulent, solitary work on the self. Many analysts of Christianity share this perspective, focusing on the individualism of Christianity. But the Guhu-Samane experience of religious transformation is irreducibly social, as is evident in their turbulent communal lives. Like so many other schismatic Protestants in the world, Guhu-Samane Christians as members of groups—of churches, of denominations, even as members of an ethno-linguistic group—schism and argue, and even vandalize other churches, with stunning frequency. What makes the communal life of Christianity so difficult? And why, if Protestantism is the religion of individualism, do Protestants like the Guhu-Samane spend so much effort and energy on getting the group right? How does a translation of the Bible into the Guhu-Samane language, predicated on a sense of ethno-linguistic homogeneity and authenticity as the key to meaningful conversion, become the basis for fractious denominational critiques?

The quick answer to the problem of denominational fighting could easily just be "politics." Indeed, most scholarly analysts see Protestant schisms as an un-Christian residue of the social—ultimately explicable in terms of the categories of secular social science. From this perspective, schisms appear as the result of a worldly will to power among church leaders, a morbid infection of earthly interests and social categories in what is supposed to be an otherworldly religious realm. But as I will argue here, schism is an integral part of Protestant religious practice. The ways in which critique produces new social groups is not always viewed positively by Guhu-Samane Christians, but they do view it as fundamental to producing moral Christian worlds. What might appear to be merely secular, social, and institutional matters—the stuff of social groups, their formation and dissolution—are for Guhu-Samane Christians infused with fundamentally religious concerns. This book takes a perspective on Christianity that brings critique, schism, denominationalism, and other superindividual concerns to the fore, one which provides a much needed counterbalance to the attention given to the individual in both Christian and scholarly accounts of Christianity. For without attention to distinctly Christian forms of religious sociality and institutionality, it becomes impossible to understand the recurrent social processes of denominationalist schism, critique, and missionization throughout the history of Christianity.

To view schism, sociality, and institutionality as un-Christian is to assume a modernist, secular understanding of religion as distinctly private. Moreover, it would not be ethnographically faithful to the ways in which Guhu-Samane people practice Christianity. If anything, captioning the social concerns at the heart of Christian religious practice as "just politics" is to capture one moment in a Christian critical discourse while overlooking the larger process. With the increasingly common mobilization of people into novel units of moral protest that do not fit neatly into categories of the nation-state, political party, or advocacy group, attention to religious formations disregarded by secular social science is a crucial component of an anthropology of social transformation.

THE CHRISTIANITY OF HISTORY IN THE WARIA VALLEY

In 2004, between my initial trip to the Waria and my later return for fieldwork, an American Jew for Jesus named Gabriel came to visit Guhu-Samane speakers for a few days to lead church services.[1] As a group of roughly ten thousand swidden agriculturalists living a few days' walk from the nearest vehicular road, the Guhu-Semane would likely have considered the visit of a foreign religious dignitary an important event no matter what he discussed. But Gabriel's sermons had a particularly strong impact on the denominationalist disputes that divide Guhu-Samane Christians into several, often antagonistic, groups.[2]

The different denominations welcomed Gabriel in their own particular ways. Members of New Life Church, who celebrate traditional culture as a God-given gift, organized a *singsing,* a dance and song of welcome, with men and women outfitted in bird-of-paradise feathers and tree-kangaroo skins. They beat handheld drums, sang a traditional but Christianized song, and slowly danced Gabriel up from the airstrip. Members of Reformed Gospel, who eschew traditional culture as much as they can, left the showy welcome to others, opting instead to run the first church service with Gabriel. Having banned the use of drums in church, the Reformed Gospel Church service featured young men strumming guitars, young women in long skirts dancing to choreographed tambourine routines, and everybody else singing Pentecostal songs known across Papua New Guinea. Two competing claims to a moral life came into sharp focus.

The tensions that exist between these churches are not always as visible on a day-to-day basis as they were during Gabriel's visit. Members of both New Life and Reformed Gospel have to contend with the fact that in their rural corner of Papua New Guinea, they are unlikely to see the kind of economic and social development that they hope for: better schools, better access to a cash economy, better governance. Everyone agrees that life would be radically improved if a road from the nearest urban center, Wau, could be built. But during church services, these shared complaints are fractured into distinct moral discourses in which people hope to establish a form of Christianity that will manifest God's favor toward them, whether that is on earth or in the afterlife.

When Gabriel preached to the multidenominational crowd of Guhu-Samane Christians, which included members of New Life, Reformed Gospel, and a number of other churches, he did so wearing the ritual garb of an adult Jewish man (including a kippah, tefillin, and prayer shawl). He spoke to the Guhu-Samane in the audience about the right way for them to pray and be Christian while also being part of a flourishing culture. In order to do so, Gabriel first identified himself and the source of his authority. He said he was a Jew from the family of Jesus, which people understood to mean that his clan line (which in this area of Papua New Guinea refers to a matrilineal genealogy) includes Jesus. Next, he praised the dance group that had performed earlier in his welcoming procession, which used Christianized traditional songs that had been sung to drum accompaniment. But then he changed his tone. Guitars, he said, are the property and the tradition of *his* group, white people. Drums and the decorations worn in the dances are the property and the tradition of the Guhu-Samane, black people. Drums and other aspects of traditional culture are God's blessings upon the Guhu-Samane, and those blessings should continue to be used today. Moreover, he said, to use guitars, as Guhu-Samane Christians do in certain churches, is to steal the blessings from his group, from white people's traditions. Gabriel said that just as he prays to Jesus as a Jewish man with Jewish paraphernalia of prayer, so too the Guhu-Samane should pray to Jesus as culturally Guhu-Samane people, using their traditional garb and instruments.[3]

When I arrived a few months later, and throughout my time in the Waria Valley, people frequently brought up Gabriel's visit and his message about the role of culture in contemporary Christian life. In the highly charged environment of local denominational differences and contestation about the role of culture in Christianity, Gabriel's sermon was a topic of endless debate. For New Life members, who celebrate the use of drums in church services, Gabriel became an important figure of authority, while the Reformed Gospel members developed extended arguments against his claims. Gabriel's visit made the stakes of denominational conflict especially clear: salvation depends on a critical analysis of the proper organization and practice of Christian groups, whether racial, denominational, or cultural.

Lutherans, the New Life Church, and the Reformed Gospel Church are the major groups in this schismatic history: the "mama church"—the colonial Lutheran mission—experienced a schism in the late 1970s that produced New Life, and in the mid-1990s New Life experienced a schism that produced Reformed Gospel. Beyond this lineage of schism, new denominations have been coming into the Waria Valley on a consistent basis since the Lutheran monopoly on church life dissolved. The alphabet soup of churches matches what is usually seen in more densely populated and ethnically diverse urban environments: Seventh-day Adventist, Seventh-day Adventist Reformed, Associated Local Churches, Church of Christ, Assemblies of God, Four Square, and Lutheran Renewal all have a presence in the valley.

Many of the Guhu-Samane experiences of denominational schism and Christian critique turn on the projects of Bible translation ongoing in this area since 1956 and run by the (Papua) New Guinea branch of the Summer Institute of Linguistics (now known as SIL PNG), a powerful organization of roughly eight hundred members mostly hailing from the United States, Western Europe, and South Korea. Its parent group, SIL International, is a linguistics and literacy NGO whose work focuses largely on the translation of the New Testament into vernacular languages around the world. SIL translators do not plant churches, as other evangelistic groups do. Instead, they hope to give speakers a "clear, accurate, and natural" version of the New Testament in the local language. Translators go through graduate-level coursework in linguistics to bring scientific backing to questions of ethno-linguistic localization. Of the estimated eight hundred languages of Papua New Guinea, SIL PNG has so far produced about 160 New Testament translations. They develop these translations as at once linguistically familiar but also religiously revelatory, a textual invocation of the fact that God has been a part of the ethno-linguistic group and that the ethno-linguistic group has the chance to respond through acts of conversion.

Translation projects in the Waria Valley have included not only the creation of Guhu-Samane versions of the New and Old Testaments but also the larger moral projects of establishing the sense of appropriate local Christianity. During Gabriel's visit, some people performed the "Baruka," one of the songs that was "translated" in the 1960s under the auspices of Ernie Richert, the SIL translator of the Guhu-Samane New Testament. This "translation" was not a translation from one language to another but the process of deleting Guhu-Samane lyrics that were about mythic or recent history and adding lyrics, still in the Guhu-Samane language, of worship or praise to God. Locally, this is referred to in Tok Pisin as *tanim singsing* (turning the song), just as more canonical forms of code-to-code translation are referred to as *tanim tok* in Tok Pisin or *noo burisi eeta* (to turn talk/speech) in the Guhu-Samane language. While the lyrics were Christianized, the dance steps, the rhythm, and the melody remained the same. As people arranged in denominationalist groups now ask, is this version of a traditional dance "Christian" enough for them to use in constructing a moral life? Is a service without such a dance local enough?

In 1977, two years after the New Testament translation was distributed to local people (and two years after Papua New Guinean independence from Australia), a major religious movement seemed to realize the localizing promise of the initial translation work. Guhu-Samane Christians, who were then members of the Lutheran Church but who participated in this Holy Spirit revival, saw it as the moment of spiritual independence, when they could form a relationship with God through their own language and outside of (post)colonial influences. Although other groups in Papua New Guinea also experienced revivals at this time (see especially Robbins 2004a on the Urapmin experience), Guhu-Samane revivalists saw the revival and its access to God in the local vernacular as caused specifically by the New Testament translation. With the scriptures in their own language, Christians were finally able to hear the voice of God and feel that God was hearing them. By the early 1980s the Lutheran church, heir to the original mission group that first evangelized in the area, had lost many of its members as people flocked to the revivalists. These newly energized Christians spoke in tongues, remade their villages along a Christian model, renounced certain traditional practices, and experimented with novel forms of divine communication.

The Lutheran leadership, both expatriate missionaries and local leaders, confronted the revivalists, took them to the village court, and had representatives of the movement travel to a synod conference to explain themselves. Eventually the Lutheran hierarchy excommunicated the revival leaders, which led these men to start their own church, the New Life Bible Church. New Life quickly became a major rival to the Lutherans. People were attracted to the promise of a form of Christianity translated into the Guhu-Samane experience, filtered through local issues, and led by local leaders, and one that experimented with new worship practices. New Life promised a responsive, ethno-linguistically defined church.

A number of commentators at the time (Burce 1983; Flannery 1983) characterized the revival as akin to a "cargo cult," a nativist movement with anticolonial undertones that often focused on the mystical acquisition of "cargo," the material goods that colonizers brought with them.[4] The main features of the revival for these authors were that people were praying for cargo and money and communicating with Jesus via Morse code sent by flashlight beams into the sky. And while the criticisms of the movement were initially external, soon people within New Life itself started to question some of the rituals performed in the dark of night.

In the mid-1990s the tensions within New Life reached a breaking point, and a group of men gathered to split from New Life and create Reformed Gospel Church. These latter-day reformed revivalists promised a more standard form of Pentecostalism, one that they felt would do a better job of policing the boundaries between traditional practices (to which most of the New Life rituals were likened) and global Christianity. Mark, one of the leaders of the new Reformed Gospel Church was then about ten years into the project (still in progress today) of translating the Old Testament into the Guhu-Samane language, and his translation expertise would bring scholarly rigor to the moral question of cultural mixture.

Christianity is certainly not the only story one could tell of Guhu-Samane postcolonial experiences. Burce's (1983) dissertation on the experimental Garaina Tea Plantation focuses on the ways in which wage labor affected gender dynamics and the gerontocratic knowledge economy. Certainly more critical attention needs to be paid to the ways in which outward labor migration, especially among younger Guhu-Samane men, has altered social relations. Likewise, colonial agents and local people have, at various points, put their hopes in cash cropping (including coffee, cardamom, and vanilla), but all of these have been foiled by the lack of a vehicular road into the area. Small-scale gold mining is currently (since 2007) consuming the lives and land of people who live directly adjacent to the Waria River, although it is unclear how long they will be able to access this gold, given the relatively modest apparatus they use. I touch on each of these issues in the chapters that follow as I track the many frustrations local people have had with political and economic changes.

In contrast to the always-shifting ground of politico-economic "development," Christianity offers Guhu-Samane people a critical perspective on contemporary rural life in Papua New Guinea. Within the boom-and-bust cycles of postcolonial activity, Christianity has been one of the most enduring projects around. As several Guhu-Samane people said to me: if before men wanted to be politicians, now they want to be pastors. Many spoke of Christianity as having a special—and an especially transformative—role in local lives. It is partly Christianity's punctuated longevity—the sense that Christian projects are forever renewable through the introduction of new denominations or technologies of critique, like translation—that allows people to use Christian history to criticize and organize conflicting narratives of transformation and stasis, unity and conflict, decline and development. I try to capture that critical energy in this book.

DENOMINATIONALISM: ON THE SOCIALITY OF PROTESTANT LIVES

There is an old joke that has a Protestant marooned on an island. Discovered by a passing ship, he gives a tour of the world he created, including his church, his house, and his barn; then he points to another building, "and that's the church I used to go to." When I have told people that I am studying problems of denominational schism, a common response has been for them to recount their own experiences with it. It seems as though most people who have spent considerable time as part of a church community have seen their church fall apart.

However, one would not necessarily realize this by reading literature in the anthropology of Christianity. Schisms and denominational conflicts are mentioned in a number of major texts (Meyer 1999; Engelke 2007; Keane 2007), but they are not problematized as primary components of Protestantism. Schism is most often treated as a problem external to Christianity itself (Jebens 2006; Werbner 2011), a matter of kin-based or politically based projects of power. There is a long scholarly inclination to view schism and denominationalism as worldly matters, divorced from matters Christian and religious (Troelsch 1931; Niebuhr 1929; and much of the church-sect literature that followed, see Johnson 1963; Swatos 1998 for reviews). To some extent, the anthropology of Christianity has maintained this primordial distinction between Christianity as religion and Christianity as social institution.

As the anthropology of Christianity has emerged as a specific subdiscipline (about which there is still significant debate, e.g., Comaroff 2010; Hann 2007; and see discussion in Bialecki 2012), theoretical discussion has instead largely focused on an important project highlighting extensive historical and ethnographic connections between Christianity and modernity. Like many other facets of anthropology that focus on the subject, this has entailed heightened attention to the morally self-responsible and self-authorizing modernist individual (Robbins 2007). Here is a subject who views institutions and the social world as a source of falsity and oppression, contaminating a sincere and immediate relationship between himself or herself and God.

The refusal of sociality, then, has become a central predicate of contemporary views of the Christian subject. Given this focus on the subject—and a secularist inheritance that still tends to find religion only in the private sphere—it is perhaps no wonder that church schisms come to be read as the outcome of politics rather than religion. Even when scholars work to stitch back together the secular/sacred divide and analyze religious forms of political action, including prayer or evangelization, the focus remains on the subject rather than on the organization of subjects into groups (Marshall 2009; O'Neill 2010).[5]

Two propositions are in play. On the one hand, Protestants do a lot of work trying to find the proper social groups of Christian life, producing a proliferation of denominations. On the other hand, Protestantism has now been equated with a modernist refusal of, or at least an embarrassment about, sociality. However, there is no contradiction in finding that a discomfort with sociality corresponds with a greater emphasis on it. It should be rather familiar, in fact, as a founding problem of political liberalism. Take, for example, John Locke's *Second Treatise on Government* ([1690] 1980). It is precisely because Locke begins with the individual that making society becomes such a problem. When one starts with individual autonomy, any change to that autonomy seems like an infringement upon it. Problems of freedom, coercion, constraint, and lack of authenticity are the results. As we see with liberalism, the difficulties of sociality do not keep people from society but rather encourage an intense attention to social groups as both a problem and potential solution (see also Wagner 1975).

In one sense, then, the Lockean tradition is alive and well in scholarship on institutional Protestantism, but only in ways that seem to render the social groups of Christianity illegitimate or unimportant. One of the most important theologians in American Christianity of the twentieth century, H. Richard Niebuhr argued in *The Social Sources of Denominationalism* (1929) that a church as an institution amounts to little more than a stultifying sedimentation of earthly social categories and traditions that keeps Christian practice from being authentic, free, and universal.[6] Niebuhr was arguing against the Protestant tendency for denominations to become identity markers, in which each denomination has its own national, racial, or socioeconomic basis. Even when Christians realize this and split from their churches to start a sect, that sectarian impulse lasts only a short while, as institutionality inevitably creeps in. Like Locke's liberal individual, an initial wager is placed on a new society as the one that might be the least "social," and yet it always turns into a tyranny of its own, threatening the universal freedom with which the individual started.

Locke was imagining his individuals primarily as owners of private property, but the comparison with Protestantism still holds. The Christian individual subject as described in the anthropology of Christianity is granted sovereign authority over himself or herself, as someone who rightfully owns himself or herself. Keane (2007) argues that any deviation from that self-sovereignty looks from the perspective of the Christian (especially the Protestant missionary in the global south) to be an abrogation of one's God-given agency. To live in a world in which objects (e.g., the animist's totem or the Roman Catholic's rosary), other people (e.g., priests), or institutions (e.g., Roman Catholicism) rather than human subjects have agency over the self-possessed person is to live in a world of fetishism. That is, Christians work to make themselves (and God) the only proper actors, and they do so by trying to free themselves from anything that seems to be external to them, even the Bible itself (see Engelke 2007).

The morally positive imagination of Christian sociality is where the comparison with Lockean liberalism breaks down. There is relatively little that is irreducibly social in the purely instrumental device of Locke's social contract. Private property owners create a society and, in doing so, give up some of their freedoms, but this is only in order to better defend and keep their individual property. Thus, while the anthropology of

Christianity has provided a valuable archaeology of the modernist individual, locating the modern in Christianity, this liberal-inflected approach misses a crucial dimension of Christianity—the social relationships through which Christian, moral worlds are formed. In this sense, Omri Elisha's (2011) analysis of the tentative, often unsuccessful, attempts at the creation Christian "relationalism" in an American Evangelical church is an important intervention. Yet it is precisely because Elisha's subjects are so enmeshed within a neoliberal world that attempts to celebrate the sociality of Christianity never quite seem to get off the ground.

Christians coming together in churches sometimes describe their communal worship in instrumentalist terms: one Christian learns from another in church or is given spiritual nourishment from the teachings of the pastor. But there is typically much more to the development of a church or larger denominational structure than instrumentalist projects of self-improvement. That is, Christians work to create or become the body of Christ in coming together with one another. Even Niebuhr, who otherwise seems to place himself within a modernist, antisocial framework, insists that Christians need to come together in some kind of group.

What has largely been overlooked in the emphasis on Christian individuals is the important role of the "body of Christ," or the Church. The "body of Christ" describes the relationship of Christians (as a group) to Jesus, who is the head of the Church. In the Pauline epistles, Christians are described as individuals as well as members of the body of Christ (1 Cor 12:12–27). Particularly after Jesus's ascension, the communal collection of Christians becomes a way to create the divine presence on earth (Mt 18:20). It is out of this fundamental sense of dislocation from God that churches, denominations, and church groups have importance as theological formations and lived experiences of worship. The notion of the "church militant" captures the sense of urgent and continuous struggle that Christians as a body engage in during this era of separation from God. (It is contrasted with the "church triumphant," which will be organized in heaven after judgment.) The schismatic impulse to perfect the church is an expression of this militancy, of the fight that must be continuously waged against sin as a contaminating force—from others as well as from the self. A church can be defined then as a Christian group that forges paths to salvation and godly connection for its members through worship practices, beliefs, and the joint creation of critical discursive fields. It can also be an evangelical formation, working to create such paths for others through missionization.

In addition to the "body of Christ," "the church militant," and "the church triumphant," the distinction between the "visible" and "invisible" church has been particularly productive for Christian theologians developing ways of talking about Christian social groups. St. Augustine first deployed the distinction between the visible and invisible church during the Donatist Controversy of the fourth and fifth centuries. The Donatist sect of the African church essentially declared that the true church could only be composed of the elect. In response, Augustine claimed that there is a difference between the visible church, which includes all church members who constitute actual communities in the world, and the invisible church, which is limited to the elect only. For Augustine, it was impossible for fallen man to know who the elect of the invisible church really were, as this is something only God can discern. The elect must coexist with the damned in the earthly visible church. For Augustine, the church developed in its members a charity toward others that defined Christian communal life (Willis 1950). His reigning demand was for peace through the feeling of charity toward others who struggle with one to become elect.[7]

While the Donatists were a relatively short-lived splinter group, the distinction between the visible and invisible church—and the question of what a church community is—has lasted much longer. Early Protestant reformers worked to separate the visible from the invisible church without claiming God's role of judgment. They argued that the church centered in Rome was trying to eliminate the distinction between visible and invisible church by making itself the sole means of grace. For example, rather than elevating man, Luther saw the Church as debasing God, by making him coextensive with the earthly visible institution (Willis 1950, xii). The early Protestants returned to an Augustinian position of arguing for the essentially unknowable extent of overlap between the visible and invisible church.

The desire to create as much overlap as possible between the visible and invisible church—to make the church militant, the earthly community that fights for salvation, as close as possible to the church triumphant that gathers in heaven—continues to reappear. The Puritans of Tudor England and colonial America can be thought of as neo-Donatists, who worked to make a community out of the virtual "community of saints" (i.e., invisible church). Separatist Puritans argued for covenants that would bind people together in common cause as the church militant, arguing that "saints without a covenant were no more a true church than bricks and lumber unassembled were a building" (S. Foster 1991, 153).

That is, as much as Protestants understand that only God will reveal the differences between the visible and invisible church, they still desire to work toward perfection in groups or as a church, as hard as this may be. If 2 Corinthians 6:17—"Come out from among them and be ye separate, sayeth the Lord"—is the "cry of the schismatic" (Gaustad and Schmidt 2002, 294), the desire is to be separate *together* with others, as the *church* militant and not simply the *subject* militant.

CRITIQUE AND COLLECTIVITY: THE SOCIAL ORGANIZATION OF BECOMING IN PROTESTANTISM

Christianity, according to Fanella Cannell (2005), is an "impossible religion"—impossible because it demands that its practitioners transcend the world while still being in it. This impossible imperative can lead its practitioners to a relentless sense of sin (Robbins 2004a), in which immediacy with God becomes the only palliative (Keane 2007; Engelke 2007). The quest for immediate contact with God appears to reduce Christian concerns about the social to at most a relationship between an individualized Christian subject and God. For example, in both New Life Church and Reformed Gospel Church, as in many other Protestant denominations, each individual prays using his or her own (self-generated, self-authorizing) words rather than using a common prayer book. Contact with God is relentlessly purified of the marks of human sociality, of social convention and custom.

But there is, of course, a gulf between this Protestant Christian rhetoric of an immediate relationship to God and its social reality. Even the work of individual purification must draw upon a differentiated social field of others and pasts (and even former selves) that have to be managed (Keane 2007). As I argue throughout this book, the organization of these others in denominational and sectarian forms is a crucial aspect of Christian practice. The acts of schism and denominational division, far from the surfeit of the social as it encroaches on the sacred, constitute practices of Christian critique and collectivity. This social field is an essential part of Christian becoming. That is to say, immediacy with God and transcendence of the social is itself produced through critical positionings of collectives and selves.

The anthropology of Christianity has focused on the ways in which an ethos of sacred immediacy is produced by Protestant Christian discourses that overtly devalue semiotic practices of mediation, in which a common prayer book, for example, is not a time-tested route to divine communication but instead a barrier to true expression of oneself to God. Put in the terms that John Durham Peters (1999) uses to analyze modernist concepts of communication, liturgical materials like prayer books are chasms that make communication impossible, not bridges that allow it to proceed. But mediation, of course, cannot be escaped. Signs are necessarily mediating entities (Peirce 1998), and so even the Protestant ideal of a direct relationship with God has to be understood as having value in a comparative frame, in contrast to the indirect, the mediate, and the social (see Meyer 2011; Bolter and Grusin 2000). When Guhu-Samane Christians debate whether traditional practices constitute God's "blessings" to their ancestors, they are engaging in a Christian critique of their culture that emphasizes the mediating, historical transformations that separate them from their grandparents or from other practitioners of Christianity worldwide. When these critical projects become institutionalized in denominational forms, Guhu-Samane sectarians create a social organization of becoming essential to establishing Christian selves.

Canonical genres of Christian critique foreground the critical work of the individual Christian subject purifying herself, while backgrounding the social field produced through the practice of critique. Primary genres of Christian practice like testimony (Harding 2000) are critical autobiographies: "once I was lost, but now I am found." The crucial before/after structure of witnessing, taking believers from a past life of darkness punctuated by a list of sinful practices into a present (and future) life of salvation and promises of redemption produce speaking selves in a Christian mold.

But critique—whether it goes under the name of Christianity, secular rationalism, or even something like cargo cultism—is an unavoidably *social* theory (Foucault 1997; Robbins 2004b). The genres and rituals of Christian critique are not merely instruments in personal projects of becoming Christian. On the contrary, critique positions one's present self in a social field and, most productively, a social field thereby potentially baptized anew as the body of Christ.

Guhu-Samane schismatics put great emphasis on their socio-temporal position, their sense of afterness: being after colonialism, after tradition, after the translation and revival. The past was an ever-present topic of conversation in the Waria Valley. For any person asking, "when did that change happen," the answer was always "when the Word of God arrived." Since that could refer to the Lutheran Mission's initial arrival, Ernie Richert's initial arrival, or the Holy Spirit's 1977 initial arrival, church leaders like Mark Timothy develop elaborate frameworks of afterness with which to judge moral progress. Being Christian, especially in a convert society, is, to an extent, predicated on being a schismatic who is coming after something else. Schisms are perhaps the most extreme forms of critique—rending apart the body of Christ to purify it. Not simply a "technique of the self" (Foucault 1997; see also Robbins 2004a), then, Guhu-Samane Christians use critical Christian resources to examine and remake their traditions, churches, and the Papua New Guinean nation.

Critical projects of coming after have a complex relationship to the problem of presence that Engelke (2007) explores so productively. Protestants aspire to immediacy, even if that goal is never quite manageable. For immediacy is a matter of historical becoming, not an achronic state divorced from all that comes before. As philosopher Gerhard Richter (2011, 4) says, "The foundational moment of historical understanding . . . would therefore not be a moment of presence, lucidity, and transparent awareness of an object that is available and identical to itself, but rather would call for a rigorous engagement with that which, within a work or text, bespeaks a radical nonsynchronicity of understanding." The tenacity of historical debate in the Waria Valley, the attention that a church leader like Mark puts into constructing a timeline of transformations, depends upon the "nonsynchronicity" of present and past. And yet this does not produce a simple equation of past to tradition and sin, since the leaders and laity of churches like New Life anchor the affective power of Christianity to linguistic and cultural localization—the fact that founder of New Life, Ulysses, began to hear the voice of the Holy Spirit only after the New Testament translation. In that sense, who they are as Christians depends upon organizing themselves into contrasting and often oppositional groups, but groups to which these Christians nonetheless have a sense of enduring cultural, historical, or genealogical connection. If Guhu-Samane schismatics are invested in a sense of immediacy, then that is only a product of the social field and the practices of critique from which this immediacy can be produced.

Through Christian critique, Guhu-Samane work to develop foundational moments of social positioning and historical understanding, debating with one another which organization of the social field, which moment, provides that sense of afterness and how best to align with it across time. As Harding (2000) notes, this before/after structure is predicated on a biblical model at several levels, mirroring the before/after world distinguished by Jesus's salvific work as well as the type/anti-type architecture of the Old Testament + New Testament Bible as a whole. It is perhaps unsurprising that a religion that binds its own sacred text to its antecedent is one that is so deeply concerned with a critical evaluation of the past.

The important role of critique in Christian religious practice may appear incongruous. Critical practice has long been excluded from the religious sphere in Western social theory. In one of Kant's most influential discussions of critique (Kant [1784] 1970), he specifically excludes the religious sphere from the domain of progressive, public Enlightenment. A cleric can write his letters to the editor as a citizen, but as a minister, he is expected to toe the denominational line and so is unable to act as a critical, rational individual. As in many Enlightenment and post-Enlightenment discussions of religion, religion is relegated to the private realm, a domain of obedience and assent to beliefs. The public sphere is where citizens use their rational, critical faculties to transform themselves and the world around them. "Christian critique" is almost a contradiction in terms from this perspective.

In one of his more recent genealogies of secularism, Asad (2013) outlines one kind of Whig history that liberals tell themselves, in which Christianity's truth-telling power slowly transformed into a secular project of rational, critical debate. Importantly, though, this version of history (erroneously) depends upon an early separation of church and state, of religion from politics. Liberal histories that take Christianity into account, then, do so only from the perspective of the critical individual. That is to say, from a secular perspective, Christian critique is only valid to the extent that speakers address themselves to other equally free individuals. Denominational forms that implicate morally defined social worlds are thus excluded from this tradition.

I argue, however, that denominationalism is a critical practice centered on remaking social life and not just individual selves. As Barker (1993, 1996) in particular has emphasized, Melanesian Christianity has been about getting the relationship between the church and society right. Joel Robbins, who is often considered the major proponent of an individualist concept of the Christian self in the anthropology of Christianity, in fact argues that Urapmin Christians in Papua New Guinea work diligently to create salvational social groups (Robbins 2004a, 300–311). However, his arguments for what he calls Urapmin "pseudo-holism" have largely been neglected in discussions of his work (see also Robbins 2012). For Guhu-Samane speakers, critique of Christian social groups is not a secular pursuit, nor is critique opposed to private religious practice. For them, social critique *is* Christian practice.

The critical reflections that motivate denominational schisms among the Guhu-Samane are predicated on the sense of coming after that provides a divine schism in the world, the self, and the community. That is to say, there is a social organization of becoming at work in the schismatic tendencies of Christian moralized tradition. Ancestors, the oft-rumored sorcerers, and fellow villagers provide contemporary Christians with tools of separation and contrast. Prior moments of sin, personal or genealogical, offer Christians the ground on which to engage in autobiographical critique. The spiritual work of critique is distributed across a range of social actors and historical moments.

In making this move from a totalized subject focused on immediate presence with God to a subject and community bifurcated through critical reflection of past and present, self and other, I hope to forge a connection to anthropologists working in non-Protestant worlds. For scholars who study Roman Catholic or Orthodox communities, individual and autonomous Christian subjects are not necessarily the ethnographic foci that they are for the primarily Pentecostal communities that have so far received the lion's share of anthropological attention. In Catholic communities, for example, priests might be responsible for most of the critical labor. Allowing for a spiritual division of labor even in Protestantism is one way to make a connection to the vast communities of Christians who are not heirs to Luther or Calvin.

TRANSLATION AND THE TECHNOLOGIES OF CRITIQUE

For the Protestant reformers who wanted to do away with the institutionalism of the Roman Catholic Church, one of the first orders of business was to reduce ritual life to a minimum. Ritual formulae came to be seen negatively as "formulaic," externally conditioned expressions of the institution rather than intimate expressions of the believing self (Keane 1997; Yelle 2013). The retreat from sociality did not mean a retreat from language as such, but a retreat from language figured as "other." Protestant and, even more so, Pentecostal language is often focused on cultivating an authentic, spontaneous, and individual voice (Luhrmann 2001, 2012; Shoaps 2002). In this semiotic ideology, language can represent the self in more and less authentic ways, and the rituals of non-liturgical churches are focused on creating a space for such representations to flourish. From the Protestant perspective, language has a privileged but not perfect route to one's heart. As "the shrine of the soul" (B. Schieffelin 2002), language is the best route humans have to other people.

The Summer Institute of Linguistics (SIL), whose members produced the Guhu-Samane New Testament, took up this model of authentic language, using it to develop an evangelical methodology of "heart language" Bible translation. Putting the Bible into the native language of every person in the world would provide potential readers with access to revealed truth and the chance to hear God's word in the most affectively powerful and intimate way. And yet at least in the case of the Guhu-Samane Bible translation, the effect has not been to turn people away from sociality toward intimate communication with God alone, but to emphasize language as a social but sacred institution.

As much as they are focused on the linguistic heart, SIL translations are also supposed to demand from receptor-language readers moments of critical reflection on the cultural traditions encoded in this language. A translation of God's word is supposed to suggest that newer, better beliefs and ways of life can be found in Christianity. The paradox of SIL translation, then, is that the translation is at once supposed to be domesticating—voicing an authentic, purely present self in one's heart language—and foreignizing—producing a critically distant reflection on one's culture (see Venuti 1995 for the domesticating/foreignizing dichotomy). In both moments, Guhu-Samane Christians have ideologized a language that is irreducibly social: in the domesticating mode, translation models a shared and sacralized ethno-linguistic group; in the foreignizing idiom, it creates a set of differentiated social positions from heathen to Christian, from past to future.

In contrast to other anthropological analyses of translation, especially translation in Christian missionization (e.g., Rafael 1993; Meyer 1999), I am less interested in the particular choices that translators made to translate any specific theological concept than I am in the ways in which translation engenders critical discussion from receptor-language readers. I follow an analytical model developed in Bambi Schieffelin's work (1996, 2002, 2007, forthcoming), which focuses on the local discourses that supplement and sometimes subvert textual translations produced by missionaries and local converts in the field. More specifically, however, I examine the ways in which scriptural translation oriented toward conversion offers readers and listeners with equivalences in one moment, only to have them be refused in the next. When Ernie Richert uses terms from the Guhu-Samane traditions of the men's house to depict Christian social groups like churches, he helps to foster a critical debate in which Guhu-Samane Christians try to determine the basis on which comparative differences are constituted. While certain choices of key terms, like the use of men's house terms to describe a church, are important, I focus instead on the larger discursive project of moral comparison that long ago spilled out over the edges of the text and into the social world, evident in the constant comparative critiques of denominational groups in the Waria Valley.

An emphasis on translation's role in critique, then, offers a different way to think about how subjectivities are formed in Christian linguistic practice. At the same time that language can work as the internal guarantor of authenticity and immediacy under modernist ideologies, it can also be the device of sociohistorical difference. Critical translation gives rise to an afterlife, "the figure of a repetition that does not repeat, a living on and after that both remains attached to what came before and, precisely through an analysis of that abiding yet often invisible attachment, departs from it in ever-new directions" (Richter 2011, 4). Traditional culture, other denominations' practices, or one's own sinful past can have a critical afterlife in just this sense of a citational, quoted response (see also Meyer 1998, Robbins 2004c).

Part of being able to take up a critical voice against something is being able to objectify it or, more specifically, to entextualize it as a repeatable, citable chunk of language that can seem to stay the same across contexts of utterance (Silverstein and Urban 1996; Bauman and Briggs 1990; Briggs and Bauman 1992). Critical entextualizations of things like biblical passages or traditional culture help draw the divisions between past and present, Christian and cultured. The ways in which both Lutheran missionaries and SIL translators focused on the Guhu-Samane men's house as a potential equivalent to the Christian church continue to inform the kinds of critical discourses that Guhu-Samane Christians engage in today. In that sense, the men's house is an entextualized object of comparison that is a condition of possibility for the circulation of Christian critique. The focus on critical Christianity via translation allows us to properly conceptualize the profusion of denominations and schisms so common in the Protestant experience. Denominational forms—and the emphasis on the social groups of Christianity—depend upon a positive valuation of entextualized social difference as a way for local Christians to track their own paths of historical transformation.

ONCE REFORMED, ALWAYS REFORMING: DIFFERENCE AND RELIGIOUS TRANSFORMATION

If denominations are important to projects of historical narrativization, denominations do not therefore become simply identitarian institutions lauding the specific achievements of particular groups of Christians, as Niebuhr and others would have it. Guhu-Samane churches are not simply identitarian institutions in part because the simultaneously domesticating and foreignizing translations produced by SIL translators both codify ethno-linguistic identity and subvert it. In the Guhu-Samane case, ethno-linguistic identity is fostered as the starting point from which conversion is measured. It is also a lingering presence in the ways in which Christianity is presented as a response to a group that perdures as a linguistic unit and thus must also be practiced in terms of that group. However, the original ethno-linguistic group is not the end point for either SIL or Guhu-Samane Christians who have been influenced by the SIL New Testament translation. In that sense, identity as such is not the primary object. Ethno-nationalist identity (Smith 1991) is predicated on a sense of enduring ethnic existence. "We" deserve political recognition because "we" have always been here. Christian identity, however, is an identity of transformation: "I" am now Christian, but "I" once was not; "we" were a culture lost to God, but now "we" are a people that can change.

Schismatic situations—and it is worth considering convert societies to be schismatic inasmuch as conversion presupposes a critical response to "tradition"—suggest that they can be something more that just identitarian groupings for more specifically theological reasons as well. I suggest that the figure of the remnant better characterizes them. The remnant is a group that exists in the aftermath of critique and one that looks forward to the horizon of final redemption. For Agamben (2005), it is specifically a group forged within a messianic timeframe. In the Old Testament, the remnant is formed out of the critique of the Israelites from God, a critique that foreshadows a later moment of ultimate judgment. In the New Testament, the remnant is the partial group that has accepted Jesus as universal savior even while others have not. It emerges from the critical work that people (in conjunction with God) do.

The New Testament figure of the remnant metonymically figures the ways in which Christians depict salvation as the gift that is offered to all but that only some will take. As the fragment of a once-whole group, the remnant admits a certain kind of defeat—that not everyone will be saved—even as it celebrates its own militant existence as the universal form of salvation. The remnant is a partial and earthly formulation of unity after the separations and distances produced through social, Christian critique. It militantly propagates difference in the shadow of the attempted universality of the body of Christ. While holding out hope that immediacy with God will one day be possible, it celebrates the mediating distances that exist among people and between people and God.

John Durham Peters (1999) argues that the celebration of mediation and distance—of the work that has to be done to communicate—has a biblical precedent, even if communicative immediacy is more usually discussed in Christian scholarly and theological texts. According to Peters, the Parable of the Sower (Mt 13:24–30, 36–43) can be read as Jesus's claim that communication does not have to produce uniform and accessible responses in his audience. To use terms from a more technological genre, the fact that communication produces difference is a feature, not a bug. The paradox of SIL translation theories is that they at once orient toward a sense of immediacy and a uniformity of response in readers (in terms of a hoped-for conversion) even as this conversion process initiates a longer-term project of developing traditions of critical, differentiating debate.

More broadly, the remnant makes room for difference—for the other—in Christian practice. The denomination in a schismatic and possibly agonistic relationship with other Christian social groups is an enduring figure of the transformation that has happened and could potentially happen to all people. The fact that the denominational remnant is, as yet, a partial group that does not partake of a heavenly universalism indexes the work that Christians have to do to approximate communion in an earthly domain. Denominational fragmentation has to been seen from two perspectives at once: as a successful approximation of godly communion and as a failure of human capacity to effect godly communion on its own. Denominational profusion is both lamented and celebrated in the Waria Valley, a reflection of the kind of double vision that the remnant creates. Practices that highlight particular Christian kinds of social otherness—denominational appropriations of traditional Guhu-Samane drums in contrast to churches than shun them—are the imperfect metonyms of heaven, emphasizing the compelling but still frustrating project of trying to make the earthly church militant into the heavenly church triumphant.

As Stasch (2009) argues, identity as the basis for a kind of communal solidarity (or *gemeinschaft,* see Tönnies 2011) is the preeminent way in which contemporary social scientists and Westerners imagine legitimate collectivities. Under the logic of identity, a group can speak with a single voice because there is an important, underlying similarity in all members of the group. Given these presuppositions, identity is doubly wrong as a term for the schismatic Guhu-Samane denominational groups. First, it ignores the ways in which the group is posited as a basis for transformation rather than lasting existence; second, it ignores the ways in which remnant groups are figures of de-totalized fragmentation. Guhu-Samane schismatics are able to speak together because of the critical work they do to create and defend divisions within themselves and their communities. Reformed Gospel and New Life members pray loudly and individually, yet all at the same time. The remnant can speak, but it does so with a cacophonous voice.

Ruth Marshall (2009), echoing Agamben (2005), says that subjects within the messianic time implied by the remnant have, at best, a form of negative identity. In this case, it would mean that local Christians are more than anything "not-Guhu-Samane." In this interpretation of remnant Christianity, politico-religious groups cannot coalesce around such instable and undefined negative characteristics. I agree that the denomination-as-remnant is often an unstable institutional form, the product of and later the object of critical debate. Churches can pop up and disintegrate with incredible speed. But the longevity of a group should not be seen as the primary index of its cultural value for either local people or for social scientists. To make that equation is to work under the assumptions of an identitarian politics predicated upon historical stability as the guarantor of political rights.

In fact, instable groups are a standard part of Melanesian forms of sociality. Sociality and groups in Melanesia are often event-based rather than identity-based (Wagner 1974, 1977; Strathern 1988). Even something like male initiation, which would seem to solidify a gender identity, is often the ritual milieu in which young men learn of the shifting contexts through which specific relationships and their attendant characteristics come to the fore: if in one stage of initiation, men learn that a sacred flute is a penis, in the next stage, they are told that the flute can also be a birth canal (Strathern 1988). Events elicit specific relationships from an untotalizable self. Under conditions of "dividual" or "relational" personhood, such event-based sociality is not problematic (other than for the structural functionalist anthropologist looking for segmentary descent systems).

In contrast to Marshall or Agamben, I argue that the value of a remnant group can be seen in terms of its capacity to create critical discourses, ones which may very well lead to the dissolution of the group, as when the Guhu-Samane revivalists, led by Mark and Ulysses, unintentionally produced a split within the Lutheran community in the late

1970s. Viewing denominations in these terms, we are able to give due consideration to the critical and Christian frameworks in which these social groups and institutions exist. In doing so, we avoid equating religion with the private and individual. Likewise, we avoid equating secular politics with the public and social. From this post-secularist perspective, denominationalism is not the failure of Christianity but its very practice. Once reformed, always reforming, as Luther said.

ORGANIZATION OF CHAPTERS

As scholars working within the anthropology of Christianity have shown, the modern, Christian individual can seemingly turn any event or phenomenon into an opportunity for self-reflection on individual responsibility and personal sinfulness. Given the emphasis on a Christian refusal of sociality, one might expect a relatively impoverished catalogue of social groups with which Christians work. As I show in the following chapters, however, this is not the case. Not only are there multiple models of how to create Christian sociality, but there are also many different media through which this critical, social work can be done.

Based upon local people's ongoing historical critique, Guhu-Samane engagements with Christianity can be divided into three categories: missions, Christian villages, and denominational schisms. I use this organization here in order to highlight various foci of Christian sociality. Missionaries from different evangelistic traditions provided Guhu-Samane Christians with conflicting models of how to construct a Christian social world, in one case denying and in the other case emphasizing the role of the ethno-linguistic group as the object of evangelism. The first three chapters use primarily historical and archival material to analyze the forms of Christian sociality espoused by different missions. The remaining chapters use ethnographic materials to examine the ways in which Guhu-Samane Christians have developed their own critical regimes and new social formations. During the revival, local people employed aspects of missionary models in conjunction with their own kin- and village-based sociality. In these initial moments of localized Christianity, critical work focused on explicit comparisons between traditional and Christian religious institutions, emphasizing comparisons between the men's house and the church, and I consider the ways in which villages have become Christian spaces in this section. Under this critical and comparative gaze, local experiments with Christian sociality continue in contemporary denominational schisms that accept, sometimes begrudgingly, the importance of social difference and social order in Christian life. Cutting across these eras of Christian group formation, language, land, men's houses, and music are some of the primary media of critical religious reflection.

Chapter 1 presents the problems of group formation in Christianity from the Lutheran Mission perspective—that is, from the perspective of the organization that first introduced Guhu-Samane speakers to Christianity. More than SIL or the local Pentecostal churches that otherwise take up much attention in this book, Lutherans have a particularly positive image of the church as an important project for Christians. Because the Lutheran Mission also had to give up on its original goal of native language evangelization when it confronted the overwhelming linguistic diversity of New Guinea, the Lutheran Mission is an important counterpoint to the vernacular language evangelization and Christian group formation of SIL and the Guhu-Samane revivalist churches that followed it. Although post-revival Guhu-Samane Christians refused some aspects of the Lutheran model, the emphasis on the critical remnant church as a primary unit of salvation has remained.

Chapters 2 and 3 examine SIL in detail. In chapter 2, I discuss SIL's methodology and translation theory, putting its development in the context of U.S. evangelical trends in the mid-twentieth century, especially the Church Growth movement. I analyze how SIL conceptualizes language and its relationship to culture and how their model of translation is both domesticating and foreignizing at the same time. Focusing on Eugene Nida's model of dynamic equivalence translation, I look at how SIL translations are meant to foster both an immediacy of native-language authenticity as well as a mediating critical sensibility about one's own culture.

Chapter 3 focuses on SIL's role among Guhu-Samane-speaking communities more specifically. I look at how Ernie Richert tried to develop a sense of the ethno-linguistic group where it had not existed before. Indeed, Guhu-Samane people were not even known by that name in colonial documents until after Richert began his work. Bringing together speakers of different dialects, elders knowledgeable about traditional customs, and younger men who could teach literacy courses, Richert created an ethno-linguistic framework for the reception of the New Testament translation that he was working on. At the same time, Richert set the stage for the critical undoing of this ethno-linguistic formation through the very practices of commensuration and comparison that were part of the translation project.

Richert's New Testament was distributed to local people in 1975, and was followed soon after by the Holy Spirit revival that began the schismatic problems that Guhu-Samane Christians still face today. In the remaining chapters of the book, I look at different aspects of Christian group formation and disintegration brought on by the revival and translation. Chapters 4 and 5 pay particular attention to the role of villages and the men's house in the critical, comparative work that Guhu-Samane speakers do in developing Christian groups. In chapter 4, I focus on the revival itself and the reformulation of the local village as a Christian space. Because Lutheranism had largely been based at mission stations, the revivalists who wanted to bring Christianity into a local space had to reconfigure the village in Christian terms. Villages were and still are considered the spaces of fractious social difference, and at least initially, people felt that villages needed to be the focus of critical work in order to become spaces of more peaceful homogeneity. In part because Richert had used the term for the village-based men's house (*guhu*) as the term for "church," revivalists set to work on a comparative project of religious reform of this space and the construction of the first schismatic church, New Life. Critique, translation, and Christian sociality combine within the context of the revival to create a new remnant grouping.

In chapter 5, I continue to use the figure of the men's house to help understand transformations under Christianity. Here I focus on how local people reflect on Christianity—and on Richert's work in particular—in terms of their altered conceptions of language use and linguistic power. While today, social life under the governance of the men's house is remembered as a time of violent, silent order, I show how a Christian conception of language-as-system, divorced from emplaced communicative events of agentive response, has made the now sacralized Guhu-Samane language into something of a power beyond any person's control. Figured as sacred, truth-telling power, language in the era of Christianity, which is often characterized as the era after wars ended, has nevertheless become the power to create division, animosity, and fighting. Here is the cacophonous voice of a remnant group, rather than the univocal presentation of an identitarian one. In both chapters 4 and 5, I discuss the schism in New Life that resulted in the creation of Reformed Gospel Church.

Throughout chapters 2 through 5, I discuss how SIL translation methodology produces ethno-linguistic groups of language-based authenticity as well as remnant groups engaged in critique that develop into denominational forms. In chapter 6, I look more specifically at the uses of the Guhu-Samane New Testament in church services. Rather than being concerned with the translation of specific terms or concepts, I show how local Christians use the translation as a way to conceptualize their own histories of transformation. That is, translation is important in church services and church life more generally for pointing to and celebrating the critiques that Christianity has engendered. I contrast the use of the New Testament translation in New Life Church and Reformed Gospel Church.

In chapter 7, I focus specifically on the problems of denominationalism and on the ways in which denominational disputes are both sources of embarrassment and objects of celebration. I show how the objection to denominationalism as "just politics" is itself a moment within the logic of denominationalism. I contrast two event-problems in contemporary Guhu-Samane Christianity. First, I look at the fights over the disposition of the former mission station at Garasa, in which all the parties involved denounced the conflation of land politics and denominational politics as the interruption of external, secular life into the world of religious practice. Second, I look at the fights over the use of musical instruments in church services; external objects like drums, guitars, or brass horns are figured in these cases not as trivial externalities but as embodied expressions of critical Christianity. These internalizations of musicality are not positively valued because of some perceived route to immediacy. Rather, they are valued precisely because they point to the long, mediating histories of critique that culminate in denominational form.

In the final chapter, I look toward one horizon of unity that exists within all of this denominational fragmentation. Guhu-Samane Christians, of whatever denomination, toy with the idea that they are one of the Lost Tribes of Israel. Focusing on the past, they hope to connect their pre-Christian ancestors to the original ancestors of divine transformation. Even though ethno-linguistic identity as promulgated by Ernie Richert and SIL methodology is an important part of the Guhu-Samane story, this final chapter shows how Christian identity diverges radically from standard nationalist models. Christian identity is an identity of sacred transformation, where being lost is valued for the ways in which people can imagine a moment of one day being found. Importantly, Guhu-Samane Christians are not the only people in Papua New Guinea to be fascinated by the idea of Lost Tribes origins. Similar claims are made by Christian groups across the country. Moreover, they are using this position of critical lost-ness to create a Christian politics at the national level. That is, people are coming together to critique the government because they all come from the same situation of having engaged in critique of their own cultures. While this might not look like the basis of politics or political groups as found in Western democratic traditions, the figure of the Lost Tribes holds out hope for Papua New Guineans that Christian critique can be used on ever-larger fields of transformation.

GUHU-SAMANE COMMUNITIES

The Guhu-Samane language is a member of the Binandere language family, although lexico-statistical analysis suggests that it is very distantly related to the other languages in this group.[8] There are presently roughly thirteen thousand speakers of the language, mostly living in the Waria Valley or in three villages near Morobe Station on the north coast. There are also Guhu-Samane communities in Port Moresby, Lae, Wau, Bulolo, and Popondetta.

According to local history and at least one colonial patrol report (MOROBE report 3 of 50/51, 4), all Guhu-Samane speakers originally lived near Morobe Station and were displaced when Suena-speaking groups moved west along the north coast of New Guinea in the mid- or late nineteenth century. Cultural features more associated with coastal communities, like matrilineality, are evident in Guhu-Samane communities.

Local norms of political organization include a tendency toward processes of political fragmentation that interacts with the migratory history local people tell. Clanship is inherited through one's mother, and clans are organized into a moiety system; intra-moiety marriages are still highly frowned upon but are becoming more common. Mother's brothers are often geographically distant but affectively close (fathers are just the opposite), and they are supposed to help arrange for the marriages of a sister's children, the use of garden land, and access to the forest. Trees are the only major resources that people inherit from their fathers. Guhu-Samane kinship and residence could most succinctly be described as matrilineal but patrilocal—linking women are often moving away from their male kin. Matri-clans cluster geographically in a single village in one generation, but when the matri-clan daughters move away to marry in the next, the clan's local geographical center dissolves.

As Turner (1957) discussed, this inherently unstable situation leads to frequent village schisms. Major Guhu-Samane regions are defined as more or less autonomous spaces through a history of feasting and migration. A

FIGURE 1. Looking north toward Titio village.

village is established as a political entity through a major feast, but slowly different factions from this village hive off and start a new village. In this kind of hub-and-spoke organization, older villages are centers to which the newer villages still have to orient. What I here refer to as political regions generally take their names from the older (in some cases, no longer extant) villages. In other words, Guhu-Samane people are long accustomed to having social groups fall apart, although I argue in later chapters (especially chapters 4 and 7) that the Christian forms of schism differ from the schismatic politics of kinship and locality.

Villages were (in some cases, still are) anchored by a men's house, a central institution that organized marriages, gardens, initiations, feasting, warfare, and religious rituals. During initiation and regularly after that, men slept and socialized in the men's house while a man's wife and children lived in a separate house. Organized into what Godelier (1986) identified as a Great Man system, the men's house had a number of specific roles (overall leader, ritual garden specialist, ritual poison specialist, negotiator, and so forth, with any person lacking a specific role considered a warrior). Young men would be slotted into one role or another at the end of the male initiation ordeals. In most cases today, this ritual division of labor is vastly reduced, if there is even a men's house in a village at all. Some villages, however, have a secular political leader and a Christian leader (that is, the church pastor). In the Muniwa region in which I was based, the men inhabiting these roles had at times an extremely contentious relationship. That is to say, a secular/sacred divide is tentative at best. I discuss the role of men's houses in the 1977 revival and contemporary Christian thinking in chapters 4 and 5.

Given local people's temporal and ideological distance from the era of more robust men's houses, I have large gaps in my understanding of what could be called "pre-Christian religion." Indeed, given the ways in which both Lutheran missionaries and the SIL translator pitted Christianity against "the *poro* cult" (a men's house is a *poro guhu*, or *poro* house), the sense in which the men's house was a religion as such has to be understood as an outcome of this comparative, critical discourse. Nevertheless, some features are relatively clear. Each men's house was inhabited by—or was the instantiation of—an overall *poro* spirit; however, any particular men's house might have a specific *poro* spirit that it was associated with. These spirits seemed to have a division of labor that loosely mirrored that of the men who organized within the house. For example, the *poro* spirit that was most commonly spoken about with me was the spirit that helped men to construct the impressive cane bridges that cross the Waria River at certain sites. Each men's house has or had a male *poro* (a bullroarer) and a female *poro* (a pair of sacred flutes). Both bullroarers and flutes are now played at major celebrations out in the open, although in the past they would have been hidden from women and uninitiated boys.

There is some debate about the origins of the *poro guhu* system for the Guhu-Samane. Some older men suggest that the institution comes from neighboring groups to the west (in the direction of Wau and Bulolo). Certainly the major feasts, called *masere* in Guhu-Samane, which were organized by men's houses, take their name from the neighboring Kunimaipan word *matere*. It may be that as Guhu-Samane communities migrated up the Waria River valley in the latter half of the nineteenth century, they took on the institutions of the groups they encountered. Simon Harrison's (1993) arguments about Melanesian borrowing cultures certainly seem apt for this case.

In that sense, then, Christianity may have started as yet another instance of such borrowing, at least by the groups in the Middle Waria, who were initially receptive to Lutheran missionary advances. But as Burce (1983) notes, other Guhu-Samane communities were extremely antagonistic to any Lutheran encroachment, especially those men's houses that were in the middle of preparing to pay off debts by hosting a major feast. When Ernie Richert arrived, toward the end of the 1950s,

FIGURE 2. Preparing piles of food for an inter-village distribution.

many Guhu-Samane were not particularly enthusiastic Christians. The Lutherans had worked to dismantle men's houses and worked to insert their own institutions of education and economic assistance in their place.

Like men's houses that tried to anchor villages that were prone to schism, the colonial center of the Waria Valley has never been stable. The Lutheran Mission initially entered the area in the early part of the 1910s, although the circuit of which the Guhu-Samane were a part was headquartered at the distant Zaka Station, on the north coast. There were Lutheran schools, run by "native evangelists" from other areas, at Ohe, Kipu, and near Garaina along the Waria River valley. These stations sometimes had trade stores and other amenities, although the stores were only occasionally stocked and open. In the 1960s the Lutherans established a station at Gaure, just upriver from Garaina. A European missionary sometimes resided at Gaure, although there has not been one there since the mid-1990s.

Ernie and Marjorie Richert first came to the Waria Valley in 1956 and were settled at their regular residence at the Kipu Lutheran station by 1957. As I discuss in more detail in chapter 3, a large group of men and

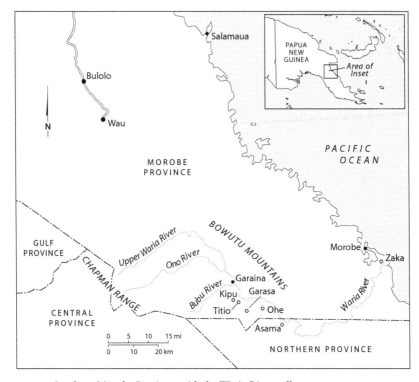

MAP 1. Southern Morobe Province, with the Waria River valley at center.

their families resided in Kipu to work with Ernie on translation, literacy, carpentry, and a number of other projects. The Richerts lived at Kipu off and on until 1974, and one of the Richerts' sons stayed for a few years after that. After the revival got going in 1977, Kipu started to shrink.

In the 1980s Garasa station, a four-hour walk downstream from Garaina, became another important locale. Ex-SIL missionaries set up the second outpost of Pacific Island Ministries (PIM). An airstrip was built there, and PIM set up an aid-post clinic, a trade store, missionary residences, and a general-purpose building (what came to be known as the *biiri* (temple), mentioned in the opening anecdote of this chapter). Some work had started on a Bible college when PIM decided, somewhat abruptly, to pull out of Garasa. From Zaka to Gaure to Garaina to Garasa, the center of colonial power has constantly moved up and down the valley.

With this history of irregular colonial presence comes a history of irregular attempts at economic development for these largely subsistence-farming communities. With an elevation of roughly seven hundred meters, coconuts grow in the Waria Valley, although not as well as at the coast. Primary staple crops are yams, taro, and sweet potato, while sago trees are harvested irregularly. Foods introduced since colonization, such as peanuts, potatoes, corn, tomatoes, snake beans, cucumbers, watermelons, and papaya round out the usual diet. Some people also grow rice, although most buy rice, as well as instant noodles, tea, and sugar, from the trade stores that are found in several different villages.

There are relatively few opportunities for engaging in a cash economy in the Waria Valley itself. As I noted above, people have at different times planted coffee, cardamom, and vanilla for sale to traveling middlemen, but air transportation is so expensive and unpredictable that most of these cash-cropping schemes have been abandoned. As Burce (1983) discusses in her dissertation, the major opportunity for wage labor in the Waria Valley came from the Garaina Tea Plantation, which opened in 1949. After closing, reopening, and closing again, it looks like Garaina Tea is unlikely to ever restart production. Most men and women who want to look for wage labor do so in Lae, Wau, or Bulolo. Remittances constituted a major portion of the cash that circulated locally during the primary portion of my research (2005–2006).

When I returned in 2007 for a month, however, a significant amount of cash was coming from people who were panning for gold on the banks of the Waria River. In certain villages, some households had almost entirely given up subsistence farming and were able to collect about $25 worth of gold per week. A new weekly market was held in this area, and gold-panning households were buying a week's worth of staple foods. During markets prior to this, women could generally collect the equivalent of $2 at most. At the gold-panning village, marketers were able to collect more, perhaps as much as $5. It was a significant increase for local people, and it seemed as though trade stores were handling more sales. Aside from gold and remittances, the other semi-regular source of cash was the sale of pigs. A female piglet could be purchased for about $25, while larger adult pigs went for higher prices (between $50 and $250).

Most children have access to primary education, and most children are expected to complete sixth grade. Going beyond this level requires passing a competitive exam and having the resources to pay the greater school fees. There were two "Top-up" schools in the area that covered seventh and eighth grades. There was no high school, so any student admitted to high school generally went to Lae or Wau and lived with kin there. Children were supposed to be taught in the Guhu-Samane language for "prep" (the equivalent to kindergarten) and first and second grades. In the classrooms that I observed, students were taught as much in Tok Pisin as in Guhu-Samane. School was therefore the place where children learned to speak Tok Pisin, although some had a passive competence in the language from living with their Tok Pisin-speaking kin. The upper primary grades were supposed to bridge students from their local language into English, but Tok Pisin was the default language of instruction. Sixth-grade graduates would be able to work through English texts (especially the Bible), but speaking skills in English were generally limited.

In other regions of Papua New Guinea, anthropologists have reported that local people did not draw a sharp distinction between Tok Pisin as an English-based creole lingua franca of Papua New Guinea and standard Australian or Melanesian English as the official language of the nation-state (e.g., Robbins 2004; Kulick 1992). This is not the case for many Guhu-Samane speakers, some of whom specifically complained that Tok Pisin was too much *antap antap* (without depth, in Tok Pisin) in comparison to the depth of either Guhu-Samane or English. English language translations of the Bible (usually the NIV) are almost as common as the Tok Pisin *Buk Baibel* or the Guhu-Samane New Testament, particularly in villages dominated by Reformed Gospel Church or villages with a large number of Lutherans. When people read along during the recitations of scripture passages during services using their different translations, they often make aesthetic claims about the different translations (Tok Pisin passages are often considered to be too long, too cumbersome, or too confusing in contrast with a sense of English simplicity and parsimony, even for speakers who have minimal English-language competence). New Life Church, as I discuss in chapter 6, has a greater emphasis on Guhu-Samane language purity in Christian contexts, and in villages where this church is prominent, relatively few people bring Tok Pisin or English Bibles to church. Yet even in these villages, people are highly aware of the differences between Guhu-Samane, Tok Pisin, and English, and use this knowledge in their critical, Christian practices of comparison.

In the postindependence, post-revival, post-Richert era, Guhu-Samane Christians were developing local forms of rituals and local means of communication, using what was roughly sixty-five years of experience with missionaries to help them do so. With a local political organization that was itself prone to schism and a number of different models of "development" and unity presented by the colonial administrations and missions, Guhu-Samane Christians soon turned toward divergent models of sociality to anchor their futures and understand their pasts.

THE FIELDWORK SITUATION

As I mentioned at the beginning of the introduction, I was originally interested in working with a group that had experience with SIL translation projects. On my first trip to Papua New Guinea, during the northern-hemisphere summer of 2001, I spent a brief period of time at SIL PNG's headquarters at Ukarumpa, Eastern Highlands Province, to speak with people there about doing research on their organization. SIL leaders and members were in almost all cases extremely welcoming, even given the long history of animosity between missionaries and anthropologists. I returned to Ukarumpa during the summer of 2003 to look at archival records from the PNG branch and to work on setting up a fieldwork situation with a particular PNG community. It was actually SIL leaders who pointed me toward the Guhu-Samane community as a unique situation. Not only had there been an SIL team there who had translated the New Testament, but local people were working with SIL's partner organization, the Bible Translation Association of PNG, to compose a vernacular language translation of the Old Testament. This project is still in process, and the opportunity to see both how a finished translation project had been received by the community and how an ongoing project worked in day-to-day terms was an important consideration for me.

When I went to Garasa with two members of the Bible Translation Association for a two-week workshop on translation procedures in 2003, I was deeply impressed by how many people showed up day after day for this event, as well as by the incredible warmth and generosity of these attendees. During this short visit, I was able to arrange to return for my primary field research. My main contacts were the father-son team who currently lead the Old Testament translation project (Mark Timothy and his son Sean). I asked the people of their natal village if my husband, James Slotta, and I could live with them. To my great delight, they welcomed us into their village, and James and I returned in January 2005.

Although I had gotten a glimpse of the denominational disputes that divided the community during that 2003 trip, I had not quite realized the extent to which living in a village that was identified as a Reformed Gospel village would also identify me. James and I were able to make connections to the Lutheran church (we had been married in a Lutheran church, so people saw us as having a connection), but it was extremely difficult to connect with members of New Life church. Because prior researchers in the area had discussed the revival in terms of the cargo-cult literature, both Reformed Gospel and New Life people were concerned that I would paint the Christian community in similar terms. Though there was no specific sense of threat or problem, there was just a general air of distrust between members of the different church communities. People from Titio village, where I lived, often accompanied me to visits with New Life members in other villages (as I discuss in later chapters, a village usually only has one major church in it). New Life people saw these acts of guardianship in negative terms, jokingly and disparagingly referring to them as my "bodyguards."

So while I was able in the end to spend time in New Life villages and with New Life people (unchaperoned on occasion), it was not to the same extent as my engagement with Reformed Gospel or the Lutherans. I feel as though I have been able to present the New Life side of various arguments in ways that members of that church would recognize, but there are undoubtedly biases that I cannot account for. As various anthropologists of Christianity have noted (Robbins 2007; Bielo 2009), there is no objective position one can take with respect to Christians who want to bring you into their communities of practice and belief.

Unfortunately, translation work on the Old Testament was largely put on hold during the time that I was living in the Waria Valley. Initially, the translation team held weekly meetings to compose first drafts of the book of Daniel. I attended these events and was always amazed by the large number of people who showed up for them. Only a few people were active participants, however, and these men later went to SIL headquarters at Ukarumpa to participate in translation courses, which effectively put a temporary halt to progress. I was not able, then, to spend as much time as I would have liked working on the daily problems of translation. But as I found out, the translation as a project was more important than just the work that was done at these sessions. People talked about the work regularly, talked about the New and Old Testaments daily, and used the translation as a productive figure of transformation. In that sense, the translation project was much larger than just the men huddled around a laptop or chalkboard.

I lived in Titio village from January 2005 through March 2006, at which point James and I went to Ukarumpa for one and a half months. There I was able to interview some SIL members, including a few who knew Ernie and Marjorie Richert. James and I returned to Papua New

Guinea in 2007 for his fieldwork among Yopno communities on the Huon Peninsula. I lived there with James for the first nine months of his fieldwork, and was able to return to Titio for a month (May 2007) to follow up on some lingering questions, get help with transcribing some audio tapes, and see old friends.

My understanding of life in the Waria Valley is influenced by the very different experiences James and I had in Yopno communities on the Huon Peninsula. Patrilineal where Guhu-Samane are matrilineal, strongly Lutheran where most Guhu-Samane long ago split from the colonial church, more similar to highlands communities compared to the coastal traits that Guhu-Samane evince, the contrasts between these two places seemed particularly stark. Although I only mention Yopno communities in passing in this book, the ideas presented here are, in part, the outcome of this unintentionally comparative project.

PART ONE

Missions

CHAPTER I

Sacred Speakers or Sacred Groups

The Colonial Lutheran Mission in New Guinea

According to the secularization hypothesis developed by Max Weber (1957) and others, under conditions of modernity, religion was gradually supposed to become a private affair, moving further off the public stage and further into the minds of private individuals. Of course, predictions of the public death of religion have been proven wrong in recent years, as fundamentalisms of all stripes—or even just publically religious people—have emerged as major forces in contemporary life.

This much is almost a social-science truism at this point. But the terms of the secularization hypothesis still hold subtle sway in much current anthropological thinking about Christianity. In particular, the focus on the religious subject as the exclusive unit of Christian practice, belief, or salvation reinscribes the division of the world into a private, individual, religious domain and a public, group-based, political one. Groups—demographic, electoral, ethnic, but especially congregational—are either ignored in studies of Christianity or are seen as not Christian in any important sense.

One could argue that ignoring groups like churches and denominations reflects Protestant realities of the highly individualized practices of the people anthropologists of Christianity have studied. Certainly the almost exclusive orientation to the individualist sacred subject has been extremely productive for the anthropology of Christianity, producing with it models of transformation, personhood, materiality, temporality, value, agency, and more (Robbins 2004a; Keane 2007; Engelke 2007;

Luhrmann 2001; Schieffelin 2002; Harding 2000; Coleman 2006; etc.). In one sense, the anthropology of Christianity came into its own when it landed on the individualist subject as its primary unit of analysis. In order to get out of the culturalist trap—in which the barest shred of cultural continuity could seem to negate arguments about the authenticity of conversions—the Protestant subject became the positive sign of cultural transformation. However, a rigid focus on the subject has meant ignoring other extremely common and striking realities of Christian lives worldwide: Protestants schism; they create ever newer denominations; and they worry about church organization. And yet these kinds of events and desires have mostly been neglected in the anthropology of Christianity. Though Protestantism has no major tradition of world-renouncing ascetics, the focus on sacred subjectivities almost makes it seem as if Protestants are nothing but desert fathers, searching for and talking to God all on their own.

When scholars see subjects forming into groups, a process of object-dissolving (Robbins 2003) starts to happen: Christian groups look too much like kinship groups, ethnic groups, socioeconomic groups, or national groups to be Christian in a meaningful sense (that is, organized around practices and theologies of Christianity).[1] H. Richard Niebuhr (1929) argued that any church is necessarily a non-Christian reduction of Christian universality organized around socioeconomic class, race, or nationality. More recently within the anthropology of Christianity, Werbner's (2011) discussion of a church schism in Botswana is mostly focused on power struggles between family members. Jebens (2006) analyses Seventh-day Adventist and Catholic denominational conflicts in Papua New Guinea as the repetition of power politics between big men (traditional leaders).

One of the most productive yet also group-renouncing veins of the anthropology of the Christian subject has been the work on the speaking subject and on Christian language use more generally. Protestants so want to lose track of the social world that they can even erase the distance between themselves and their divinities, having coffee with Jesus or engaging in other intimate moments (see especially Luhrmann 2001, 2012). Protestant talk—even Protestant ritual talk like prayer—is supposed to be direct, unadorned, natural, authentic, off-the-cuff, and without influence from others (Keane 2007; Shoaps 2002). The sacred speaking subject of Christianity is self-contained and self-referring, a native speaker voicing authentic prayers to a native God. It is a linguistic imminence that is readily parodied as religious solipsism.[2]

I counterpose the sacred speaking subject with Protestant groups for a reason. Especially when viewed by church historians under Weberian influences (e.g., Troeltsch 1912; Niebuhr 1929), Protestantism was supposed to have replaced the authority and hierarchy of the church with the (individually read) Bible. That is, the opacity of institutionalism was supposed to be replaced by the transparency of Bible reading and biblically inspired individual speech. But the troubling fact of church organization never receded as much as modernist theologians like Niebuhr would have liked. The Bible—and the speaker-reader of it—wasn't able to do away with churches, denominations, and other forms of religious sociality. New churches are created by the thousands every year in the United States alone. Learning the alphabet soup of denominational acronyms is now a standard part of fieldwork for anyone with more than a passing interest in Christianity.

From the perspective of the subject, much Protestant theology is expressed as a refusal of distance (Engelke 2007): of God, of a sacred but alien language, or of a hierarchical order. My own interest is instead with the ways in which mediations—social and semiotic projects of creating distance—are central to Christian worship. Without them, it is impossible to understand the recurrences of schism—of critical distance—that punctuate Christian lives in so many communities, or of the later struggle to produce unity in the wake of Christian criticism. As I argue below, the church as a Christian group mediates a temporary but theologically and socially important distance from God.

In this chapter, I argue for the central place of religious groups in studies of Christianity, and I want to raise a number of questions. To use some of the terminology of groupness that Christian theology provides, what does it mean to Protestants to be the Body of Christ? How does one do it? What is the relationship between the Body of Christ and the sacred speaking subject? Why is the Body of Christ, as instantiated in any one Protestant church or congregation, so seemingly unstable and prone to schism? While I approached some of these issues in general terms in the introduction, here I want to examine these issues in terms of the specific problems that Lutheran missionaries encountered in colonial New Guinea. Although they initially hoped to create sacred speakers by translating the Bible into vernacular languages, the extraordinary linguistic diversity of the north coast of New Guinea made that impossible. Soon a model of sacred church organization became the primary focus instead.

Although I use material from the Zaka circuit that Guhu-Samane communities were a part of in this chapter, this is not a history of early Guhu-Samane engagements with Lutheranism. Burce (1983) provides a detailed, rigorous account of that history, and I do not want to duplicate her work here. Instead, I use this as an opportunity to examine Lutheran mission strategies specifically in terms of regional and interethnic Christian interactions.

THE BODY OF CHRIST: CHRISTIAN GROUPS AFTER CRITIQUE

In the era of Protestantism, separation from God seems to demand both a militant critique of others through separation and a similarly militant union with others through worship. Paying attention to this moment of unity is important for differentiating Christian groups from other liberal forms of individualist selfhood, since schism and Christian group formation as described by Niebuhr (1929) looks very much like liberals dissolving and reconstituting the social contract. For example, Puritan and nonconformist debates about church structure focused on a congregation's freedom to dissent from larger Episcopal structures or freedom to choose its own pastor. As voluntary associations, Protestant churches are hard to disentangle from a liberal tradition in which groups, while important, do not detract from what Dumont (1986) calls the paramount value of individualism.

However, I argue that Christian practices can exhibit a more complex notion of groupness, particularly through models of the Christian remnant—the group that is partial but looks toward a horizon of eventual unity. Unlike the Old Testament remnant that was shattered by others, the Christian remnant, as I use it here, is the product of critique made possible by the ethical demands of Christianity. Robbins (2004b) and Meyer (1999) both discuss the ways in which Christian critique constitutes a social whole—"the past" or "tradition" or "our culture"— from which to engage in critique and form this remnant. Some of the most interesting anthropological work to date on the formation of Christian groups focuses on the ways in which the relationship of "church" to "society" is a product of critique (Barker 1993, 1996; Robbins 2004a, 2012). American evangelicals likewise emphasize Christian critiques of social forces, even if this leads to the failures, for example, of charity groups to maintain momentum or even organizational existence (Elisha 2011).

A tradition of critique does not, of course, separate Christian groups from liberal ones. However, critique and the regimentation of separateness through the differentiation of Christian groups is not the end of the story. Christian groups only become the Body of Christ in their enactment of Christian unity, a partial enactment of the unity imagined in the remnant made whole—the "church triumphant" in heaven. While certain elements of the liberal tradition have similarly positive models of incorporation (early Marx's image of "species being" to be realized in communist communities might be equivalent), political liberalism largely sees groups as instrumentalist means to individualist ends.

In the colonial New Guinea context, Christian group formation was a central part of missiological work. As I discuss below, the goal of Lutheran mission organization was to foster and then partly overcome acts of critical separation. Separation might first be from one's immediate intra-village neighbors, but then separation had to be suspended at the level of interethnic group relations. Unity—and Christianity— existed in Lutheran New Guinea only when ethnic-group animosity was suspended. This critique-separation-unification movement was supposed to be fostered by a complex organizational pattern of districts, circuits, and congregations that forced New Guinean Lutherans to walk across mountains, rivers, or valleys in order to become Christian. As I will discuss more in the second half of this chapter, the image of the separating remnant makes possible this positive formulation of Christian critique and groupness.

LANGUAGE AS TOOL VS. LANGUAGE AS SACRED SUBJECTIVITY IN COLONIAL NEW GUINEA

As I discussed above, native-language authenticity is one of the most important aspects of developing a "semiotic ideology" (Keane 2007) of immediacy in Protestant practice. In order to speak to God in the way many Protestants hope to do, one must speak as naturally and "freely" as possible. Missiological practice takes this model of freedom and fluency into spiritual territory by making native-language authenticity an attribute of true communion. Language is thus "the shrine of a people's soul" (B. Schieffelin 2007) or the "heart language" through which Christians' innermost selves can be addressed (Handman 2007). The Summer Institute of Linguistics (now known as SIL International) is a linguistics and literacy NGO that has brought this model of Christian linguistic immanence to most corners of the world. By placing teams in every extant language community in order to translate the New Testament (as well as other literature) into each person's heart language, SIL brings this model of sacred linguistic subjectivity to its methodological conclusion. Making the Gospel sound as natural as possible in the heart language in which a team works, SIL translators want to erase any sense of the translation's foreign origins. SIL teams want the New Testament to produce new Christian communities without the mediating influence of churches or organizations, and SIL as a whole has a policy against church planting.

As heirs to Luther's sanctification of vernacular languages, one might expect the Lutheran missionaries in New Guinea to give support to this sort of model of vernacular language sacredness and authenticity. And they do at certain moments, as when the 1948 Lutheran Mission New Guinea Conference Minutes includes a resolution from the executive committee affirming "the mission policy *that a tribe be evangelized in its own language*" (Conf Min 48, RES 48–71, emphasis in original). But Lutheran history in New Guinea does not always reflect this affirmation. Faced with the stunning linguistic diversity of the north coast of New Guinea (there were over two hundred languages spoken in Lutheran territory),[3] Lutheran missionaries began promulgating lingua francas with which to evangelize local people. In comparison with standard models of Protestant language, non-sacredness—as opposed to linguistic sacredness—was the calling card of the church languages that the Lutheran Mission employed.

By "linguistic sacredness," I refer to the ways that divine revelations come in specific linguistic forms (e.g., Hebrew or Arabic) or the ways that linguistic subjectivities of sincerity and authenticity can be used to make the Word "real" or affectively powerful to specific kinds of speakers (one could say, following SIL, that as a native "heart language" speaker of English, the Gospel in English speaks to me in specific, sacred ways). By any of these means, some kind of specificity is given to the language or to a speaker's subjective orientation to the language. Without this kind of specificity of linguistic form or subjective orientation, communication with God is assumed to be either impossible or extremely difficult. "Linguistic non-sacredness," as I am calling it, thus would have to be seen in the non-specificity, the lack of particularism, of a language.

When the first Lutheran missionary, Johannes Flierl, arrived on the Huon Peninsula as a representative of the Neuendettelsau Mission from Bavaria in 1886, he began working with local languages. But as the mission grew and the missionaries learned more about the ethnic and linguistic diversity of the north coast, new Lutheran communities were slotted into one of two tracks: Austronesian or non-Austronesian. Speakers of Austronesian languages were missionized in the Austronesian church lingua franca Jabem (or Yabem); speakers of non-Austronesian languages were missionized in the non-Austronesian church lingua franca Kâte. The separate Rhennish Mission, also from Bavaria, worked largely out of Madang, starting in 1887, and its missionaries promulgated the local Gedaged (also called Bel or Graged) language as a church lingua franca. After World War II, during which the Lutheran groups lost a significant number of missionaries, American and some Australian Lutherans resuscitated the beleaguered organization. The Rhennish Mission was folded into the structure put in place by Flierl, and the language of mission memoranda and reports became English, even though many of the missionaries were more comfortable in German (for more on Lutheran Mission New Guinea history, see Frerichs 1959; Reitz 1975; and Wagner and Reiner 1986).

The Lutherans thus instituted three non-sacred and non-particular church languages that would be used in its three main districts: Gedaged language in the Madang district, Jabem in the Jabem (coastal Huon Peninsula) district, and Kâte in the Kâte (interior Morobe) district. These languages were learned by missionaries and then taught to other New Guineans in Lutheran schools and churches. Kâte (pronounced COH-tay), for example, went from having two thousand speakers at the end of the nineteenth century to having roughly one hundred thousand people claiming some level of competence by 1959 (Kuder brief, 4). As the missionaries themselves admitted, competency in Kâte varied enormously, from fluent first-language speakers to those with minimal passive knowledge. The goal was not to give speakers a relationship of sacred specificity to the church languages but to enable interethnic communication and constitution of a Christian community.

Each language-defined district shared in a generalized exchange of people and resources that was made possible by the use of a lingua franca. Underneath this uniformity of language, however, there was an extensive organizational structure that divided district members into many different kinds of groups. As I note below, missionaries constantly lamented people's lack of interest in sending their young men out as evangelists or contributing to distant projects within their district. That is, the mission both codified a series of differences (outline in the next paragraph) and insisted that Christian practice meant overcoming those differences to produce a lingua franca–enabled district unity.

Districts were the largest organizational unit below the level of the mission as a whole. Districts were composed of circuits, which ideally had at least one European missionary resident. Circuits could be enormous, and the missionary might tour his circuit only two or three times a year. If a group lived far away from the circuit station, the missionary was a rare sight. Beneath the circuit level were congregations, which usually incorporated several villages. Major Sunday services would be held at the congregational seat and people would have to walk (in some cases, for several hours) in order to attend. "Native" evangelists from other circuits within the district would staff the church and school at the congregational seat. This meant that, in general, the only language the evangelist and his flock shared was the church lingua franca. Villages had elders, some of whom organized morning or evening prayer sessions and some of whom did more or less nothing.

As can be seen from this brief sketch, Lutherans were not shy about hierarchical organization and institutional bureaucracy. The Lutheran church in Papua New Guinea today retains much of this structure, a point of pride for Lutherans otherwise surrounded by the flat structures of independent Pentecostal churches. While the national creole, Tok Pisin, has largely taken over as the church language from Kâte, Jabem, or Gedaged, the use of a supra-local language to navigate this organizational order is still necessary.

The non-specificity and non-sacred character of the Lutheran church languages can be seen most clearly in a brief given to the New Guinea administration in 1959 by the Lutherans when colonial education policy was shifting toward English. The New Guinea administration had always depended upon the mainline missions (Lutherans and Catholics) to provide most of the education services and had given the missions a relatively free hand in devising curricula and methods. Lutheran Mission schools taught village children in whichever church language was used in that district, creating a younger population that was literate in the church language, able to recite Bible stories and other liturgical materials, and able to learn basic skills like numeracy. In the mid-1950s, the New Guinea administration decided that English must become the language of the colony (and the language of the eventually independent nation-state), and that education should be aimed at teaching more secular skills. The Lutheran Mission was rightly terrified that this policy would decimate not only their school system but also their church organization as a whole.

In a brief to Minister for Territories Paul Hasluck, dated October 22, 1959, the president of the Lutheran Mission, Paul Kuder, laid out Lutheran objections to the coming English-only policy, trying to make the strongest possible case for the continued use of church languages in education. Much of the brief that addresses specifics of the language history of the mission is in fact taken from an internal mission memorandum "prepared by a senior missionary on [their] staff, a man born in New Guinea, with long experience in dealing with her people and having the confidence of New Guineans and Europeans alike" (Kuder brief, 2), likely Wilhelm Flierl.[4] This was the Lutherans' primary opportunity to defend the church languages' important role in New Guinea. And yet even in this document, Kuder and Flierl give, at best, lukewarm support of the church languages, focusing only on their practical use.

In fact, Kâte and the other church languages are defended mostly for their total lack of specificity within the New Guinea context. The church languages are, for all intents and purposes, perfectly equivalent to other New Guinea languages. Given that this argument appears in a brief about the "language problem" in New Guinea and details the long struggle the Lutheran Mission had with languages, the argument adopted in the brief ironically makes language as such into something of a nonissue.

> We should get rid of the idea that the tribes lose anything when we give them a different N[ew] G[uinean] language which is "ideologically" and in most cases even structurally perfectly equivalent to their own and in which they find the equivalent of every little shade of difference of meaning which is contained in their own vocabulary. What is the difference whether "eternal life" is juju-sangang (Kâte) or gogo-gäneng (Mape) or kepkep-sili (Kuat-Hube) or andeandekatik (Komba) or mama-karingang (Naba) or alaala-tatanga (Kipu) and so forth?—When one of these languages dies out (as fortunately some of them have), no one loses anything except the linguist-anthropologists.

The "Kipu" language mentioned here is now called Guhu-Samane. In contemporary Guhu-Samane, *alaala-tatanga* is still the phrase for "eternal life" (in current orthography that uses a *q* for the glottal stop, it is spelled *qaraqara tatanga*), although it literally means "strong life." While I have not been able to check on the other languages mentioned in this quote, other Lutheran communities, such as Yopno, similarly use "strong life" to calque "eternal life" (*egapegap tebai*, James Slotta, personal communication), and it is likely these other languages do too. That is, when Lutherans did engage with the vernacular languages, they tried to make them conform to a regional standard.[5]

Note, however, that this effort to construct a language for religious discourse along lines similar to work in Africa (Meyer 1999) is, in this case, mentioned in the context of an argument against making any language sacred. Each of these languages could die out, says the author, no harm no foul (except for those secular scientists of language and culture—the linguist-anthropologists). Indeed, a reduction in the multiplicity of languages in New Guinea could only help develop both a democratic state and an ecclesiastic structure. This point is emphasized again a few pages later, when the author argues that New Guineans can learn other New Guinea languages much more quickly than they can learn English, because "[a]ll New Guinea languages have practically identical thought categories, ideas and concepts" (Kuder brief, 8). The only specificity to the New Guinea languages is their uniform distance from English.

Far from the linguistic sacred, church languages in the Lutheran Mission perspective are simply instruments for effective communication. Kâte, Jabem, and Gedaged were the best instruments to use, given the years of work that Lutheran linguists had put into devising theological vocabularies, developing and printing language-learning materials, and teaching the language to parishioners across the Lutheran territory. As a practical matter, the turn to English-language education would require institutional reorganization, retraining of personnel, and reworking of curricula.

In 1960, the colonial administration in fact mandated English-language education. Since most of the Lutheran teachers and evangelists had no knowledge of English, and since the Lutherans had few education materials for English-language curricula, their funding was slashed and their institutional organization was thrown into disarray. The mission felt betrayed by the administration that had up until that point backed and often depended upon the mission, and even many years later, the transition was still a sore spot (see Johnson 1977, 445; Hage 1986, 409).

As I mentioned above, Lutherans counted one hundred thousand people as Christians and Kâte speakers in the Kâte circuit, even as they recognized that only about thirty-five thousand of them spoke Kâte with any fluency (Kuder brief, 4). As opposed to the model of the sacred Christian speaker, the Lutheran mission was populated with sixty-five thousand semi-speakers who could nevertheless be called Christians.

For Lutherans, the goal of an independent, autonomous, and thriving church was not going to be reached through talk, or at least not through talk alone. The independent church could be reached only by creating tight linkages across the different mission circuits, with native evangelists crisscrossing Lutheran territory in a wide-ranging movement aimed to get local people beyond ethnic boundaries and into the universalism of Christian faith. But if New Guineans were to partake in this freeranging theological, economic, and geographical exchange, this sacred public could be formed only with non-sacred church languages.

I want to now turn to the ways in which the church as a hierarchical, regional, and multiethnic institution was seen as sacred and as an integral part of creating Christians and Christianity in New Guinea.

SACRED INSTITUTIONS OF UNITY

Church organization was a sacred project, one to which other forms of sacredness, like language and the speaking subject, had to be sacrificed. The Lutheran Mission decided to promulgate non-sacred church languages after World War I, when there was suddenly a great opportunity for mission expansion into the New Guinea highlands (Kuder brief, 3). Quoting again from the Kuder brief to the administration, the urgency of the post-WWI moment is clear:

> In such a dilemma, what should the mission have done? Stop the [post-WWI] expansion by force, at a certain stage, until every little tribe that had been won was neatly fitted out with every miniature institution necessary for its subsistence as a little Christian church of its own? There were missionaries who strongly favoured such a development. If they had had their way, the Lutheran Mission would probably look very nice today and make a good impression on visitors, but certainly have no part, to speak of, in the winning of New Guinea for Christ. Thank God that our mission had men of sufficient vision, initiative and energy to conceive of and carry out the one and only solution of the problem in such a super-multilingual country as the coastal parts of New Guinea, namely the development of church languages, comprising a multitude of tribes, church languages which can serve as transport systems for the lifeblood circulation of at least 50,000 or 100,000 member churches instead of 2 or 3000. (Kuder brief, 3)

The author presents the counterfactual history of Lutheranism as a parody of church organization. "Every little tribe" with "every miniature institution necessary" producing "a little Christian church of its own" is a nice dream of the ethno-linguistic sacred, but one that simply was impossible in the case of New Guinea.

SIL would disagree, of course. When SIL's Ernie Richert moved into the Zaka circuit, which included the Waria Valley, in 1957, the resident Lutheran missionary realized the challenge that SIL's "heart language" Christianity posed: if the SIL translator continued to turn the Kipu language (that is, Guhu-Samane) into a liturgical language, the local people would no longer need to be a part of the system of generalized exchange within the Kâte district that enabled congregational life (1958 Zaka Report). The Lutheran Mission was much more concerned to create not "miniature institution[s]" of Christian micro-nationalism but rather macro-institutions of church organization.

Practically, the mission required such an organization so that local evangelists could be sent out to missionize in areas beyond the reach of European missionaries, a practice that began in 1907 (Frerichs 1959, 260) and continues to this day. Theologically, this super-ethnic organization was the actual embrace of Christian universalism.

> Of much greater avail was the fact that through the church languages a large number of tribes who had been enemies or even total strangers to one another, were joined together into one large community. It is true, God had effected the union through His Word and Sacraments and through His Holy Spirit. However, that union would remain an abstract one, as it were. It could not have been properly experienced and enjoyed, nor utilized for mutual edification and for common enterprise, without personal intercourse, which was only made possible through the common language. Only that language gave the former enemies the chance to worship together, to serve one another, and to work together. (Kuder brief, 4)

Missionaries constantly emphasized cross-circuit linkages in their reports and, it would seem, in their discussions with their flocks. Missionary Schuster's 1958 report for the Zaka circuit makes this point.

> A highlight at Zaka was also the visit of Bro. Scherle and W. Fugmann on the "Mula" [a recently acquired ship] with native delegations from Malalo and Sattelberg, to our circuit meeting at the beginning of June. . . . It was symbolic: [these were] Delegates from the two congregations from where Christian evangelists had been sent to Zaka years ago: What we wanted was more contact with the Malalo congregation and if possible exchange of pupils on the Primary school basis. Although we saw that many of our natives still do not think beyond their own circuit or district it was at least one step beyond that thinking to have such a meeting. And we hope this will continue. (1958 Zaka Report)

An important statistic for annual station reports was how many evangelists each circuit had sent out to work in other Lutheran circuits. Missionaries constantly searched for suitable candidates, sent them to the appropriate Kâte- or Jabem-language evangelist schools at the coast, and hoped that they would be able to work well and for a long time in a cross-cultural situation. Many candidates, at least in the Zaka region with which I am most familiar, quickly came back, unable or uninterested in effecting the "mutual edification" that the Lutheran Missionaries so hoped for (see, e.g., 1958 Zaka Report). The laity was also supposed to contribute to this project in the form of donations to other circuits or in offering their young men up as evangelists.

When missionaries in Zaka felt that congregations were being too stingy with their money or their people, they saw this not only as a renunciation of Lutheran Mission institutions but also as evidence of a lack of true spiritual development. Note how, in the following quote from a Zaka-Garaina annual report, Missionary Dahinten is able to move from church structure to personal comportment in three quick sentences: "At some places I noticed a rather egoistic thinking as far as the stationing of church workers is concerned. There is also a lack of community amongst the people, especially in the Bubu valley. Some cases of polygamy are found and there are always illegitimate children" (1964 Zaka-Garaina Report). What keeps these three sentences from being non sequiturs is the sense that, for the Lutheran Mission, church organization itself was a sacred project, as important and as personal as the decision to be monogamous or to give birth to children in wedlock.

While the Lutherans viewed tithes of money and people as a sacred responsibility for any church hoping to one day become independent, the people of the Zaka circuit often saw such an emphasis on cross-circuit giving as a tax. Missionary Horndasch fought with his Zaka circuit members, who too often equated the sacred circuit with the secular colonial administration. Missionaries had to collect tithes when they traveled around their circuits, a process that looked to local people very much like the colonial administrators who collected taxes while on patrols. Especially for the inland groups in the Zaka circuit, who saw administrators or missionaries only a few times a year, the differences between the administrators based at Morobe Station and the missionaries based at Zaka could seem paltry. Brother Horndasch, a native German speaker, expresses his frustration at being taken for a colonial administrator in his somewhat stilted English: "But this year it was harder than ever before to get the money out of their hands for Elcong-[6] and Kâte-District-Treasury. They offer from one hand into the other and the money is still theirs. What kind of offering is this we think?— Because the missionary is the only one who collects the money for

Elcong and District Treasury they call him: 'tax-collector'. A nice name for a missionary, isn't it?" (1960 Zaka Report). This is an important moment within the archival record of local people's criticism of the Lutheran work. At the same time, we can also understand this complaint from within its Lutheran orientation to establishing a sacred unity. The problem is not a lack of individual belief or sacred speaking subjectivity but is instead a problem of refusing to overcome differences in the practice of church-constituting charity, as Augustine would call it.

Like the non-sacred vernacular languages of New Guinea, culture was largely considered an obstacle to evangelistic universality. Any particular emphasis on local culture in Lutheran Mission strategy was often oriented toward the destruction and negation of that culture. Christian Keysser—a Lutheran missionary whose influence was second only to that of the founder, Johannes Flierl—thought that culture and kinship bonds, as opposed to individualism, were especially strong in Melanesia. Therefore, conversions should be group affairs, and missionaries should initially not be too strict about dogma (Lawrence 1956, 75). After the group as a whole converted, the subtleties of Lutheran theology could follow. Keysser was, however, focused in particular on the cultural attributes that he felt were destructive and inhibiting, like sorcery.

For some areas, the greatest legacy of Keysser's non-individualist approach to Christian conversion was a general animosity toward cultural practices, usually focused on men's houses, that missionaries felt kept groups from experiencing conversions. The Lutheran missionaries referred to all men's house systems as *Balumskulten* (*Balum* cults). According to Missionary Lehner ([1911] 1935), *Balum* was the name of the men's house cult among the Bukaua people on the Huon Peninsula. Apparently *Balum* became a quasi-technical term among Lutheran missionaries for any men's house system, with special emphasis on the initiation ordeals to which elders subjected young boys. Note, then, the ways in which Lutheran analysis created the interchangeability of New Guinea languages and culture.

In the instances where men's houses were destroyed or had their sacra shown to noninitiates, local cultural practices were understood as competing against Christian influence (Tomasetti 1998; a similar example of showing men's house objects to noninitiates is in Kulick 1992, 164–65). Burce describes a Zaka missionary, Rev. Mailander, as "being engaged in an all out spiritual battle for people's souls against a powerful entity that he sometimes referred to as 'Herr Balum'" (Burce 1983,

195). As both Waria people and their missionaries suggest, the spread of the mission came with the destruction of local men's houses.

In Keysser's ideal, only a few aspects of local culture needed to be changed—like men's houses and the sorcery or feasts that they sponsored—while in other respects he felt that people could remain within their cultural milieu. This seemingly practical approach was still very transformative. First, the anchors of local villages—men's houses—were destroyed or were made substantially less powerful. Second, Keysser's technique of missionizing the society as a whole meant that even people who had not shown any particular interest in the mission were still encompassed by it, especially in the congregational structure that was supposed to organize local people, at least with respect to the mission. Although there was an initial flurry of interest in 1922, a few years after Rev. Mailander's entrance into the Waria Valley (see Burce 1983, 195), local people soon cooled to the mission and confirmations were few and far between. There was, however, little possibility of a total renunciation of the mission. Not only were many of the men's houses destroyed and sacra buried or burned, but daily life was starting to orient more and more to the mission stations. The Lutheran Mission was rapidly building practical institutions—health services, education, commerce—even if the sacred institution of the church was slower in its formation.

THE REMNANT: GROUPNESS IN A RELIGION FOR SOME AND YET ALL

Alfred Koschade, a Lutheran missionary to New Guinea, developed theological arguments for church organization as part of a Lutheran response to anticolonial Christians urging missionaries to leave their fields. Koschade works to define a church and especially an independent church in his book on the New Guinea Lutheran situation, *New Branches on the Vine* (1967). It is helpful to examine it here insofar as it focuses on the nature of Lutheran unity as an integral component of a Christianity that exceeds individualist subjectivities. In particular, Koschade argues for the importance of the church as an actual, this-worldly entity, emphasizing two points in particular. First, the visible, actual church instantiates Christian unity, but second, the visible, actual church can do this only if it is preceded by a moment of separation, what Koschade speaks of as cultural critique.

Throughout the book, Koschade pays particular attention to the moment in 1956 when the Lutheran Mission New Guinea officially became the Evangelical Lutheran Church of New Guinea. He writes that even if individual New Guineans had been in the process of becoming members of the Body of Christ since Johannes Flierl's first conversions at Simbang village in 1899, it was not until 1956 that New Guineans became a church as such. Echoing Augustine's distinction between the "visible church" of actual congregations and the "invisible church" composed of only the elect, Koschade argues that the invisible church ("the congregation of saints and true believers" [Koschade 1967, 13]), while important, is not sufficient. New Guineans—and all Christians—must also join together to constitute an actual existing community and to create an actual existing unity across difference. Koschade sees the constitution of the church body at Simbang in 1956 as a miraculous transformation (especially given his use of the primitivist trope of cannibalism so common to discussions of colonial New Guinea): "Within fifty years they had learned to look upon each other, not as potential *hors d'oeuvres,* but as brothers in the blood of Christ. Such things cannot be wrought by the power of men. It is the work of God!" (Koshade 1967, 14).

In the archival materials I consulted, a constant lament is the insufficient interest in constituting the church in exactly these ways. Potential congregational leaders are dismissed or derided for not wanting to walk for days across rivers, mountains, and valleys in order to instantiate the colonial circuit at regional meetings (see Zaka Reports for 1958, 1961, 1962, 1964). Insofar as the circuit was defined by fiat—by the church language used within it—this circuit contained within it multitudes of ethnic differences that needed to be negotiated.

But Koschade's argument covers more territory than just a call to constituting churches. He is interested in the ways in which the third-world churches (to use the language of the time) would contribute to global Christianity. "Constituted churches" are necessary to enrich the world's understanding of the Christian revelation, as each such constituted church has a perspective on the Gospel unique to its cultural and social milieu that must then be witnessed in evangelism.

This believing community exists in its own peculiar environment as it is influenced by the various sociological factors within that environment. In response to the Gospel and for the sake of its witness to the Gospel, it establishes itself as a constituted body. The proclamation of the Word to the society in which the church exists makes it necessary that this be done. The phenomenon of the younger churches, then, has been brought about under the guidance of God for the sake of the church, that is, for the preaching of the Word and the administration of the Sacraments. It is not merely a matter of organization or of autonomy or of historical development. It is a matter of theology—of the comprehension of the Word and its proclamation. For this is essentially what theology is all about. It is the church from its particular position in history and in the light of prevailing social and cultural conditions examining the Word of God which brought the church into being, for the sake of proclaiming that Word to the world. (Koschade 1967, 20–21)

This is certainly a clichéd paean to multiculturalism, given the never-specified content of the "prevailing social and cultural conditions" providing each group's unique perspective. But it is, nevertheless, an important argument for churches as the necessary institutional formations through which Christian understanding and, importantly, evangelization take root. Like Puritan arguments that Christians without covenant are so many dissected organs of the Body of Christ, Koschade enunciates Lutheran Mission sentiment that emphasizes the theological importance of what Augustine called the visible church.

Koschade later cites and agrees with the pseudo-multiculturalist missiological theories of Donald McGavran, a conservative American evangelical who had a major influence on mid-century missionary work through his books (e.g., *Bridges of God,* 1955; *Understanding Church Growth,* 1970) and his position as founder of the School of World Missions at the Fuller Theological Seminary in California.[7] McGavran (1970) actually argued against mainline missiology of the sort the Lutherans practiced. He felt that people should be converted from within their "homogeneous units" ("HUs"), what SIL would call "people groups" and what anthropologists used to call "cultures." SIL, in fact, is populated with many graduates of (or simply devotees of) McGavran's School of World Missions. McGavran's missiology closely resembles SIL's model of the ethno-linguistic sacred, in which people are converted through their heart language and constituted within a sacred speaking subjectivity. It is a model that rejects the importance of difference, or in McGavran's terms, of "crossing boundaries." How then does Koschade—a Lutheran missionary devoted to precisely this practice of crossing as a theological necessity—square his McGavran-like multiculturalism with his Lutheran insistence on confrontations with others?

Koschade is able both to emphasize "prevailing cultural and social conditions" as producing unique perspectives on the Gospel and to justify, theologically, the necessity of mediating church institutions by working with a concept of the remnant. As in Romans 11:5 and echoing Isaiah, the remnant "chosen by grace" is the shattered remains of a once-whole group. The remnant is also the group in the process of trying to reconstitute itself, what might also be called the "church militant" fighting to achieve salvation.

> [The Gospel] can never be manipulated in such a way that the [indigenous] church, which is the product of the Gospel, is made into an institution recognized and accepted by all members of the society, or with which they all identify themselves. It is the character of the Gospel that it is "a stumbling block to Jews and folly to Gentiles, but to those who are called, both Jews and Greeks, Christ the power of God and the wisdom of God" (1 Cor 1:23–24). . . . There must, therefore, always be a tension between the church and society, for the people of God are a remnant people, a pilgrim people who are but strangers and sojourners in the world. (Koschade 1967, 39)

As opposed to the ideals of SIL or McGavran—or to the models of immediacy that attempt to remove society altogether from Christian practice—the remnant emphasizes the ways in which both the church and the church's only partial overlap with society is important.

Discursively, the remnant insists on the central role of criticism—criticism of one's traditions, culture, language, or church. To return to Koschade one last time, the remnant that looks to Jesus is the group that is organized around critique. "[Christ] is both in and of the world, a product of a particular human society with all of its cultural institutions, speaking a particular language, practicing particular customs, sharing the history of a particular people; and at the same time he stands over against the world, society and culture, rejecting it and being rejected by it" (Koschade 1967, 40).

Criticism is often the engine of schism and sectarianism, producing more and more Christian groups among independent churches. But it was also important to the Lutheran missionaries, who, of course, were not trying to create schisms (at least not within the Lutheran mission). Rather, missionaries like Koschade saw the divisions within the world—many of which were established through Lutheran missionary organization—as helpful tools with which Lutherans or potential Lutherans could develop theological insights. Young evangelists sent to other circuits could recognize differences with their home circuits and use these to council their new charges. Guests at circuit meetings could help village elders understand how things were done in other parts of New Guinea. And as much as the gentlemen's agreements kept inter-mission hostilities to a minimum, Lutheran missionaries were still happy to see fights with their Roman Catholic counterparts at frontier zones become opportunities for (what they thought of as) critical work.

For example, Goilalans, whose land abuts that of Guhu-Samane communities, were officially in Roman Catholic mission territory, but the Lutheran Mission tried for years to see if the Goilalans could be convinced to come into the Lutheran fold. Missionary Schuster, usually at the request of a few local Goilalans, tried throughout the 1950s to evangelize in this area, with only occasional success. When he did have a small group to baptize, he focused on the importance of the public ritual as an engine of comparative, critical work for other Goilalans in attendance: "Then, this baptism of the first 30 Lutherans in the Goilala area was a great event in September, with many heathens and R.C. [Roman Catholic] adherents attending, of whom many of the latter returned their crucifixes given to them by the priest to him declaring they would from now on, join the Lutherans" (1957 Zaka Report). For Missionary Schuster, the public baptism service gave heathens and "R.C."s (not coincidentally paired together) a chance to engage in a critical comparison between Lutheransism and their culture or mission.

Most importantly, the remnant provides a space for understanding groups within what is otherwise a universal religion of brotherhood. The remnant is a fractured and partial group—shattered from a unity and universality—into which Christians work to place themselves. The remnant church allows for the church as an instituted community to move beyond the individualism of the Christian on the one hand or the universality of humanity on the other. The remnant church inserts distance between people simultaneously as a proof of and performance of a constituted allegiance to a critical process of transformation (Agamben 2005).

Moving back to the archival materials, the experiments with groups and with churches can be seen as different attempts to make the remnant visible, public, and constituted in the militant fight to create paths to salvation. In 1962 in the Zaka circuit, Missionary Horndasch describes a village in which the elders called roll at morning prayers, punishing those who were absent without proper excuse. Horndasch admitted it was "a bit legalistic" (i.e., Roman Catholic), but he permitted it because the village seemed to be a thriving spiritual community. Likewise, the village also conducted public confessions, a practice that caused a lot of commotion, given the tendency of local people to primarily confess sexual sins like adultery (1962 Zaka Report).

It would be easy to discount this as not even a Christian moment. Certainly scholars like Jean Comaroff and John Comaroff would consider this more an event of colonial resistance, of taking the power of the roll book from a colonial officer and putting it into local hands (e.g., Comaroff and Comaroff 1991). And indeed, that aspect of the practice cannot be ignored either at this point or in its more dramatic manifestations during the 1977 Holy Spirit revival (see chapter 4). But it is also a moment of Christian experimentation with the proper constitution of the group through which salvation might emerge. Like the circuits developed through the promulgation of church languages, the Lutherans were more than just willing to create new groups. They saw it as imperative to do so—in order to create that difference between "society" and "the church," between the critical remnant and the potential universe of Christians. A small group of New Guinea Lutherans had engaged in the roll-book experiment in an attempt to make that relationship clear.

. . .

The terms I have used in this chapter from Christian theology or history—visible/invisible church, church militant, remnant—are all terms that get more use in either Roman Catholicism or the early Reformation churches (Anglicans and Lutherans). It leaves open the question of if this emphasis on groups is really applicable only in such cases; that is, if it ignores the Pentecostal and evangelical traditions so central to the anthropology of Christianity and to later Guhu-Samane history. Is it simply the case that churches are interested either in church organization or in the sacred speaking subject?

The Lutheran Mission framed its own history as a choice between sacred speakers of the sort associated more with Pentecostal and evangelical Christianity on the one hand and sacred organization of the constituted church on the other. However, not every Lutheran missionary saw these as opposed forces. I noted at the beginning of this chapter that the Lutherans passed a resolution at their 1948 conference affirming the importance of native-language evangelization, even though they rarely worked with native languages in the Kâte district. Other facts also point to ambivalences about languages and linguistic authenticity in the Lutheran archival records. First, early Lutherans were great scholars of Huon Peninsula anthropology and linguistics (Otto Dempwolff, the first person to suggest the Austronesian language family, was actually a doctor with the Lutheran Mission who studied the linguistic research of his mission colleagues). Christian Keysser, as I noted above, believed in working within the terms of local culture to enact conversions, although that often had the practical effect of creating a missionary focus on finding the right cultural practices to banish (Lawrence 1956; Tomasetti

1998). Lutheran missionaries used local languages for evangelization in the highlands, where speech communities tend to be larger. And other than the problems in the Zaka circuit, Lutherans were very supportive of SIL's work in New Guinea (see 1960 Conference Minutes).

Further, the remnant is not just a Lutheran concern. Even McGavran's or SIL's models of linguistic imminence presuppose moments of separation in which a remnant is forged. McGavran argues that each generation within each culture (or "homogeneous unit") must engage in its own revival in order to maintain a vibrant and authentic (read: noninstitutional) Christianity. Likewise, SIL argues for the importance of native language evangelism from within the linguistic economy of power and prestige of the nation-state. The critical act of empowerment for minority cultures within a nation-state is the sacralization of the ethno-linguistic group that takes place through New Testament translation.[8] Odd as it may seem from a secular perspective, both McGavran and SIL members (e.g., Nida 1954) saw their missiological models as anticolonial, in that they provided local peoples with spiritual tools of emancipation and critique (Handman 2010b). That is, the remnant is a widely available model for Christian critique and group formation.

I followed Troeltsch, Niebuhr, and any number of Western Christians in pitting church institutions against linguistic authenticity, but is this necessary? If the Lutherans, on the one hand, develop their theologies of remnant groups, and McGavran and SIL, on the other hand, can depend upon the authority of native language and culture to anchor their work, is there any use to this distinction?

I argue there is a useful distinction here, although it requires a slight reformulation of some of the terms. The major difference between Lutheran and SIL missiology might instead be the ways in which the remnant is memorialized and carried through time (see Agamben 2005, 53 ff. for a slightly different discussion of the temporal aspect of the remnant). For Lutherans, cognizance of the separation and attempts at reunification are crucial. The church remains a mediating force throughout Christian life (at least on this earth) as the institution that performatively enables separation and unification. For SIL or other McGavran-inspired groups, the goal of native language authenticity of Christian discourse suggests that once completed, the critical act of separation can be sublimated in attempts to forge connections with God. What Bialecki (2010) refers to as the opposition between church and revival here needs to be understood in terms of the ways in which Christians conceptualize their own processes of transformation.

The ethnographic case of the Guhu-Samane—heirs of the Zaka circuit discussed here—helpfully points to the ways in which both emphases can be present in a Christian community. In the forty-five years since most Guhu-Samane schismatically split with the Lutheran church in the wake of an SIL-inspired Holy Spirit revival, new churches have appeared with a regular insistence. Sometimes the post-revival lack of unity is lamented. Today people scoff at how strange and foreign the Kâte language sounds as a language of prayer, but still they appreciate the district-wide unity and connections that were made possible by it. And yet the qualities of the separating remnant, of the militant fight to create the group through which salvation can occur, is not something they would give up. Schism is their form of critique—political, religious, and organizational.

Guhu-Samane Christians work to maintain a sacred speaking subjectivity that emphasizes immediacy through their history of SIL Bible translation. But they also maintain this spirit of Christian critique, given institutional form in the models of groupness developed by the Lutheran mission, where sacred church structure trumped the sacred speaking subject. Guhu-Samane Christians oscillate between enjoyment in and shame in the denominational fights in which they engage. In their moments of enjoyment, they seem to be harkening back to the kinds of organizational theologies with which the Lutheran mission first introduced Christianity to them. And as I argue in chapter 6, even their translation work does not erase the historical mediations of denominational splits. In fact, the practices of translation in Guhu-Samane churches highlight the ways in which they have historicized their own heart language through ongoing translation work.

Ruth Marshall (2009, 143–44, 163–64) argues that born-again Christianity in Nigeria does not project an identity. Within messianic time, as discussed by Agamben (2005), being a Christian is, if anything, the negation of all identities. But as Marshall also notes (165), this renunciation of identity is not equivalent to a renunciation of community—nor, I would add, of the importance of groups like churches. Churches certainly can be identity groups. In fact, that is usually all they are assumed to be. But as I have tried to argue here, churches can be other things entirely: constituted perspectives on Christian revelation that bring others to greater understanding, places from which to launch critiques, mediating institutions that historicize the possibilities of salvation, partial constitutions of divine unity.

Identity groups often tend to assume or aim for stability and permanence. Protestant churches do not necessarily have the same goal.

Stephen Foster (1991, 185) says that it was a Puritan axiom that "separation did not automatically beget reformation," holding out the hope and possibility for further schisms to come. "Once reformed, always reforming" as Luther put it. As the long history of Melanesian anthropology has taught, the duration of a group's existence should not be seen as an index of its importance. Groups organized around events rather than ethnic identities are, in fact, the Melanesian norm (Wagner 1974; Strathern 1988). Protestant Christianity has been partly responsible for the sedimentation of ethnic groups in Melanesia, but practices of Christian critique have made the remnant—the ongoing work of separation and reunification—possible as well. This is evident in the many denominations and schisms that occur in Melanesia and across the global south. It is because of their impermanence and overwhelming capacity for proliferation that I attend to these churches in the following chapters.

CHAPTER 2

Linguistic Locality and the Anti-Institutionalism of Evangelical Christianity

The Summer Institute of Linguistics

In the contemporary memorialization of the 1977 Guhu-Samane Holy Spirit revival, people emphasize the power of the SIL New Testament translation to bring on the revival. Just as important, people also speak about the effectiveness of the translation-inspired revival to bring about "real change" as contrasted with the utter ineffectiveness of either the colonial administration or the Lutheran Mission to do the same. I leave it to later chapters to focus on what speakers mean when they are talking about "real change." In this chapter, I want to approach the methods and theologies of SIL through the comparison set up by the memories of the revival. Why do people conflate a colonial state and a colonial mission on the one hand, and why do they contrast them with a Bible translation in a local language on the other? How do states and state-like institutions come to be compared with a vernacular language biblical text?

I argue here that when Guhu-Samane Christians memorialize the revival in these comparative terms they are voicing aspects of SIL and evangelical missiology rooted in an anti-institutionalism and a rhetoric of liberal choice. For SIL and other midcentury American evangelical movements focused on the developing world, conversions had to be created outside of the coercive forces of the state, since according to missionaries, such conversions tended to keep people un-Christian, turn them into syncretists, or make them susceptible to other malignant forces in global politics (Communism and violent nationalism, in particular).

SIL's ambitious project of having New Testament translations in every viable language in the world required a delicate balance between locality and universalism.

I refer to this form of missiology as Christian liberalism. It is liberal in the sense that it depends upon critical debate, either with oneself or with others, to be successful. In this model, adults are all equal in the sense that one person cannot legitimately determine the religious choices of another person. Rather, a person must come to Christianity on his or her own, through a process of informed inquiry and the search for answers. Colonial churches that divided up colonies by gentlemen's agreements—making this part of New Guinea Lutheran and that part Catholic—took this form of freedom away from potential converts.[1]

If all adult humans are equal, this is largely because they are all equally less powerful than God. Unlike secular forms of liberalism that confine the dramatis personae of rational, critical debate to humans, Christian liberalism allows for other kinds of agents to influence subjects through processes like inspiration, in addition to rational thought. That is, God can compel a person to convert. Even with the addition of God (or the Holy Spirit) into the drama of conversion, however, liberal Christian missiology could still be considered a practice that tries to avoid coercion. When scholars speak of coercion they most often speak of the illegitimate use of physical or social force. But if one's sociology includes God, then God's use of direct intervention in a person's life (by way of inspiration or direct communication) cannot be coercive. As the King of Creation, in this model, God cannot act illegitimately. Making someone open to hearing God's voice and reading the Bible without coercion from *other humans* is the central concern.

In addition to a commitment to avoid coercive force, Christian liberalism shares another basic tenet of secular political liberalism: an emphasis on developing the linguistic conditions of possibility for rational debate. Enlightenment thinkers and their heirs have a long history of defining the formal terms of critical thought through analysis of language and culture. From Locke (1979) to Ogden and Richards (1923), from Herder (1966) to Whorf (1956), people have long tried to establish the conditions for the most rational possible language or the ways that language influences rationality. For SIL, this emphasis on the conditions of possibility for rational debate centered on creating linguist-translators who would be able to put God's word into local peoples' languages and, to a lesser extent, their cultures.

As I argue below, language becomes an organizing principle of people that is both God-given and natural. Different languages might be a punishment for the hubris of building the Tower of Babel, but those languages are still outcomes of God's intervention in the world and therefore still have some relationship to the divine. That is, God's creation of linguistic diversity makes translation both necessary and possible. But just because something is God-given does not mean it cannot be considered part of nature. Indeed, for nineteenth-century evangelicals, nature was one of the premiere places to meditate upon the enormity of God's creation. As a natural phenomenon, language can be understood using the scientific principles employed for the study of other natural phenomena and can be free from the taint of human coercive influence (even if it is used by humans). The years of work required for this kind of missiological strategy was deemed necessary for the cultivation of a noncoercive, anti-institutional, and even anticolonial form of Christian evangelization.

In this chapter, I argue that SIL has to be understood in terms of Christian liberalism, in the sense defined above. I do so first by examining aspects of the "church growth movement," a parallel twentieth-century missionary methodology that elaborates aspects of SIL principles. The church growth movement hoped to allow potential converts to "be themselves" while also becoming Christian. That is, they wanted to avoid coercive political or social institutions like churches and missions and instead foster what they considered natural structures of local life that would allow for authentic and noncoercive conversion. This leads to a problem: which aspects of the self, configured in terms of social structure or linguistic structure, can remain throughout this self-critical project of conversion? Can social structures that appear, from the missionary perspective, as immoral be used in this conversion process? SIL methodology develops a particular answer to this question based upon the disciplinary boundaries of American linguistics. By maintaining language and linguistic structure as the core of the self, through which knowledge and understanding of God's Word can develop, SIL methodology establishes the parameters of authenticity and constancy. By following Bloomfieldian models that largely left culture outside of the definition of language, the linguistic self could then critique the cultural self.

Eugene Nida developed the "dynamic equivalence" model of translation that SIL teams used for much of the twentieth century. At first glance, it seems to be a textbook example of what Venuti (1995) terms "domesticating translation." A domesticating, dynamically equivalent translation works to put the translated text into local terms rather than asking receptor-language readers to understand the text in its own, foreign terms. However, this moment of domestication is just the first moment of engagement with an SIL translation (at least, under ideal circumstances). Part of the goal of a dynamically equivalent translation is to create a text that produces in the reader the same response that "original" readers had to the text. In the case of the New Testament, this should be a response of critical questioning of one's life and one's cultural practices. In that sense, SIL translations are "foreignizing," inducing in the reader a comparative and evaluative habit. The New Testament has to have an "afterlife" of citation, comparison, and analysis (Benjamin 1968a; Richter 2011), although that depended upon a translation that was "domesticating."

Nida's model of translation depends upon both a scientific sense of linguistic structure as well as a specifically Christian sense of Godly inspiration. "Clear, accurate, and natural" translations of the New Testament are made possible through the scientific, universal meta-language of linguistic description that allows the linguist to compare different languages with one another. At the same time, though, divine inspiration is necessary to help ensure that New Testaments structured by local terms are still capable of producing the effect that the New Testament had for the "original readers," that is, conversion to Christianity. Scientific concepts of structure mean that the New Testament can be transmitted in noncoercive, noninstitutional terms, while theories of divine inspiration mean that New Testament readers can feel the effects of God's (legitimate) demands upon their hearts. This latter project—not necessarily encoded linguistically—then creates the conditions for readers' critical reflections upon their own local circumstances, cultures included.

If the foreign translator depends upon his or her own access to linguistic science and divine inspiration in order to create a successful translation, this translator also depends upon a model of linguistic subjectivity that secures authenticity via a speaker's native language and not necessarily the local culture. The domesticating aspect of SIL translations depends upon a concept of an immediate and intimate linguistic self, such that talk produced in one's native language (what was at one point called one's "heart language" in SIL terms) is affectively powerful and denotationally accurate. Using the two functions of language most commonly ideologized in American discourse, it sets the ground for referential and emotional understandings of the New Testament. The foreignizing aspect of SIL translations, however, depends upon a concept of mediating distance between the linguistic self and one's cultural practices. With the proper understanding of the text, potential Christians (that is, New Testament readers) can embark on projects of critical reflection. Dividing the task of translation into these two domains, in which linguistic immanence motivates the reader himself or herself to engage in mediating cultural critique, allows SIL translators to engage in what they consider a noncoercive, non-colonial, and anti-institutional form of liberal evangelism. They provide the text in terms that make it comprehensible to local readers, and those local readers do the rest.

CHURCH GROWTH AND CHRISTIAN LIBERALISM: LOCALITY IN NONCOERCIVE EVANGELISM

Mid-century American evangelical missiology was framed as a response to the nineteenth-century model of mainline missions figured as welfare states (the Lutheran Mission New Guinea would be a perfect example). As opposed to the perceived excesses of the older model of colonial institution building, postwar American missionization did not want to be colonialist. Local people would be offered a choice in religious affiliation, and in thus avoiding the coercion of state forms, they would also remain authentically themselves. The use of the local language helped to guarantee this. The only operative forces would be the power of the Bible itself and the guiding hand of the Holy Spirit.

> A translation of the Bible provides the best foundation for missionary work. With the Word of the Lord in the vernacular of the people, "the missionary says . . ." gives way to "God says . . .". Then babes in Christ grow as they feed on the "milk of the word." Then believers have a victorious "It is written . . ." for the time of testing. Then native teachers are armed with "the sword of the Spirit which is the word of God." Then are founded indigenous churches on the "word of God which liveth and abideth forever."[2]

The coercion of the colonial missionary is replaced in this model with the self-authorizing, internally persuasive Bible in the local language.

Although SIL's initial formation in the 1930s and incorporation in 1942 precedes some other cognate missionary movements originating in the United States under the name "church growth" (for major titles in this field, see Nida 1954; McGavran 1955, 1963, 1970; Tippet 1967, 1970; Kraft 1979; but also Allen 1912), these other movements share a number of overlapping members and objectives. The focus in SIL was on language as the key to authentic conversion (as I discuss in the second half of this chapter; see also Handman 2007), while the primary focus of the church growth movement was on understanding local social structures as objects not to be overcome but to be used in Christian conversion. In either case, the key to this authenticity was the structuredness of local life. When the (universal) content of Christianity was put into the structure of local language, the transmission of the message would be much more successful than missiological techniques that (coercively) force people out of their linguistic and cultural structures.

Donald McGavran, the main force behind the church growth movement, felt that previous missionaries had tried to work against culture, and they had therefore not been very successful in creating new Christians. "Tribal structure everywhere is the enemy of church growth—till the church gets inside the tribe, when structure often becomes its great friend" (McGavran 1970, 132). Getting missionaries "inside the tribe" would create astronomical growth of Christianity. For both SIL's language focus and the church growth movement's anthropological focus, scientific study of "native" people would be the key. The native is no longer the one who needs education; the missionary is instead.

The church growth movement was initially focused almost entirely on the developing world. So much so that after it became a major force in American evangelical missions, McGavran's supporters insisted that his major work, *Understanding Church Growth,* be revised to be relevant to a project of re-churching the developed world. He did so in 1980, but it was his protégé at the School of World Missions at the Fuller Theological Seminary, C. Peter Wagner, who really took up the project of church growth for the developed world. Both McGavran and Wagner came under criticism from mainline Christians for their heavy use of statistics and numerical counts of church growth, which struck some as being too much like a business model to be appropriate for Christianity. But in the evangelical world, the church growth movement was mainstream by the 1970s, when some of its main principles were ratified in 1974 by the First International Conference on World Evangelization (a.k.a. the Lausanne Congress, which produced the Lausanne Covenant), Billy Graham's conservative Christian response to the World Council of Churches. United States mega-churches organizing members of into small groups of identity-based believers (small groups for Christian teens, Christian cat lovers, Christian dog lovers, ad infinitum) is a further elaboration of the church growth model that was originally aimed at local cultures in the developing world (see Bielo 2009 for an ethnography of small group Bible study in the United States).

In this section I outline the missiological methods of the church growth movement. Both SIL and the church growth movement come out of the same American context and have a number of institutional and personnel overlaps.[3] But because the church growth movement is more elaborate and more idealistic in its discussion of the process of conversion and subsequent church formation, I use the church growth literature to connect SIL's theory of translation to evangelical anti-institutionality that creates ethno-linguistically defined churches. Put another way, I show how language and social structure are ideologically constituted as "natural" objects such that ethno-linguistically defined churches are seen as anti-institutional and post-denominational configurations of Christians.

Eugene Nida (1914–2011) is institutionally and intellectually a bridge between SIL and the primary leaders of the church growth movement. He worked initially via SIL in Mexico but left (for reasons discussed below) in order to head the American (later, United) Bible Society. He published *Customs and Cultures* (1954) as a primer in the relatively new field of anthropology for missionaries about to do work overseas. His book goes over some of the main topics of mid-century anthropology (myth, ritual, social organization, etc.) and demonstrates how strange practices can actually make sense if placed within an overall, structured context. In fact, he says, many of these seemingly strange practices can express Christian concepts like love or charity.

Nida argues that many of the things that Americans think of as important and universal aspects of Christianity are actually manifestations of Western culture rather than biblical truth. As with SIL methods, Nida suggests that it is the Western missionary who must educate himself (to use the pronouns of the day), not the "native." Missionaries have to educate themselves on two scores: first, in understanding the cultural—rather than biblical—reasons for many Western Christian traditions; and second, in understanding the cultures of local people. Christianity could be respectfully imparted to these natives if missionaries would work with the local culture's proto-Christian practices rather than force on them Western versions of Christianity.

Donald McGavran, who grew up in and missionized in India, wrote a series of books (most importantly *Bridges of God* [1955] and *Understanding Church Growth* [1970]) that focused less on anthropology as such and more on developing a strategy of localization in which missionaries target "homogeneous units," groups of people who are living within a single social and cultural milieu. McGavran's antagonists in these books are the missionaries of mainline denominations who evangelize from overbuilt mission stations. Mission stations that focus on health and primary education merely try to make Westerners out of the natives. This not only separates potential converts from their families and coresidents (often by making the mission station the center of their lives), but it also makes people "cross boundaries" beyond their homogeneous units, something that McGavran felt people rarely want to do. McGavran focused on how to convert people without making them cross geographical, social, or cultural boundaries—how to find Christianity in place.

The timing of the church growth movement is important to understanding how it came upon culture or social structure as the key to globalizing Christianity. Both McGavran and Nida began their books by commenting upon the new era in which missions would have to be conducted. They were at a "hinge of history" (McGavran 1970, xvii), a moment when the masses would have more political power than ever before. With Europe weakened after World War II and chastened by decolonization, these men felt that it was up to America to make allies and converts of the masses. They would not and, given the political situation, could not do so using the rough tactics of colonialism, and so they would have to act in ways that would be recognized by local people as polite, respectful, and locally appropriate.[4] Moreover, with Communists ready to swoop in to align new nations with them, there was a Cold War urgency to the entire task. The main authors of the church growth movement wanted to create a form of missionization that would allow Christians from the developed world to move into an area, convert people without alienating them from their local culture, start a revival that the local people themselves would maintain, and then move on. Culture became a theological and methodological key to postwar conversion efforts. Although the SIL methodologies required a much longer stay in a given era, the SIL goal was similar to McGavran's: offer nothing but the Bible in a locally appropriate fashion. *Not* providing health care, economic aid, or church structures the way the Lutheran Mission New Guinea did became a more humane, less colonial form of missionization.

This kind of missionary practice was based on the assumption that Christianity existed in two different forms: universal or essential Christianity, as described in the Bible, and actually existing groups of

Christians who intertwine essential Christianity with their own cultures. The problem is not, though, culture as such. The problem is culture that parades as a universal, as in mainline liberal missions that go overseas to create good Christian citizens of Europe, rather than good Christian tribalists of "Africasia" (McGavran's ungainly blend of *A*frica, Latin Am*e*rica, and A*sia*).

Using a line from cultural anthropology, these men argued that every culture has been perfectly adapted to fit local circumstances. That is, every culture answers a set of universal questions or needs in ways that make sense for a given context (Oates 1992; Kraft 1979). What the missionary has to impart is that God and Christianity can answer these universal questions better (e.g., in giving eternal life) and yet can do so in ways that accord with the local context.[5] Part of the way in which missionaries allow essential Christianity to answer local questions is by giving people minimal biblical teachings. The process of revelation and development is then appropriate for the people of that area, because the only entities involved will be the local people, the scriptures, and the Holy Spirit. Adherence to essential Christianity was guaranteed, because these authentic local people—who had not been confused by being forced to become Western at mission stations—would be able to hear the guiding voice of the Holy Spirit (McGavran 1970). Maintaining authentic local identities also means creating authentic Christians through revivalist movements. As in the multiculturalist discourses in settler states that Povinelli discusses (2002), local people have to "remain themselves" even as they conform to nonlocal demands to change.

These men often went back to a Pauline precedent, emphasizing the methodology of being "a Jew to Jews, a Greek to Greeks," as 1 Corinthians 9:20 puts it (see also Allen 1912). Because the Old Testament was God's revelation "translated" into Jewish cultural forms, Jews need to maintain their Jewishness in order to fully understand it. Because the New Testament (especially the corpus of Pauline epistles) was God's revelation "translated" into Greek forms, Greeks need to remains Greeks. Because tribal people of Africasia are like the ancient Jews (a common refrain in American evangelical missions, elaborately addressed in Kraft 1979, see also Handman 2007 and chapter 8, below), they can read and understand the metaphors and idioms of the Old Testament best. God is figured here as the first domesticating translator, adapting his message to suit his audience. Since God's nature does not change, the Old Testament, combined with the revelation of Jesus, can be just as conducive to creating Christians as the (Greek/Western) New Testament can be.

In such a framework, culture and social structure seem to be less like institutions of human authority to which issues of choice and coercion would apply and more like locally specific contexts of natural life. That is to say, the more culture could be construed as part of the natural world, the less it seemed like something that needed to be attacked as an enemy of liberal self-determination. Nevertheless, culture was not entirely off the hook. Even if culture is a God-given and universal fact of human existence, it is still partially a product of man's free will, especially the free will to be moved to immoral acts and customs. In that sense, aspects of culture would have to be changed in order for Christian principles to flourish.

Unlike many of their contemporaries in cultural anthropology (see Robbins 2007), McGavran and others believed that radical cultural change was possible, specifically through the interventions of the Holy Spirit. As cultures change, each generation will create its own church through its own revival movement. Each such church will have a slightly different insight into the nature of God, and eventually cultural differences will be reduced as everyone benefits from the diversity of local ethno-theologies that offer unique but integrateable perspectives on God's total revelation (Kraft 1979; Sanneh 1989). Cultures will converge as all Christians come to outlaw practices like polygamy, an example discussed by Nida (1955), McGavran (1970), and Kraft (1979). All of the authors agree that men could be accepted into a church while still polygamists (a departure from previous mission practice), but that this practice should be allowed only in the first generation of a church. Not only would this save women from being thrown into prostitution, as happened sometimes when a mission required that a polygamist divorce multiple wives, but it would be another way in which Christianity was being offered to people without having them "cross cultural boundaries." Of course, this proto-multiculturalism has its limits and certain practices were deemed absolutely unintegrateable with a Christian life (then, as now, an important limit of multicultural acceptance was female genital mutilation [Nida 1955]).

In this image of missionization, there are no historical denominations or large-scale institutions supporting these bundles of believers, just locally appropriate versions of Christianity that emerge from revival movements in each context. It is a post-denominational world where changing generational and cultural contexts keep churches from ever being institutionalized, made into static identity markers rather than active groupings of Christians swimming in the transparency of local context. Every church is a sect (Niebuhr 1929; Weber 1978), a revivalist voluntary association in which Christianity and contexts are perfectly matched, with new churches formed for each generation.

Local people convert to Christianity as part of their social groups in large-scale revival movements, making group-based "multi-individual decisions" to convert (McGavran 1970), a phrasing that tries to split the difference between the reification of culture as the appropriate and naturalized target of Christian evangelism and the individualism that Christianity demands. As natural entities that can be parsed through scientific analysis, these people groups in which conversions occur are transparent: missionaries can compensate for local particularities with adjustments to how the Christian message is transferred. As natural entities that are autochthonous, these people groups are not subject to coercion: local people can continue to "be themselves" while they convert.

The church growth movement is an idealistic model of minimalist missionization. The actual work of evangelism requires much more than what McGavran suggested in his seminal books. SIL translators, who come close to instantiating a church growth model, usually spend more than a decade on a New Testament translation. And yet the principles of church growth—autonomy, liberal choice, and anti-institutionalism—are strongly visible in SIL methods. Moreover, SIL's focus on language as the natural context for conversion seemed to help translator-missionaries to avoid some of the moral issues of a more culture-focused approach, which could be construed as supporting what missionaries thought of as immoral practices such as polygamy. That is, language did not seem to have the same inherent moral charge that culture did. It could more easily fit into a scientific perspective of naturalized, and thus noncoercive, context. In the rest of the chapter, I look at how SIL uses language and linguistics in particular to put some of these Christian liberal principles of missionization into practice.

THE LINGUISTICS OF CHRISTIAN LIBERALISM: EVANGELISM WITHOUT MISSIONIZATION IN SIL

SIL narrates its own history by beginning with its founder, William Cameron Townsend, selling Bibles in Guatemala during World War I and realizing that national languages like Spanish were inadequate for reaching vernacular-speaking indigenous populations. As enshrined in SIL history, one Guatemalan indigenous person challenged Townsend, asking, "If your God is so great why can't he speak my language?" (Benge and Benge 2000, 57; for more on Townsend, see Wallis and Bennett 1959; Svelmoe 2008; Aldridge 2012). How can people participate in rational, critical debate about their spiritual futures if they do not even have access to a comprehensible version of the text to be considered?

From this encounter, Townsend imagined an organization that would translate, print, and distribute New Testaments for languages that sat far below the top-and-center standard languages of nation-states. He eventually hoped that his organization's work could provide New Testaments in all the world's unscriptured languages, a patchwork of small, subnational, and often "tribal" communities. "We are seeking the lost tribes, the remote, unreached, the unnoticed peoples of the world, including the small tribes."[6] New SIL members all went through a survival-skills course called the "Jungle Camp" in the early years, since the target communities for SIL work were assumed to be in rural, out-of-the-way, "jungle" places.

In 1934, Townsend convened the first summer camp in Arkansas to teach students basic linguistic analysis. At the next summer sessions, in 1935 and 1936, Eugene Nida and Kenneth Pike, soon to be the guiding lights of SIL, attended, and they returned in subsequent years as teachers at the camp. Every year the camp attracted more students, who quickly began work in Mexico with indigenous communities. From these modest beginnings (which are covered in more detail in Aldridge 2012), the Summer Institute of Linguistics has grown exponentially. As of 2014, there are 5,500 members of SIL worldwide, who are actively participating in 2,590 language projects (involving literacy and script development as well as translation) reaching a potential audience of 1.7 billion people.[7] With roughly 800 SIL members in Papua New Guinea, SIL Papua New Guinea is one of the largest branches of this global organization. I discuss the beginnings of SIL in (Papua) New Guinea in the next chapter.

If Anderson (1991) equates the beginnings of the imagined communities of nation-states with the production of orthographies, books, and other print-capitalist media, SIL was organized to create the sociolinguistic context of micro-nation-states for each tribal community in which it worked. However, Townsend was not trying to foster micro-nationalist movements (SIL has a policy of cooperation with host governments [see Stoll 1982; Aldridge 2012]). The organization of a language into something equivalent to a national standard at the local level was an unintended consequence of what Townsend and others thought was just a process of providing access to scriptures in local languages.

Creating institutional forms of any kind—either sacred ones like churches or secular ones like nation-states—was anathema to American evangelical missionization.

An important component of SIL's ability to operationalize the conflicting demands of the church growth model of missions is the partial separation of language-based issues of immanent understanding through heart language translation with evangelistic ones of mediating, critical debate about Christianity and culture. Language is imagined in this model as a noninstitutional, authentic core of the self that determines the conditions for proper understanding of the revealed truth of the Bible. The translation project has two component parts: domesticating translations allow vernacular-language readers the chance to understand the Bible, and this understanding leads to critical reflection. Translations need to be domesticating in order to access this linguistically defined authentic core of the self, but the proof that they have reached this core self is the critical self-reflection that they engender. This theoretical bifurcation of the translation project has an institutional existence that allows for certain tensions and ambiguities within the SIL family of organizations.

One of the most controversial binaries of SIL's existence is its organizational one. Most (but not all) members of SIL are also members of the Wycliffe Bible Translators (WBT). The dual membership is as strategic as it is controversial. Members of SIL are known in their home countries largely as members of WBT. They generally raise funds for themselves as Bible translators specifically. However, members of SIL are known in their host countries largely as members of SIL. In this role, they are part of a worldwide scientific literacy and linguistics NGO helping host governments by creating literate citizens with a healthy sense of ethnic pride from of the "tribal" peoples who might otherwise be disaffected from national life. The contracts that SIL (but not, note, WBT) sign with host governments may mention that Christian literature will be translated, but in controversial cases, like SIL's relationship with Peru, the Christian aspects of SIL's work can be heavily downplayed in the contract (Aldridge 2012).[8] (In Papua New Guinea, the government celebrates and encourages SIL's Christian work.) Legally and financially, SIL and WBT are separate entities. Moreover, SIL and WBT have different models of communicative interactions: SIL works within the world of linguistics as science, creating the conditions for engaged citizens who can participate in national life; WBT works within the world of Christian communication, where God, the Bible, and forms of sacred inspiration may (legitimately) compel people to convert or be born again.

Given the vastness of the SIL/WBT family of organizations (which includes aviation and other support services), SIL members often argue that SIL itself is not a particularly coherent organization. What they mean by this is that SIL translators largely spend their time away from other SIL members in their local allocations and are largely on their own to fund their own work via personal networks of home-country donors. From the outside, SIL seems to have a considerable institutional presence in places like Papua New Guinea, and its members have considerable similarities via their Christian and linguistic training. However, my own interactions with SIL members suggests that they largely see themselves as a very loose-knit organization of people with a wide range of Christian commitments. This ambivalence about their institutional existence, I argue, is an outgrowth of a larger methodological commitment to language as a natural, scientifically analyzable entity that does not share the same kind of institutional (that is, coercive) features of churches, missions, or other colonial groupings.

In the mid-twentieth century, SIL leaders described the explicit projects surrounding languages as ones that simply organized an element of nature (language). Even though, as I argue here, many languages in which SIL works are constructed through translation projects, SIL translators thought of their work in terms of simply "reducing" speech to writing (e.g., Pike 1947; and see quotation below)—of transposing language from one medium to another without having any effect on the language other than adding biblical texts to its corpus. This agnostic relationship to language emerged, for example, in a 1956 meeting between Paul Hasluck, then minister for territories in Australia, and a number of SIL leaders who were negotiating SIL's entrance into New Guinea. "At one stage in the interview, Mr. Hasluck asked if we advocated trying to preserve the native languages. Our reply to this was that we did not regard it as our duty to either preserve or to destroy the best native languages, but simply use them, as long as they existed, as the best possible bridge into the benefits of our language and heritage. We said that we felt we had no right to take away from the natives the heritage of their own language."[9] Although reminiscent of the Lutheran mission's pragmatism detailed in the previous chapter, this comment depends upon a different model of the role of language in missionization. Local languages will not be saved, but they will be used wherever they are in use. Local languages are then part of the "natural" local context that secure a form of personal authenticity, not projects in and of themselves. Of course, language becomes a project soon enough, and I hope to document how this happened in the Guhu-Samane case in the following chapters.

Wanting to avoid the institutions of churches and missions, SIL members focus primarily on language as a natural entity available to scientific, structural analysis. By policy, SIL is not a church-planting organization, and members shy away from associating themselves too closely with any one church in areas where several churches are already established. When James Dean, the head of the nascent SIL New Guinea, came to the 1960 Lutheran Mission annual conference, his explanation of the organization's goals was noted in the conference minutes in these terms:

> *Building the Indigenous Church:* The SIL is not interested in direct Bible-teaching. Of course, teaching takes place in discussion of the Word around the translation table. Normally it is the believers who have helped in the translation work who become the leaders in the new tribal Christian community. In the Tzeltal tribe of Mexico a strong church has developed in this way. "We feel we must specialise in language reduction and Bible translation if our task (to give the Bible to all the world's tribes in their mothertongue [sic]) is to be completed."[10]

SIL members are equipped to promote skills such as literacy and to disseminate information, which generally is the New Testament. In the same document quoted above, Dean describes SIL methodology: "The SIL is a service organisation to the tribes, to governments, and to missionary societies. The linguists' aims are limited to linguistics, Bible translation and person to person witness. The main steps are: reduce the language to writing; prepare literacy materials; teach reading; translate the New Testament and parts of the Old Testament" (59). While working with and through these other groups, Dean sees SIL work as limited to language-related issues, even if team members cooperate with governments and missions. In other words, SIL members see themselves as not creating churchly institutions of their own.

In addition to an organizational split between SIL and Wycliffe Bible Translators that allows for an emphasis on language in host countries, SIL training also helps translators to develop a focus on language issues, as opposed to theological or evangelistic ones, through the linguistic coursework and assignments translators have to complete. Indeed, Aldridge (2012, 108–9) notes that members of SIL voiced complaints in the 1950s that there was no theological training for translators even as the linguistics training became more and more thorough. Though professional linguists sometimes disparage the quality of SIL-produced grammars, it is important to point out that SIL's emphasis on scientific linguistics is unparalleled in evangelical circles. The emphasis on language and linguistics in evangelical missions is not an obvious one, and I hope to briefly sketch some of the influences at work in the history of American evangelicalism that led to this language-centric idea of missions practice.

In the late nineteenth and early twentieth centuries, modern American evangelicalism was coming into being, in part as a response to the emerging liberal theology that would eventually take over such major U.S. seminaries and divinity schools as those at Princeton and the University of Chicago. This liberal theology is itself traced back to the hermeneutic tradition of Higher Criticism coming primarily from Germany. One of the goals of Higher Criticism was to discover the historical relations between various books of the Bible, for example, the idea that Mark was probably the source for Matthew and Luke. That is to say, it deconstructed the Bible into various sources, some hypothetical and not in the canon, and as such, it turned the Bible into a historical text. To use Latour's (1993) terminology, Higher Criticism theorized that the historical authorizing "center" of the Bible might not be in the Bible itself.

In response to this perceived decomposition of the unity of the Bible, conservative theologians responded with a new evangelical movement that made belief in the divine authorship of the Bible a theological prerequisite. Conservative Christian scholarship, unlike Higher Criticism, assumed the unity of the Bible as, almost, a single linguistic utterance, interpretable within its own terms. That is to say, it projected the Bible as a unitary, given entity in need of objective analysis. Under conservative scholarship, the Bible was its own center of authority (see Crapanzano 1999; Harding 2000).

As Latour (1987, 1993) has discussed regarding the emergence of experimental science, nature, under Enlightenment assumptions, is an autonomous object and, in that sense, an object that authorizes itself. Scientific experimentation should simply make visible the secrets of that autonomous, natural world. Conservative Christian scholarship looked toward science as a way to provide the Bible with autonomous authority. A famous example from the beginning of the twentieth century was the rise of dispensationalism. According to its adherents, dispensationalism was a Baconian experimental and inductive science that took the facts at hand (i.e., the Bible) and was specifically contrasted to the deductive, theoretical, and hypothetical work of Higher Criticism (Marsden 1980, 55). Dispensationalism's goal was to "divide and classify" the ideas in the Bible, as opposed to the humanistic, philological work of Higher Criticism. In that sense, liberal Christianity became associated with interpretive disciplines in the humanities, whereas conservative Christians oriented their biblical studies toward science, in particular, natural science. Though dispensationalism itself has come in and out of popularity, some of the basic tenets that underlie it—divine authorship, unity of the biblical text, the Bible as object of scientific analysis—have remained central to the continually shifting definition of what an evangelical is in the United States (Marsden 1987).

As American scientific linguistics emerged in the early twentieth century, primarily through the work of Boas, Sapir, and Bloomfield, we see again the positing of a "natural" entity, language, which needed to be analyzed on its own terms. Linguistics, as opposed to the historical interpretive work of philology, was emerging as precisely the kind of science of language that could fit into the conservative side of the conservative/liberal divide that dominated American Christianity at the end of the nineteenth and beginning of the twentieth centuries. William Cameron Townsend, who corresponded with Edward Sapir, pushed his early students, notably Kenneth Pike and Eugene Nida, toward this scientific version of language study as an essential precondition to successful and comparatively fluid Bible translation. Townsend thought that having the skills to scientifically analyze languages would make translation easier and more accurate. The science of biblical analysis then dominant in conservative Christian circles and the science of language would be the best way to ensure translations of good quality.

With this scientific background, SIL translators have a specific image of themselves as not being missionaries in the conventional sense of the term.[11] SIL's rigorous training program for its translators is focused on linguistics and language learning, as these forms of knowledge are the most instrumental in attempts at local-language evangelism at the center of the Bible translation organization.

Today SIL schools take students through the same levels of linguistic analysis (phonetics/phonology, morphology, syntax, semantics, and pragmatics) that other graduate programs in linguistics do, although translation principles are sometimes taught alongside semantics. Translators may also take several anthropology courses and courses on the Bible, meaning that they often spend about two years in training before going to their "allocations." SIL translators also have BA degrees, either from secular universities or from Bible colleges, where recent graduates often have studied Hebrew and Koiné Greek. Once they have settled into their allocations, SIL PNG translators will have to write three linguistics papers (referred to as the organized phonological data, grammar essentials, and grammar sketch papers), one sociolinguistics paper, and two major anthropology papers (referred to as the social organization and worldview papers), as well as take exams in the language into which they will be translating the New Testament and compile a dictionary of it. It is recommended that translators spend five years after allocating just learning the local language and studying the local social and cultural situation. Scholarly knowledge has to be put in the place of native linguistic knowledge for SIL translators. When one is not communicating to or about God in one's own language, the education of the translator will be the key to opening the door.

As a liberal, procedural problem of finding the right linguistic conditions to allow for critical debate, the emphasis on language is relatively straightforward: people need to understand the Bible in order to be persuaded by it. And yet referential adequacy is not all that SIL seems to be after. In Papua New Guinea, for example, many people are fluent speakers of the lingua franca Tok Pisin, and the Bible in Tok Pisin *(Buk Baibel)* is used in churches around the country. However, the procedures of a specifically *Christian* liberalism require more than just referential adequacy; they require a route to a subjective core of the self, the self that will respond to God's interventions.

"Heart language" is the term used in older SIL materials to describe the kind of naturalized linguistic subjectivity that would be most conducive to allowing the listener to understand the Bible and its message.[12] It is one's native language, ideologized here as the path to one's heart and pointing to the idea that language is at the heart of the self. Additionally, a heart language connects language not only to the "whole self" but to a whole community of selves—for SIL, it defines the boundaries of communities (Cowan 1979, 62–63). In this sense, it is close to the Saussurian concept of *langue,* in particular, Saussure's image of language wherein each speaker has an individualized dictionary in his or her head. As later analysts have pointed out (e.g., Weinreich, Labov, and Herzog 1968), Saussure's famous dictionary metaphor constituted a foundational formulation of the relation between individual and group. That is, the group is simply an outgrowth of the fact that many individuals have similar forms of knowledge, rather than the group being an outgrowth of interactional histories. Weinreich, Labov, and Herzog criticize this dictionary metaphor as one of the reasons why historical linguistic change had not been properly theorized in terms of its social (rather than simply structural linguistic) processes.

However, I would suggest that part of the reason why heart language is such an attractive concept is precisely that it points the evangelist both to individual speakers and linguistic communities ("people groups" in missionary terms). That is, it defines groups through the knowledge that individuals have. If language constitutes a social bond, it is not so much because of a speaker's identification with or social interactions with the other members of the group but because each speaker has the same linguistic knowledge stored in her or his head. As such, heart language is both the site of epistemic ethno-linguistic group authenticity and the site of personal, interiorized truth. As a group definition, it delimits the breadth of access an SIL translator will have for a given translation program. As an individual definition, it identifies the self of the potential convert or reader. Heart language is a way to establish the people groups around which evangelical practice is structured, as well as a way to engage individual speakers. In contrast to the naturalization of culture and social structure that McGavran advocated, naturalized heart languages seem to have only positive moral valences. That is, from this scientized perspective on language, language as system and subjective core does not have much to do with the specifics of something like polygamy.

SCIENCE AND INSPIRATION AS PRINCIPLES OF TRANSLATION

If SIL organized an institution around the linguistic heart of authentic and meaningful translation, it was not until Eugene Nida (1968) developed his model of "dynamic equivalence" translation that there was a specific translation theory to accompany this organizational setup. However, the institutional bifurcation into SIL and WBT has allowed a number of ambiguities about dynamic equivalence to persist in practice and in analysis of this translation model. Nida saw the two sides of the organization—linguistic study and evangelism—as necessarily conjoined, but in many cases, both within and outside of SIL, these two emphases have been viewed as much more separable. Paying attention to this ambiguity is important to understanding the ways in which language, even within SIL, can be seen as both the immediate source of authentic selfhood and the mediating condition of critical self-reflection that, from the evangelist's perspective, ideally leads to conversion.

In dynamic equivalence translations, the source text is decomposed into underlying sentences that include the background knowledge that is assumed by the original author. It is then translated in this form into the receptor language and finally reconstituted at the "surface" level according to local genres and local readers' needs. The translation is brought to the receptor community by putting idioms and events in local terms, rather than bringing the receptor community to the translation by changing the receptor community through education or Westernization. As a theory of translation, it parallels McGavran's model of missionization.

To give an example found in a handbook used for training Papua New Guinean translators through SIL's sister organization (*BTA Handbook* 1995, section 3, 38–41), the dynamic translator can take a verse such as Mark 1:4—"John the baptizer appeared in the wilderness, preaching a baptism of repentance for the forgiveness of sins" (Revised Standard Version)—and decompose it into the following implied events and participants: "John PREACHED (a message), (John) BAPTIZED (the people), (the people) REPENT, (God) FORGIVES (the people), (the people) SIN." Putting this information into a sentence again, the dynamic translator arrives at a *revised source text sentence* on which he can base his translation: "John Preached: (people) (must) REPENT and (people) (must) be BAPTIZED so that (God) will FORGIVE (the people) who have SINNED." This process, a cornerstone of dynamic translation principles, depends upon a kind of universalization of semantic roles and assumes that these roles are, in one form or another, capable of being expressed in all languages. The method is vaguely based on transformational grammar's bifurcation of language into surface structures (the sentences we speak and hear) and deep structures (the universal grammar of all languages), wherein language-specific processes (transformations) turn the latter into the former (see Chomsky 1965 for an early statement on transformational linguistics). In this case, the original source text sentence from Mark 1:4 would be the "surface structure" while the revised source text sentence would be the "deep structure" equivalent. From this revised source text the translator could translate into the receptor language in a structurally, semantically, and culturally appropriate fashion.

Nida caused a major controversy in SIL when he seemed to move away from the standard fundamentalist claim of biblical literalism with his dynamic equivalence model of translation. Nida argued that translators work from a literal underlying text but that surface-form texts were not necessarily literal. Instead, translators must use godly inspiration to help produce an *equivalent* text—where equivalence is able to be guaranteed through structuralist linguistic principles—but not necessarily a *literal* one. "Lamb of God" might not have much effect in the Canadian Arctic, but "Seal of God" is structurally equivalent and able to produce a similar emotional and cognitive response for Inuit people that "Lamb of God" did for the initial Semitic readers/hearers. Importantly for Nida, the similar emotional or cognitive response would be a turn toward Christianity.

Ken Pike—who divided his time between SIL and the University of Michigan anthropology department—argued continuously for the importance of the scientific linguistic perspective as the way to make the Christian message available to "unreached" people groups. Linguistic science would allow translators to understand the local perspectives of the people in SIL allocations. Pike is perhaps best known within anthropology for expanding the emic/etic distinction from phonological theory into a more general model of culture (Pike 1967). An "emic" perspective is one that uses distinctions and values that are organized around a particular, local system, linguistic or cultural. An "etic" perspective is one that uses universal distinctions and values, only some of which might be in place in a local system. Structuralist linguistics allows the translator to get to the emic level, to see the world as vernacular language speakers do.

Nida's dynamic equivalence theory of translation said that understanding the emic perspective of local people is only one step in the translation process. The next step requires that the translator then move the Christian message into the emic perspective (making "Lamb of God" into "Seal of God," to use this example again). "Words are merely vehicles for ideas. They are symbols, and as such they usually have no special significance over and above the actual objects which they symbolize" (Nida 1947, 12, quoted in Aldridge 2012, 111).

But for some SIL members, this changed the Bible too much: how can the Bible be literally true and inspired if it can also be changed into an emic perspective? Do the critical demands of Christianity stay the same if they are put into an emic context in this way? From Nida's perspective, SIL members who were upset by his move away from literalism (toward dynamic rather than strict equivalence) were simply not connecting the two sides of the organization together. Scientific analysis of local conditions of communication had to be brought together with a Christian, prayerful, inspired translation, one that would produce in the reader a critical sensibility only after having developed a frame of linguistic immanence. The institutional separation from the overtly Christian and overtly scientific sides of the WBT/SIL family of organizations made it possible for controversies like this to exist. As Aldridge notes (2012, 123), Nida wanted to be a Christian scholar, not just a Christian and a scholar. Nida left SIL in 1953 in part because of the controversy around his movement away from literalism and in part because of his discomfort with the organizational separation dividing SIL from WBT. The two causes can be seen as one, however. Nida saw SIL as separating a rational but emotionally authentic perspective on language from an evangelical, critical Christian one, but dynamic equivalence theory, and translation-as-mission in general, requires their unification.

Pike and Nida, while the leading developers of SIL methodology, were controversial within SIL circles. SIL members have, at different times, felt that the organization was losing its Christian focus, given this emphasis on science, and especially given the requirements that Pike insisted on in the early years to publish a large number of papers in academic journals (Aldridge 2012, 92–93). The science of linguistics did not leave enough time for the practice of evangelism. At the same time, SIL members have also rebelled from the synthesis of Christianity and science that Nida used in dynamic equivalence translation. From Nida's perspective, the more (religiously) conservative SIL members who were concerned about the move away from literalism, which is necessary within a dynamic equivalence model, were refusing to acknowledge that God is the ultimate domesticating translator, who had already adapted his message into two different forms—in the Old and New Testaments— but who had nevertheless been able to create the critical response required by the convert.[13]

Lawrence Venuti (1995) considers Nida's dynamic equivalence theory to be a perfect example of a "domesticating" translation, one in which all of the work of mediating difference is performed by the translator rather than by the reader. Venuti considers domesticating translations, in many cases, to be a translation-based form of colonization. Particularly when the target language is a global force like English, a domesticating translation makes it seem as though the world perfectly reflects the norms and structures of English and its speakers. But even when the target language is an indigenous vernacular, Venuti suggests that domesticating translations, by blurring differences between languages and cultures, evince a colonial politics. He contrasts domesticating translations with "foreignizing" ones that highlight the structural, historical, and semantic disjunctures that trouble the translation process. He follows Benjamin (1968a) in finding the beauty in disfluencies. While Benjamin considers this part of a messianic project of redemption, Venuti secularlizes foreignizing translation into a project of linguistic decolonization. Critique, Venuti argues, is produced through foreignization, not domestication, where the reader must work to navigate difference.

In contrast to Venuti, Nida saw domesticating translations as the less colonial, since they do not make potential readers "cross boundaries" or have to become Western. Domesticating translations are, for Nida, populist translations for the uneducated. Dynamic equivalence translations of the Bible presume a form of missionization that would not require the local reader to do much other than learn about Jesus. The domesticating translation would put the Christian message into local terms, such that rational discussion of the pros and cons of conversion from the local religion to Christianity would be an uncoerced and self-motivated outcome. As Venuti also notes, this domestication of a translation tries to mask the origin of the text to suggest that it easily and naturally fits into the receptor language and context. For SIL teams intent on producing "natural" translations, foreignizing seems to be anathema. Christianity needs to fit like a glove with the local context so that it can be understood with the least effort by local people and so that it can seem disconnected from coercive colonial and state contexts of mission-station education. In one sense, then, SIL succeeds when ethno-linguistic groups find something extremely familiar in the Christian God. When Amazonian Piro speakers "forgot" that they had converted (Gow 2006) after an SIL translation, they essentially made God so domestic as to be unremarkable.

At the same time, foreignization of the receptor culture is the desired response. The pure presence of heart language translation is simply the first step toward Christian critique. In that sense, Piro forgetfulness is a failure of SIL work. Readers must be engaged at their linguistic core, which requires domestication. But readers are engaged in this way in order to create the context for a noncoercive process of criticism of the reader's self and culture. Just as Nida's critics within SIL did, Venuti ignores the ways in which Nida's project tried to stitch back together the two sides of SIL and WBT that are institutionally separated. The continuing ambiguities of the relationship between language and sacred revelation contained within Nida's translation theory leave open the possibility for local languages themselves to become sacred institutions of revelations and divine connection, as I argue in the following chapters.

. . .

Both the church growth movement and SIL display a very specific kind of liberal attitude toward the procedures of conversion, a point I want to make with a brief comparison between J.S. Mill's *On Liberty* and the version of evangelism outlined here. Mill's political liberalism is based upon a utilitarian answer to the question of continuing progress in the West. How can progress be maintained? For Mill this meant primarily allowing geniuses—men of pure individualism—to be examples to others, especially the unmotivated "masses" then constituting the middle class (Mill [1859] 1978, 62). Through their exceptional examples of free thinking, these geniuses could guide the masses, hopefully persuading them to want to achieve more than their present mediocrity. The masses of Europe and the rest of the world were in thrall to the power of tradition, and until the force of tradition could be defeated, progress would not be possible. "The despotism of custom is everywhere the standing hindrance to human advancement, being in unceasing antagonism to that disposition to aim at something better than customary, which is called, according to circumstances, the spirit of liberty, or that of progress or improvement" (Mill [1859] 1978, 67). Education is necessary to liberate oneself from opinion makers enough to think critically about the issues geniuses are discussing. That is, one needs to be educated enough to be able to distinguish illiberal coercion from liberal persuasion.

Mill's vision of progress was distinctly secular (Christianity having a particularly strong despotic hold on believers). Nevertheless, many other missions used a similar model. As Keane (2007, 83–112) argues in his Sumbanese case, Calvinist missionaries figured themselves as the purveyors of moral rationalism in the colonies, even if Dutch secularists saw them more as Mill might have. For the mainline missions in New Guinea and for secularists like Mill, progress was a product of education and the decline of tradition.

Nida, McGavran, and others in the church growth movement developed a missiology that contrasts sharply with both Mill and the mainline missions of New Guinea. The first issue to confront here is how cultures and traditions can go from being despotic to being the keys to missionization. This crucially involves the creation of a science of structure in both linguistics and anthropology that can act as the "natural" (rather than social) context of communication. Given mid-century

UNESCO statements on both race (1951) and vernacular education (1953) that focused on human mental plasticity and capacity for learning in local languages, culture and language were for SIL and church growth practitioners the keys to a science of universal communication rather than despotic carriers of tradition. Custom/culture is not a sign of essential difference between peoples but a historical accretion of mental particularities. Note that SIL does not trumpet languages as necessarily constitutive of mental difference (as in certain versions of the Sapir-Whorf hypothesis, but see Aldridge 2012, 85), but rather as objects of pride. Having books in one's vernacular language merely gives a speaker self-respect, enabling one to more easily engage in rational debate.

In moving from Mill to the missionaries, custom goes from being a hindrance to being the scientized context for universal communication and the first step on the path to rational discussion. While Mill focused on "the despotism of custom" as the force denying progress, both SIL and church growth practitioners focused on the despotism of the colonial state and mainline mission as the force denying Christian conversion. In place of geniuses rationally persuading masses about the path to progress, the Bible, the Holy Spirit, one's interlocutors, and one's own burgeoning critical capacity inspire and persuade one to convert.

A number of differences between SIL and the church growth movement exist. While church growth methods of missionization are concerned to evangelize minimally and then move on, SIL translators tend to work within a given area for ten to twenty years in order to get inside the linguistic and cultural structures and make Christianity as easily adopted as possible. This time commitment requires a certain amount of organization and interaction with government and mission agencies, and SIL often promotes itself as a group that aids governments by creating literate populations. In that sense, they are quite different from the ideal church growth form of drop in/get out missionization (indeed, it is not clear that any mission group could ever instantiate those ideals). Nevertheless, these methodological discrepancies underscore the extent to which SIL is organized around a notion of language as the primary force in conversion, where the message is internally persuasive when it is correctly understood. SIL is willing to work with the organizational, bureaucratic, and institutional constraints of colonial governments or other missions since, for its members, the only thing that matters is (a naturalized conception of) native language.

To summarize, SIL and church growth literatures both connect evangelical anti-institutionality and postwar anticoloniality with what

Venuti calls "domesticating" translations, whether those are thought of in linguistic or cultural terms. This is true in two senses. First, by providing Bible translations to linguistically defined populations, evangelicals feel that they are allowing local people to remain in their own cultural and linguistic contexts. This contrasts with the reorganization of local space and sociality toward the mission station in Lutheran and mainline methodologies for conversion, what McGavran vilified as "boundary crossing." The natives no longer bear the burden of education, except for what is needed to become Bible readers.[14] Second, by naturalizing local languages and cultures as their own centers of authority, these translations project ethno-linguistic identities as similarly "natural" organizations of Christians in a post-conversion context. The ethno-linguistic group becomes a de facto denomination, but one whose institutional basis is masked, at least in SIL and church growth ideologies.

However, there is still a component of dynamic equivalence translation that stays closer to Venuti's concept of foreignizing translation. While Venuti and Benjamin put the burden of foreignization on a radically non-idiomatic translation (Benjamin seems to advocate translations that look essentially like interlinear glosses), SIL translators depend upon the message of the New Testament to be the origin of a radically self-critical project. And yet because the "selves" in these self-critical projects are ethno-linguistic selves, the ethnic group comes to have a particular salience in Christian projects of critique. In that sense, there is a direct link between theories of translation and the social organization of Christianity into cultural denominations, a point that I will return to in chapter 4, on the revival. In the next chapter, I move from a more general discussion of SIL and church growth to a discussion of the SIL experiences in the Waria Valley.

CHAPTER 3

Translating Locality

The Ethno-Linguistics of Christian Critique

The popular model of translation is that a preexistent text is reproduced in another code in order to be or mean "the same thing." Various theories or critiques of translation argue that this kind of reproduction is impossible. As the French formulation would have it, translations are, like women, *les belles infideles*—either beautiful or faithful, but never both. The question then turns to the kinds of transformations that translations generate.

In the last chapter, I used Venuti's dichotomy of foreignizing versus domesticating translations to characterize Nida's dynamic equivalence theory of translation as initially domesticating; that is, as trying to make the translated text fit as perfectly as possible into the receptor language. The translator, rather than the receptor text reader, does most of the work to make the text comprehensible. With SIL's goal of "clear, accurate, natural" translation, the New Testament will seem as if it has always already been available for any given people group. It is a methodological extension of the premise that the possibility of Christian salvation is universal, especially when it is properly localized into particular ethno-linguistic terms.

Many anthropologists and historians have demonstrated the ways in which colonial and missionary scholarship helped to produce order out of what seemed to colonizers to be endless and uninterpretable difference. Romantic models of *folk* were exported to Africa to produce ethnic groups (e.g., Harries 1987; Comaroff and Comaroff 1991; Meyer

1999); imperial models of civilization were exported to Asia to produce dynastic orders similar but inferior to their European counterparts (Cohn 1990; Chakrabarty 2000). Colonial linguistics helped to develop a modular concept of ethno-linguistic identity that could be transported across the globe (see Errington 2001; Irvine and Gal 2000). Ethno-linguistic identities that emerged from these colonial projects have become the bases for nationalist politics predicated on a sense of enduring existence (Smith 1991; Woolard 1989; Blommaert and Verschueren 1998). In the Pacific, anthropologists have pointed to the ways in which speakers index Christian or otherwise modern identities through the use of one language or another (Watson-Gegeo and Gegeo 1991; Kulick 1992; Besnier 1995).

However, given the ways in which SIL domesticating translations are supposed to feed into moments of self-generated cultural critique, the model of ethno-linguistic identity as a political formation with colonial origins is not especially useful in the case of the Guhu-Samane. As much as SIL translation practices helped to develop a Guhu-Samane ethnolinguistic identity, they also set the stage for a continual process of subversion of that identity. The development of a Guhu-Samane ethno-linguistic identity has produced neither a micro-nationalist politics nor a cargo cult (cf. Kaplan 1995). As I argue more fully in later chapters, local speakers think of the Guhu-Samane language as a sacred language, but one whose sacred power comes from possibilities of transformation rather than continuity. Guhu-Samane speakers are not indexing an identity of one sort or another in pointing to the sacred powers of their language but are constituting a position from which to critically produce new versions of themselves and their culture.

In this chapter, I examine the specific procedures and theories that the Guhu-Samane New Testament translator Ernie Richert used in developing a particularly Guhu-Samane ethno-linguistic identity. Richert wanted to make the New Testament translation as easy to read and as affectively powerful as possible. I focus on two consequences of this methodology. First, Richert had to actually construct a sense of ethno-linguistic identity during his time in the Waria Valley. For people who had been known—up until his arrival—as simply "Waria people" or "Kipu speakers" (referring, respectively, to the geographical region and the name of one the Lutheran centers in the region), a specifically ethnic, rather than geographic, ethnonym and identity had to be constructed. At the same time, the ethno-linguistic identity needed to be naturalized, so as to be the authentic and noninstitutional context for liberal evangelism, in the sense of "liberal" that I discussed in the previous chapter. Because SIL translators and other evangelical missionaries thought of institutions as oppressive and inauthentic, language was emphasized as a "natural" feature that anchored locality and yet seemed to do so without the more pronounced moral conflicts found in local culture.

The second consequence of Richert's domesticating translation project is the way in which it actually created the space for critical Christianity to flourish. Richert wrote about the process of using Guhu-Samane language and culture to develop a more natural and accurate translation as a process in which potential reader-converts go from puzzlement to pleasure. Getting the domestic feel of the translation right, with local language idioms and borrowings from traditional culture, meant turning on the salvational light bulb for Guhu-Samane people. While this was the case at least in part during the translation-inspired 1977 revival, Richert's incorporation of traditional elements also laid the groundwork for the endless controversies over the morality of tradition that punctuate denominational disputes today. The "judicious selection and blending" (Richert 1965a, 85) of Christian and local concepts that Richert used did not lead to a form of irenic Christianity or even to a form of irenic syncretism. Rather the space for the traditional—codified as specifically Guhu-Samane ethno-linguistic tradition—became the space for competing possibilities of Christian group formation.

In chapter 1, I analyzed the model of trans-ethnic community developed through Lutheran Mission policies of lingua franca–based districts. Being a Lutheran meant overcoming the ethnic and moral boundaries of traditional life. Lutheran Mission methodologies emphasized how New Guinea Christians should overcome locality. Before getting to Ernie Richert's work in the Waria Valley, I examine the colonial administration's approach to the problems of governmentality, in which economic and geographic criteria help to classify, divide, and rule New Guinea colonial populations. As will be clear, the ethno-linguistic identity promulgated by Richert was a novel way to organize locality.

THE CIVILITY OF VILLAGES: ADMINISTRATIVE TRANSFORMATIONS OF RURAL NEW GUINEA

The New Guinea colonial administration had the modest goal of turning primitive people into governable subjects living in villages (see Stasch 2010, 2013 for similar colonial processes in Melanesia; also

J. Scott 1998, chap. 7, for a more violent instance of villagization in Africa). In the Middle Waria area, this was a matter of reconfiguring villages rather than constructing them from scratch, but the colonial administrations nevertheless imposed important changes on local residence patterns. As Burce (1983, chap. 6) discusses, the early German control of the area meant that pacification by and large took place in the first two decades of the 1900s, and after that, villages were able to expand into larger, less defense-oriented communities. Given the administrative focus on the north coast further to the west of the mouth of the Waria River, the early exploration and pacification of the area was exceptional. The Waria River valley was, in fact, the only inland part of mainland New Guinea to be pacified prior to 1914 (Firth 1982, 95).

The reason for this relatively exceptional interest in an inland area was gold: miners, starting from both the Australian and German sides of the island, were working gold claims along the Waria River up until around 1910, when miners decided to try more fruitful claims, eventually focusing on the extraordinary lode at Eddie Creek, near Wau (Burce 1983, 180). The interest in the Waria area brought colonial forces in as well as private miners. Because the Waria River flowed back and forth across what was the international border between German New Guinea and British Papua, miners and colonial officers occasionally ended up on the wrong side. A Mixed Boundary Commission between the Germans and Australia led to the construction of the Morobe Patrol Post at the mouth of the Waria River in 1909, at the edges of German territory (Firth 1982, 95).[1]

Prior to sorting out the confusion about the boundaries, Middle Waria people were subject to violent intrusions and forced labor from both Australian and German miners and colonial officers. Men were forced to work as carriers, while garden produce and pigs were stolen for food. Burce also cites scattered evidence of sexual violence against local women (1983, 183, 190). Pacification diminished the threat from other New Guineans (fellow Guhu-Samane speakers as well as Goilalans and Kunimaipans to the south and west), but the larger, more visible villages produced because of it became the sites of colonial violence.

If pacification meant that local people of the Middle Waria were able to form larger villages, it also meant that the German administration was able to conduct its labor recruitment more efficiently. Centralized villages had the advantage (for the Germans) of gathering together large numbers of young men, often in age-graded initiation sets in the men's houses. These young men were taken from their villages and brought to coastal plantations for terms of indentured service. From this early moment of pacification up to the present, a large percentage of Middle Waria men have been "absent at labor", a colonial administrative category for men whose names remained on village census books but who were working in other parts of the territory. Initially they worked at coastal plantations, and later they did so in urban centers throughout the country. These dual consequences of pacification—the capacity to organize in large, permanent villages and the capacity for men to work well in a capitalist context of wage labor—became the primary characteristics of Middle Waria interactions with administrations. From these two qualities the Australian administration saw Middle Waria people as relatively more "civilized." This actually translated into less attention from the administration, since other groups in the area became priorities for administration activities.

The relative importance of village formation in administrative interactions is best seen through a comparison with the other groups who were visited during these patrols. Officers stationed at the Morobe Patrol Post were responsible for patrolling the Lower, Middle, and Upper Waria regions, as well as the Ono and Bubu Valleys. The Lower Waria region included the three remaining coastal Guhu-Samane-language villages (Epa, Zinamba, and Paiawa), as well as ethnic Zia and Suena areas. The Middle Waria region covered scattered Mawai-language villages and the rest of the Guhu-Samane-language villages from Biawaria to Bapi, who primarily lived along the temperate grasslands of the valley floor. The cold and mountainous Bubu, Ono, and Upper Waria Valleys branched off at or upstream of the Garaina area. The ways in which Middle Waria people (i.e., today's Guhu-Samane) stood out from this hodge-podge of ethnicities and regions played a large part in the treatment colonial officers gave them.

McArthur (2000) notes that Kunimaipan peoples of the Upper Waria and Ono and Bubu Valleys lived in dispersed settlements and only constructed larger villages for the purposes of periodical massive feasts (*materes*) that would collect large numbers of guests from across the Kunimaipan social field (sometimes including Middle Waria guests). These feasts would last several months, and during that time the guests became semi-permanent residents at the feast site. Halvaksz's (2006) description of nearby Biaru people's penchant for this regional travel as what they call "local tourists" is a contemporary continuation of this kind of feast-based mobility. This is not true of Middle Waria people, who had men's houses anchoring villages, even if these were surrounded by smaller settlements of schismatic family groupings.

Throughout the patrol reports from the end of World War II until independence, Australian Patrol Officers consistently complained about the mobile populations of the mountain regions—particularly the Bubu and Ono populations at the top of the Chapman Range, who would cross back and forth between Papua and the Territory of New Guinea. The mobility of these people was a constant source of friction. Although the Australians did not go to the lengths that the German administration apparently did, they nevertheless consistently chided these groups for their lack of settlement in appropriate social and residential formations. Not only did this represent cultural backwardness, but it was also unhealthy, according to the Australians. In fact, one could say that the latter point was simply an indication of the former, since hygiene was such an important index of civilization for Australians.

Even when patrol officers thought they were making progress with these mountain populations, they found that the latter used administration regulations for exactly the opposite of the intended effect. One officer was at first grateful to see not only that Ono and Upper Waria people were then living in villages, but that the villages were also fenced in. Unfortunately, he found out that the fence was not built for the purpose he thought it was: "All villages have an elaborate fence around the outskirts and there is no disputing the fact that these are pig-proof but investigation reveals that their purpose is to keep pigs in the village not out" (MOROBE report 2 of 62/63, 3). These villagers seemed incapable of civilizing their residential patterns even when they built and lived in villages.

In contrast to this, the Middle Waria people were consistently described in glowing terms: "The natives who really captured my interest were the Middle Warias. I have no hesitation in saying that their health and standards of living are more advanced than the Lower Waria natives. My opinion is that these natives have really heeded the instructions of the Government Officers and done their bit, and it is now up to the Government to do something really constructive for them" (MOROBE report 4 of 50/51, 4). Note that "health and standards of living" in the quotation above are ways of referring to Middle Waria residential patterns, since colonial officers thought of villages primarily in terms of the quality of life that it brought when they created real "communities." The Middle Waria people are stable, living in cleared villages, with pit latrines and domestic animals in their appropriate places. Unlike the cold, windy mountain climates around them, the Middle Warias live in a relatively low-lying, temperate area with many streams and rivers, making daily bathing both welcome and easy to do. This made the administration even more besotted with them (see MOROBE 4 of 50/51). In addition, Middle Waria people live in an area where the geography and soil conditions are such that there is abundant arable land for gardening nearby. Although some people garden in distant, mountainous areas, most gardens are near the main walking track through the valley. During the colonial era, this meant that people could live in settled villages close to the administrative patrol route without having to build additional shelters ("garden houses" or "pig houses") in remote corners far from government control.

These physical conditions were essential to developing a settlement pattern that made the Middle Warias seem the most civilized of the populations patrolled from the Morobe Patrol Post. In the quotation above, they are compared with the people of the Lower Waria more than with the mountain-dwelling Ono, Bubu, or Upper Waria people, since the assumption was that the earlier-contacted Lower Warias would be more "advanced" than the later-contacted Middle Warias. (All things being equal, the civilizational scale was supposed to be based on time spent in contact with Europeans.) For the patrol officers, neither the coastal nor the mountain groups could compete with the clean, decorated, and healthy Middle Waria villages. "These natives are perhaps the best that the writer has visited and they are always eager to improve themselves. Villages visited were always clean and well cared for and did not often show traces of only just having been cleaned prior to the writer's visit. In most cases ornamental shrubs and plants decorate the village area" (p. 6, MOROBE report 2 of 53/54).

This overall glowing characterization of the Middle Warias—a formation defined by hygiene standards and residential patterns more than language or culture—gave them a reputation that was further burnished in their colonial labor activities. At the beginning of the colonial era, as Burce notes (1983, 191–93), Middle Warias had to be coerced into road maintenance or indentured labor at coastal plantations. During World War II, however, men from this area made names for themselves for the quality and quantity of labor they provided in the war effort. Middle Waria men spanned the range from carriers for Australian and American troops to noncommissioned officers in the Pacific Islands Regiment, some traveling as far as Sydney.

Their participation in the constabulary and the war contributed to the impression among colonial officers that Middle Waria people were "the best sort of native," making the Middle Waria a popular stop on labor-recruiting trips. Local men were laboring at many different tasks, not just police work, and doing so all across the Papua and New Guinea territories, not just in nearby urban centers.[2] From before the war and well into the postwar period, Middle Waria "able bodied men" were absent at labor in much higher percentages than the administration's recommended 30 percent. After the postwar rehabilitation of administration property in Lae was completed, the continued high percentage was due to voluntary labor migration rather than administration-sanctioned (or administration-enabled) recruiting (MOROBE report 4 of 50/51).

Administration worries about levels of male absenteeism remained constant throughout much of the time covered in patrol reports (from just after World War II to 1973). At issue was the continued strength and possibility of "development" for rural villages, balanced against the need for capitalist production in towns. On the one hand, absenteeism needed to be—and would be—kept low as villages became sites of small-scale economic schemes. The district officer in Lae, A.R. Haviland, put it succinctly to the then-resident patrol officer in a comment on his report: "As the economic development of the area improves more and more, people will be satisfied to remain in work at home." In countering the patrol officer's worry about absentee men, the district officer expresses a blithe faith in rural development. If anything, he points to the ways in which the Middle Waria situation of extreme absenteeism was uncommon. On the other hand, Haviland did not want to send too many men back to their natal villages, since he was also concerned to bring people into a cash economy: "However, in encouraging this [i.e., village-based development], the overall Territory labour requirement must be watched. It is no use producing unless there is a consumer and this state can only be had if labour is available for outside enterprise."[3] The administration's goal was to enable enough urban capitalist production to inspire village populations to gain access to the cash needed to purchase the emerging staples of rural consumerism: salt, soap, sugar, tea, rice, and canned fish.

The main efforts at economic development then were village based. Men were needed to start the various cash-cropping schemes that the Department of Agriculture, Stock, and Fisheries thought up for this area. These included crops of tea, coffee, and cardamom, and stocks of chickens, cattle, and fish. Middle Waria men, however, were and continue to be reluctant to engage in cash cropping. Burce (1983, 221–22) argues that this is because of a cultural value on individually prized knowledge that was understood to be an outcome of paid labor rather than agricultural work.

The most devastating problem for local economic activity, however, is the lack of a vehicular road into the area. The administration had high hopes that they would be able to pay back the Middle Waria people for their WWII service by providing a road (see the earlier quotation that refers to the government doing "something really constructive" for the Middle Waria), but no road ever materialized. Once the administration finally admitted that a road would never be built over the rugged Biaru mountains from Wau unless a considerable mineral deposit was found, higher-ups also admitted that there would never be anything but modest forms of "development" for the area (unpaginated letter from A.R. Haviland to Director of Native Affairs, dated September 25, 1957, in MOROBE 4 of 56/57). Relying on sporadic and expensive air-cargo transport, the cash-cropping schemes all failed. Today, the Middle Waria area is dotted with overgrown coffee trees and the rusting remains of barbed-wire fences that once held small herds of cattle. Politicians annually come through the valley, telling local people to get their coffee trees back in order since the road will be built "next year," but so far, none of these plans have panned out.

With the administration's goal for a modest modernity in rural New Guinea based on cash cropping, the Middle Waria people seemed to be well positioned to, at best, tread water. They might have been the "best sort of native," but this beneficent recognition was not getting them much in return. At the same time, the Lutheran Mission was pushing people toward Christianity, doing so through the negation of local culture. Into this mix, Ernie Richert offered a sacralization of their locality and a demand for great change.

ERNIE RICHERT AND THE MAKING OF THE GUHU-SAMANE LANGUAGE AND PEOPLE

In the early 1950s SIL was starting to branch out from Central and South America into the Pacific, including the Philippines and Australia. In 1955 an Australian SIL leader named J. Robert Story traveled to different Western Pacific islands to investigate the possibility of starting work in that region. At that point SIL leaders estimated a thousand languages in need of scriptures, and William Cameron Townsend's goal was to have translations in all of them by the end of his life. Story addressed the biennial conference of SIL/Wycliffe Bible Translators in the United States with the disturbing news that there could be as many as a thousand additional languages on the island of New Guinea alone (Wallis and Bennett 1959). SIL Australia strongly urged that this need be attended to as soon as possible, especially since the administration and other missionaries in the colony seemed happy to have a group that would help with the language problem.

Plans for an SIL outpost in New Guinea moved quickly—this was exactly the kind of tribal, multilingual situation that SIL was organized to handle—and by August 1956 SIL had a lease on five hundred acres in the Eastern Highlands District (now Province) that had already been alienated from traditional landowners as part of the Aiyura Agricultural Station. Ukarumpa, as the station came to be known, is now a thriving, sprawling compound from which translation work is organized and supported, a dense social network of its own (analyzed in Roberts 2006). Initial "allocations" of translation teams started in 1957, and ten teams were allocated within the first two years.[4] The initial areas of interest were groups located in the Eastern Highlands near the Ukarumpa base, groups in the Markham Valley south of the Huon Peninsula, and groups in the Waria River regions. The first four allocations were in the Eastern Highlands, after which the Richerts allocated to the Garaina area.[5] I am not entirely sure why these places were selected for the first teams, except that these were Lutheran Mission areas and the Lutherans appear to have helped SIL with logistical support, particularly aviation support, in these early years (on the Lutheran/SIL relationship, see below).

Originally from Southern California, Ernest and Marjorie Richert (and children) had been working with SIL in the Philippines before coming to New Guinea. Ernie, as he was commonly known, was a tall, imposing man, according to SIL members who overlapped with him in New Guinea. Highly motivated in the missionary and translation aspects of his work, Richert finished the Guhu-Samane translation in seventeen years, even as he created some peripheral projects in the Waria region. He is remembered by SIL members and the Guhu-Samane alike for his bullishness. In the early years of the perennially overtaxed aviation department, when the Richerts were stationed in the Waria, Ernie rarely scheduled pickups or drop-offs in advance like other teams. He would get on the two-way radio in the morning and demand service by that afternoon. Both the Guhu-Samane and SIL members mentioned this fact, since aviation department protocol is only rarely and in emergencies flouted.

Tall, imposing, and perhaps a bit overbearing in the eyes of his fellow SIL members, Richert was an even more outsized personality in the eyes of local people in the Waria, who express respect for him even as they consider him to have been overwhelming.[6] Richert started his work with a bang. Within the first year of allocating to Kipu, Richert had translated the Lord's Prayer into Guhu-Samane, and interest "soared" among local people, who had until then been worshipping and dealing with the Lutherans in Kâte (J. Harrison 1978, 1).

The Richerts originally tried to settle in Sopa village, close to the Garaina Station; however, they soon moved down to Kipu, a Lutheran station that had the only permanent materials church in the area. I am not sure exactly why they moved their base of operations out of Sopa, although Richert may have seen that it would be easier to attract a number of assistants and helpers from a Kipu mission-station base than from a traditional village.[7] Although I argued in the previous chapter for an SIL/church growth antipathy to mission stations, I think that Richert may have realized that the mission station was relatively neutral territory in local land politics, and thus his co-workers would be more willing to relocate there. As I discuss more elsewhere, Guhu-Samane people tend to narrate their residence patterns in the valley as "following the footsteps of [one's] ancestors." For those who had no such paths to Sopa, relocating there to help with Richert's translation work might have been difficult. But this narrative of pathways is less operative with respect to colonial spaces, such as the Kipu station, and relocation there might have been easier to negotiate. Alternatively, the Richerts might have been the ones hoping to avoid the politics of land.

Richert began his work by trying to find assistants from whom he could learn the language, which was identified in SIL records at this time either as "Waria" or "the Kipu language," just as the Lutherans had referred to it. Richert did not limit his informants to those near Kipu. Some of his first assistants were from Au and Aro, about a three-and-a-half-hour walk downstream from the station. In addition to specific language informants, Richert also asked older men to come to Kipu to teach him about their myths and customs. Only two men from this original committee of elders were alive during my fieldwork in 2005–2006; both were in their late seventies or early eighties. At the time of the work with Richert, these two were considered so young as to almost be upstarts, unworthy of being on a panel of distinguished elders in this gerontocratic community. This suggests that Richert's committee of "elders" included men in their fifties or older, including many men who had been alive in the precolonial era. In later years, this group of men helped to check the rough drafts of the biblical texts in a process that is now called the "village check."

According to people from the Muniwa region near Kipu, Richert expressed some dissatisfaction with his initial group of translation helpers and put out another call for informants. Eventually he called upon Timothy from Muniwa to be his assistant, and that partnership lasted throughout the rest of their lives. Timothy was known as "a great hunter" (a phrase, in English, repeated many times to me about Timothy) who spent his days alone in the forests, searching for wild boar. One Muniwa man who now works on the Old Testament translation suggested a parallel between Timothy's hunting and his translation work. In both fields, Timothy was well respected and well known, but in both cases, it was for work that kept him far from the center of village life, sequestered in the forest on hunting trips or in Richert's translation house for language exercises. In addition to his work as a hunter, Timothy was also a carrier for Allied troops during World War II. He spoke Guhu-Samane, Kâte, and probably some Tok Pisin, although he seems to have been literate only in Kâte at the beginning of the translation work (there was no Guhu-Samane literature and very little Tok Pisin literature at this time).

Richert learned Kâte, and he and Timothy worked on Guhu-Samane language materials through this medium. As described by Timothy's son Mark, who now leads the Old Testament translation project and who worked with Richert at a later point, Richert would sit with the Koiné Greek original and various English translations of the Bible, while Timothy would sit with the Kâte translation produced by the Lutherans in 1939. Timothy would suggest a possible Guhu-Samane translation, which Richert would compare with the Greek and English versions, and a rough draft would come from this multilingual, comparative process.

Under normal circumstances, translations go through several drafts as native speakers offer their opinions on the felicity of particular verses. Drafts are also checked with other SIL staff, who query the translator about the accuracy and consistency with which important key terms have been translated. Roberts (2006) provides a detailed discussion of standard translation-checking procedures at SIL PNG. While Richert followed versions of these procedures, some of his Guhu-Samane coworkers remember his stubborn streak. They often struggled to convince him that a particular word, phrase, or morphosyntactic construction was ill suited to a particular context. Richert would argue with them, they recall, insisting that he was right in his translations or in his definitions for the Guhu-Samane dictionary project.

Richert also began a number of projects aimed at sedimenting a notion of Guhu-Samane language and culture as forces that the Christian message would have to work through in order to be understood. The first of these projects stemmed from Richert's understanding of the socio-geographic dialects of the language. Dialects of Guhu-Samane are distinguished by a number of phono-lexical variants. For the most part, the phonological differences are products of relatively simple consonantal transformations, for example, the different surface forms of a voiced coronal obstruent as /dz/ from Bapi to Garasa, /d/ from Wakaia to Asama, and /j/ in the Papuan Waria; or the variations in the voiced bilabial as /b/ inland and /w/ at the coast. Lexical differences include a number of suppletive forms. Some of these suppletions can be traced to neighboring languages, like the Kunimaipan Gadzili and Weri dialects, and some have no obvious history of borrowing.

Not only did Richert do a sociolinguistic survey of Guhu-Samane, but he also asked speakers of each dialect to come to Kipu and help him with his language research. At Kipu, Richert was constituting the language community, bringing into being a unified object to be called Guhu-Samane. In later years, when Richert's literacy program was in full swing, there were adult literacy courses in almost every village,[8] and young men from each dialect were trained at Kipu as literacy teachers. For some present-day Guhu-Samane members of the Lutheran church (who, like the revivalists, see Richert's New Testament translation as the root of the Holy Spirit revival that eventually took members from the Lutheran church), this constitution of the language is Richert's most positive achievement. One Lutheran man from the Papuan Waria in Oro Province said that Richert "brought our language together," but he wished Richert had not gotten involved in the Christian work.

At some point in this history (most likely around 1971), Richert also requested that any old men's house artifacts still extant (i.e., hidden from Lutheran purges) be brought to Kipu and displayed in a makeshift museum. At one end of this building, a war club was displayed upside-down, placed in this inverted position to indicate a time of peace and unity. The men's houses that the Lutherans had been so opposed to were here given space to at least be valued within a framing context of Christian work and training.[9] As I discuss below, the men's house became a key comparative reference point for Richert's linguistic translation work.

Like the collection of men and dialects, Richert's artifact collecting also seems to have given people a sense that he was creating a new level of political-religious order that had not been operative before: the ethno-linguistic group. This is not to say that people had no concept of speaking the same language as others, but rather that people had not necessarily thought of the boundaries of the ethno-linguistic unit as encircling a space of unity and shared interest through linguistic similarity. To a large extent, communities had been defined by men's houses and the alliances between them, as I discuss in the next chapter. And during the first half of the twentieth century, the colonial administrations and Lutheran mission had operated in terms of patrol areas or circuits and congregations. But Richert's literacy schools extended only as far as the boundaries of the language, and Richert's interest in men was defined only by their speaking abilities or cultural knowledge.

Richert needed to constitute a literate audience for his translation work, and he started literacy courses well before he was himself very knowledgeable about Guhu-Samane language (J. Harrison 1978, 1). Twelve hundred people went through Richert's initial literacy classes, using the first primer *Ana Hiire Isaisa* (Richert n.d., but likely 1959), although only two hundred emerged as readers. According to J. Daniel Harrison (1978, 2), during the 1963–1964 literacy campaign 850 people were enrolled and 350 finished with usable literacy skills. Richert was then also publishing a vernacular language newspaper (by 1973 it was sixteen pages long), called *Qaru* (Messenger), and 250 copies circulated for each edition.

Richert even created a level of administrative oversight such that young leaders in the literacy project would patrol the region, stopping by each literacy school to make sure courses were running smoothly. Like Anderson's (1991, chap. 4) civil servant pilgrimages, this mobilization of young men conducting language work was a central part of the emerging consciousness of "the Guhu-Samane language and people." Importantly, two men involved in inspecting literacy courses who went around to each school on these patrols became competing leaders of the post-revival churches: Ulysses, who founded New Life was a literacy school inspector, and Mark, who founded Reformed Gospel, was a trainer for the literacy inspectors. Not content to limit themselves to the subregional boundaries of men's house political organization, these two men have fought for the politico-religious control of the ethno-linguistic community as a whole (see chap. 7). J. Daniel Harrison, an SIL literacy consultant, came to Kipu in 1973 to see how Richert's project was developing. In several places in his short report, he notes that ethno-linguistic consciousness was one of the more obvious and important outcomes of the Richerts' work. "The programme has helped to bring the Guhu-Samane people together as a social unit and has fostered a national consciousness and pride" (J. Harrison 1978, 1).

Richert was starting to constitute a group of people organized by linguistic and cultural materials. After initially using the Lutheran names—"the Kipu language" or "the Waria language"—Richert was either using "Mid-Waria (Guhu-Samane)" or else just "Guhu-Samane" to describe the language and the people. Although attested in one early Lutheran document that I have seen (as "Gugusaman"),[10] the ethnonym "Guhu-Samane" was not commonly used prior to Richert's arrival.

Local people understand the name "Guhu-Samane" to refer to a story about the original men's house. At this time in Guhu-Samane his-tory, there was only one men's house, signaling the unity of men in social life. One day, a group of young men killed a pig and, instead of returning to the men's house to share the meat, they cooked and ate it in the bush. On their return the spirit of the men's house smelled the pig meat on their breath. Angered that the young men did not share, the spirit punished all of the men—guilty of the pig eating or not—for their lack of unity by traveling down to the coast and drowning all the inhab-itants in the ocean. From that point on, it became conventional for there to be a different men's house in each village. "Guhu-Samane" literally means "many men's houses" or, metonymically, "many villages." The geographically defined "Middle Waria" people came to be ethnonym-ically identified under a single name that actually refers to their political fractiousness.

From 1966 to 1971 the Richerts were away, dealing with medical issues, and returned to find the literacy programs stalled (J. Harrison 1978, 3). To counteract this, Richert organized a literacy academy (known locally as the "Akatemi") at Kipu to teach prospective literacy teachers, although it also became something of an excuse for the Rich-erts to invite their friends and supporters to spend time in the area and teach courses on a hodge-podge of topics seemingly based on the idio-syncratic expertise of these people (e.g., astronomy, Morse code, sew-ing).[11] During this time, the Richert's focus changed from the elders who helped with linguistics, anthropology, and translation to the young men who taught literacy courses and took the Academy's random offerings of classes. Richert also set up a carpentry workshop where young men made small pieces of furniture to sell in Lae.

DZOOBE ...

TTOTTA RIKATTO (Ernest
L. Richert, BA, PsD, DD)
Noi hee, Nike Akatemiho
baura khooba erake moo-
rare. Oi teqaha baura
gattiqa oonidzara, bamu.
Oonihe bodza nohoio ho-
teqani. Oho quba baura
oke moomi teqaha sukuru
kharanipamuho isaki oo-
dzaranihe oi isaisa abi
nokoke beedzaenomaitaqu
ooqaho isaki ooni. Qate
tii temuta qesaho isaki
peite oorai nokoi ipi-
bidzakoi. Dzoobe mooro!

SASE MAGARITTA (Marjorie)
Trulin Richert, LVN, Tech)
Noi hee, Nookare. Paima-
ne noko apumane nokomeho
hobihobi bagenoma naata
qubake nana Akatemi oho
neta baura oke eetorai.
Ota khameto ma noko gama
sinasina nooka qupadzo-
maqi qesamane nokomeke
hoobire qaarakoi. Oonoma
eetemi abi ma paimanema
mutu ma khata oi gamaqa
tete bagenoma oke aima
qgarakoi. Ohonga Dzoobe!

...▶

FIGURE 3. Introduction to the
*Kipu Akatemi (Academy)
Booklet*, 1971. Photo of the
booklet by Courtney Handman.

HELLO ...

Doctor Rikato (Ernest L.
Richert, BA, PsD, DD). He says,
You are looking here at the base
of the Academy's work. It is not
small work, no. But its time is
short. See this work, it can take
years but it can give great power
to the literacy men. So, in about
two years they will come up
[here] and come together again.
Thank you for reading!

Older Sister Margaritta
(Marjorie Trulin Richert, LVN,
Tech). She says, Listen. We are
working here to make women
good helpers for their husbands.
Here women and children all
learn advice and they help their
loved ones. Doing so the entire
family lives on the good path.
Thank the Lord!

Richert published a photo book of the Academy's activities in 1972, which shows Guhu-Samane from across the Waria working together on various projects. Figure 3 shows the introduction to the book, featuring welcome messages from both Ernie and Marjorie Richert. Other photos show local men using telescopes, playing musical instruments, using carpentry tools, or teaching their children about God. The photos also show Marjorie Richert helping the wife of one of the male students to read. The images from the booklet present the Academy as providing a wide range of knowledge—technical matters, science, religion, and home economics—to the men and women convened at Kipu through the Richerts' work.

Richert was teaching the young men involved in the literacy project to become Christian leaders. According to Mark, Richert taught men how to pray in an evangelical style and encouraged them to volunteer to give the sermons at Sunday services in the Kipu Lutheran church. Mark remembers one lesson from Richert in particular: a good Christian leader will always be ready to lead a service, and Richert would occasionally give these young men only a few minutes to prepare a short sermon or prayer session as a test of their leadership capacities. In addition to these lessons on public Christian speaking, Richert encouraged a different approach to music. Not only did he translate traditional Guhu-Samane songs into Christian ones, but he also seems to have encouraged his young men to react more vigorously to sacred music with energetic dancing or to react more vigorously to sermon talk with energetic calls of "Amen!" The emphasis on evangelical worship styles that contrasted strongly with what was then the Lutheran norm was a major issue in the revival that started just after Richert's departure.

Richert was able to draw a large number of men and their families to Kipu, bringing together the disparate ends of the Waria Valley populations through literacy, schooling, and manual labor. But it was his translation work that so successfully developed an ethno-linguistic identity and that made possible both the revival and the denominational conflicts about the morality of tradition. I turn now to his translation work specifically.

RICHERT'S TRANSLATION THEORY

Beyond the movements of men, sacra, and literacy knowledge, Richert's construction of "the Guhu-Samane" as an ethno-linguistic identity is centrally realized in his translation practices. Richert appears to have been focused on the translation aspects of his work from the beginning. J. Daniel Harrison (1978, 1–2) reports that by 1959 the first eight chapters of Mark were in circulation (see also comments from the Lutheran Missionary stationed at Garaina[12] and Pence [1962], which suggest that more than just Mark was in circulation by this point). Richert worked on James and the gospel of Mark during these first years, which were published together in 1966 as a booklet, but he also worked on Galatians, Ephesians, parts of Genesis, parts of Luke, and selected Psalms.[13] These portions circulated on mimeographed sheets. From 1959 to 1963, however, the Richerts produced very little and may have been on furlough during some of that time.

The majority of Richert's publications come after 1963, when he was putting out literacy primers (several from 1963 to 1966), translations (1966), a linguistics paper (n.d., but likely around 1963), and papers on translation theory and practice (1963a, 1963b, 1963c, 1964, 1965a, 1965b). Richert's production of short statements on translation demonstrates his commitment to this aspect of the work, a rarity in SIL PNG.[14] Richert was interested in theories of translation in addition to the practical work of providing a translation for the Guhu-Samane. In fact, after finishing his work in Papua New Guinea, he returned to the United States to start a Christian think tank working on English language "versions" of the New Testament in contemporary speech styles. This American English translation will be discussed more below.

Even before Richert had done much work on these translations, he was apparently promoting the local language at the expense of the Lutheran lingua franca, Kâte, or at least that is how the Lutheran missionary saw it at the time. In 1958, only one year after Richert's allocation to the Middle Waria, the German Lutheran missionary Rev. Helmut Horndasch, stationed at Zaka, was obviously upset by Richert's valuation of the local language. Horndasch expresses this in his somewhat stilted English in his year-end report for 1958.

> The preparations for baptism, Confirmation and Holy Communion are insufficient and the examinations are moreless [sic] formal. The [B]ible stories are barely known. Because many of the people do not know the Kâte language the biblical instruction has to be done in their local language. In this connection I must mention that because of the presence and the activity of the Wiclif [sic] Bible Translators our people are not interested in Kâte any more. One of that group lives at Kipu and translates the New Testament into the Kipu language. And what are the consequences?- Kâte is not used in their devotions and [word unclear] services and more. We encourage the people to learn Kâte and those [SIL] people tell them that learning Kâte is nonsense. And what do we say from our evangelical-lutheran [sic] standpoint?[15]

Horndasch is upset not only by the lack of progress in disseminating Kâte as a church lingua franca—and thus by the lack of progress in the spiritual development of the congregation—but he also sees Richert's work as an attack on the Lutheran mission as a whole. Horndasch's last question seems to suggest a certain amount of doubt about the appropriateness of using Kâte as a lingua franca given Lutheranism's historically positive attitudes toward vernacular Bible translation. For Horndasch, SIL seemed to subvert the Lutheran organization of people in lingua franca–based circuits.

However, the tension expressed here may have been between Horndasch and Richert personally, since the Lutheran Mission was, in general, supportive of SIL's work. At the 1959 Annual Conference, Horndasch inquired about expelling Richert from the Zaka circuit, but was met with mostly positive statements about SIL from the rest of the Lutheran missionaries assembled. Their only, rather tepid, advice was to see if Richert would be willing to relocate to the adjacent Goilala area, where the Lutherans were then locked in a contest with the Roman Catholics for control (1959 Annual Conference Report, 15). If this suggestion was ever put to Richert, he obviously refused. The one outcome of Horndasch's complaints seems to have been that the Lutherans invited the SIL New Guinea head, James Dean, to discuss their activities at the next conference in 1960 (from which I quoted in the previous chapter).

These rare complaints about SIL suggest that the conflict may have been due mostly to Richert's tendency toward confrontation and Horndasch's own seemingly excitable personality (given the tenor of his yearly reports). Richert was simply voicing standard SIL policy, although perhaps in more strident tones. Richert was a strong advocate of the heart language as the optimal medium of biblical instruction and was committed to Nida's domesticating theories of dynamic equivalence translation. In a comment in SIL's *Notes on Translation,* Richert (1964, 11) concludes by noting, "So it is that in translating the word of God into Mid-Waria (as into all primitive languages) the real issue is not concordance of the words, but *comprehension* of the *message!*" (emphasis in original). In other words, the most important aspect of a Bible translation was its ease of understanding for receptor-language readers.

As Aldridge (2012, 122 ff.) notes, translation theory took a backseat to linguistics training in the mid- to late 1950s. Both Eugene Nida and William Wonderly, the main translation theorists in SIL, had left the organization, in part because of their controversial stances on divine inspiration and literalism in translation. Wonderly argued that a translation, especially a dynamically equivalent one, is "the best substitute that we can produce for a divinely inspired message" (quoted in Aldridge 2012, 14). This was enough to force Wonderly's resignation. Richert's vocal advocacy for a dynamic equivalence model, particularly at a time when no other SIL PNG members were focusing on translation theory, suggests that Richert was a fearless devotee of this model.

As a way to understand Richert's translation model, it is useful to look at how Richert understood his translation theory to work for contemporary American English. In 1977, two years after the family's return to the United States, Richert self-published a "version" of Paul's letter to the Romans as *Freedom Dynamics* (organized by the "Burbank Committee" of Richert's Southern California–based Thinker House group, of which Richert had the title "Chief Translator"). The title of the translation is particularly important: using Nida's theory of dynamic equivalence could set one free to fully understand and be affected by the biblical message. Without the coercive forces of religious institutions or the constraining limitations of temporal or cultural distance, the Bible could speak to the reader in a new way. Not only would the translation be free (i.e., not literal), but the reader would also become free (i.e., saved).

In an attempt to make Romans "as relevant, readily understood and esthetically appealing to American readers as it was to the original addressees," Richert made his translation with the belief that "God is seen as being just as eager to communicate his loving forgiveness to American people today as he was to the various ethnic groups of Rome in the first century" (v). Richert provides a direct link between the different nodes of mid-century conservative evangelism discussed in the previous chapter when he notes his indebtedness to SIL, Nida, the church growth institutions at Fuller Seminary, and generational translators like J.B. Phillips.[16] Also mentioning the importance of findings in behavioral science, Richert locates his task within a science of communications that aims to reproduce in the minds of contemporary readers the reactions of the "original" hearers of Paul's letter.

More than just developing a domestic receptor text, Richert also felt that the "source" text was only partially the source. For him, the real source of the New Testament is the underlying form or underlying message that Nida's dynamic equivalence methodology of logical and semantic deconstruction brings forward. Any one specific source text has to be treated as only a skeleton onto which hangs one cultural version of the universal meaning of Christianity. "It is for reasons of this sort that the Greek words of the text (Nestle's in this case) are regarded by the translators as the extant 'fossils' of Paul's message. The committee's orientation is that the full, living import of the Hebrew author's message is *occasioned* by the Greek words, but is importantly greater than they are. The translators must grasp that fuller significance and communicate it in the most cogent form of today's language of which they are capable" (vi, emphasis in original). Richert brings the underlying source text into existence through the process of translation and yet does so while still arguing for the source text qua origin.[17] With a slight intertextual relation to the Greek text (a message that is "occasioned by the Greek words, but is importantly greater than they are"), Richert argues for an original message in the source text that is essentially coming from heaven, one that did not necessarily exist in previous (human) translations.

Along with transformations to the source text, the receptor text also has to be put into the correct cultural framework primarily through reference to "emic" words and expressions that index the receptor context, in this case, American life in the late 1970s: *the bomb* instead of

Paul's "sword" or *Appointed, Designated, Chief Minister, Divine Deputy, Executive, Representative, Messiah, Agent,* or *Stand-in* as substitutions for "Christ." (For missionaries returning to the United States after a few decades overseas, it was apparently a society indexed by Cold War management gurus.) Richert (vi) notes that "failure to employ such compensating devices is to rob today's readers of the full value of the message and create dissatisfaction, guesswork and error in understanding." The contemporary English approach is signaled at the very beginning, when Paul's greeting to the church is rendered in part as sender's and recipient's addresses, as if the text were a business letter. The first page of the translation is reproduced below using Richert's formatting:

Paul, Aid to Jesus
Appointed International
Ambassador

Cenchrea, Greece
C.E. 58

The Brotherhood of Believers
All Ethnic Groups
Rome, Italy

My Friends in Rome,

God loves you dearly and has selected you for full membership in his growing family of Believers. My colleagues join me in relaying loving greetings from our Father the Heavenly Majesty. 7

I have been praying for you and want you to know how pleased I am to hear you have come into vital relationship with Jesus. People everywhere are talking about how dedicated you are. 8

I am requesting that God will grant me a safe tour to visit you soon. He knows I serve him with all the facets of my being for I remain alert to every opportunity to share with others the good news about his Son. I am eager to see you and share personally with you my deeply felt convictions and am sure our contact will be mutually inspiring. 9–11

I am planning to visit you dear friends to motivate you further in your developing Christian experience. It has already been my privilege to stimulate other societies, but to date I have found it impossible to come to you. I feel obligated to assist you more advanced Greco-Romans as well as those of simpler cultures among whom I work. I long to communicate my message to you in person when I get to Rome. 12–15

A number of features are crucial to creating Richert's "idiomatic" English translation. First, the business-letter format as well as the marginalization of the verse numbers removes the text from the genre conventions of a sacred or religious text. The sender's and receivers' addresses at the beginning also present the contemporary reader (i.e., the "implied overhearer") with the sense that Paul and the people in Rome are at least addressable in contemporary terms—they are just like us. (In this respect, note the anachronistic descriptor of Rome as part of the nation-state Italy.) Finally, we can see Richert trying to use phrases of 1970s business jargon, such as "vital relationship" or "contact [that] will be mutually inspiring."

In both the American English and Guhu-Samane translations that Richert produced, he parlayed this interest in "dynamic" comprehension into an interest in functionally equivalent idioms, equating the "loose" translations that Nida advocated with linguistic non-compositionality. Idioms were a major focus of SIL investigation. SIL linguists at this time were post-Bloomfieldians, who saw the lexicon (as opposed to the grammar) as an accumulation of arbitrary cultural meanings. Culture is found in language in the lexicon, not in the productivity and analogy-building machinery of the grammar that was emphasized in American linguistics. Thus, non-compositionality was the key signal of cultural knowledge. One of SIL New Guinea's major linguists, Alan Healey, published an article on idioms, using the term to include "any group of morphemes or words whose meaning cannot be deduced from the meanings of its parts" (Healey 1968, 71). This means that, for Healey, English idioms include things like "after all," "nevertheless," and "How do you do?" in addition to the more commonly cited non-compositional verb phrases like "kick the bucket." This emphasis on idioms in Bible translation continues to this day—one of the first things that every person involved in the Guhu-Samane Old Testament translation said to me was "our language has a lot of idioms" (in Tok Pisin, *tok ples bilong mipela i gat planti idiom*). Roberts (2006, 237–38) also emphasizes the central place of idioms in current SIL manuals and training materials.

Richert's "idiomatic English" in his 1977 version of Romans was primarily indexed through words and expressions, and he focuses on these in his translator's introduction (e.g., "Jesus" as "Chief Minister"). Richert was really trying to create a speech style that encompassed the text as a whole, beyond just the use of certain phrases. He consistently focused on specific words and phrases (idioms) rather than larger textual phenomena, although the business letter format in *Freedom Dynamics* is an important counterexample. This version of Romans was particularly textually coherent because he was able to use his considerable knowledge of American register forms to successfully approach the genre of business-speak (although one might still quibble with his sense that a business-letter format would have a particularly large affective impact). But in his Guhu-Samane translations, where he could not depend upon such a deep well of knowledge, his focus on idioms as the central way to create an enculturated biblical text meant that he often sacrificed text coherence for idiom-inflected language. That is, even though he focused on idioms (as words and phrases), he did not construct an idiomatic text (as a register phenomenon).

As with other descriptions of heart language (Cowan 1979), Richert argued that intellectual comprehension often gives way to affectively loaded understanding through these idioms. In one submission for *Notes on Translation* (1963a), Richert describes his work in translating and revising Mark in Guhu-Samane and the ways in which bad, literal translations led to his informants' puzzlement and confusion while good, idiomatic translations led to his informants' happiness. "When the [bad] form was altered or replaced in such a manner as to convey the intended message [the Guhu-Samane] people reacted with anything from relief or comprehension to sheer pleasure" (Richert 1963a, 4). The idioms selected for exemplification in the article suggest a progressive incorporation of elements of lived experience in the Waria Valley, from learning how kinship terms index respect to the best way to express how one warms oneself by the fire. Richert was starting to equate non-compositional language and culture to comprehension, pleasure, and ultimately salvation.

But while non-compositionality in idioms was an index of culture, that culture could itself be seen as structured, as McGavran (1970) noted when he said that church growth missionaries need to get "inside" tribal structure. In Richert's final article about Guhu-Samane translation (1965a), language and culture become structured matrices through which thought and conversion happen. Richert describes a number of rituals and their affiliated idioms that are centered on the men's house "cult of *poro*." After providing a number of details about the *poro* cult, Richert segues into his discussion of translation practice:

> There is no doubt it would be folly for the translator to adopt wholesale the terms and concepts of poro in his translation of the Bible into Guhu-Samane. The message of the divine Word is *revolutionary* and cannot be bartered. On the other hand, it would be equal folly for the translator to be ignorant of, or to ignore, the prominence poro still occupies in the thinking of the people. They have gained a measure of enlightenment and sophistication through

contact with the white man and through the elements of the Gospel which have filtered through to them via another language [i.e., Kâte]. But the core of their perception is still in the old matrix.

This produces a dilemma. Does one employ terms foreign to the experience of the people at the risk of indefinite or even irrelevant meaning? Or does one employ terms familiar to the people at the risk of *wrong* meaning? The answer lies not in an either-or choice, but in a judicious selection and blending of the two. This, in fact, has been the constant aim of the work which has gone into the translation thus far. In the panel discussions on specific issues, all of the elements which are considered relevant are weighed before a collective decision is made. At the present stage none of these decisions is considered final, but honoring the background and the suggestions of the Guhu-Samane members of the panel is paying off. (Richert 1965a, 85, emphasis in original, footnote removed)

In contrast to the colonial administration's mostly glowing reviews of the level of civilization of the Middle Warias, Richert is less effusive in his praise. The Guhu-Samane have only gained "a measure of sophistication" while "the core of their perception is still in the old matrix." *Poro,* the article suggests, is at the heart of this matrix. Competing against this matrix of traditional thought and perception is Christianity. But as Richert puts it at the end of the article, if *poro* is mostly about magic (and more—it is a matrix after all), then "the translation should be free from suggesting to the readers and hearers that the Bible is nothing more than another form of magic which can be manipulated to serve people's selfish ends" (Richert 1965a, 87).

Taking on the contrary characteristics of the fetish (Pietz 1985, 1987, 1988), *poro* is powerful as magic and matrix and yet also powerless in the face of Christianity. Richert posits both the equivalence of Christianity and *poro* as matrices of thought as well as the inequality of *poro* to stand up against the Christian revolution. *Poro* is, in that sense, a perfect example of the domesticating-but-foreignizing impulses behind the dynamic equivalence translation theory. Linguistically, Richert can tap into this matrix of thought to bring the biblical message to the Guhu-Samane in familiar, domestic terms. Culturally, this process of bringing *poro* and Christianity together provides scripture readers with the tools of contrast, of a foreignizing critique of traditional practices and beliefs: "all of the elements which are considered relevant are weighed before a collective decision is made" but "nothing is final." Throughout both of these processes of linguistic immediacy and cultural critique, "the Guhu-Samane" are brought into being as a group bounded, above all, by linguistic and cultural qualities.

In all of Richert's writings about translation, the emphasis is on "clear, accurate, and natural" translations that are derived through the best possible choice of words and expressions. These idioms and phrases are, for Richert, the difference between comprehension and puzzlement, salvation and ignorance. In Richert's main translation article, he primarily includes Guhu-Samane noun phrases that can stand in for Greek or English NPs, for example, *dzuube abi* (literally, "knife man") for "priest" or *poro tongo* (*poro* bond) for "testament." In addition to substitutions of English-language words, longer English-language idiomatic expressions were given Guhu-Samane flavorings. For example, the mark of successful completion of *poro* initiation, *qaraqaraho barei* (flower of life), which is slipped into an initiate's armband, represents the gift of eternal life from God in James 1:12.[18]

1	Qate	abi	teei	toronata	battigara	naate	qaaraqu
	But	man	one	test-LOC	strength	AUX1-PRES	continue-INF
2	oio	bagenoma.					
	DEM	good-ADJ					
3	Oi	teeho	bahe	apenei	Ohongaho	dzaodzaoke	eetorai
	DEM	one-GEN	NEG	who-SUB	God-GEN	desire-OBJ	AUX2-IMP
4	Ohongai	qaraqaraho	barei	nokoho	matubata		
	God-SUB	life-GEN	flower	3PL-GEN	armband-LOC		
5	dzeebidzakoiqi		hiireta.				
	slip.through-FUT-SS		say-PAST				
6	Oonita	torona	bamu	naatemake			
	then	test	NEG	AUX1-IRREAL/DS			
7	abi	oi	oho	barei	dzeebire		qaarakoi.
	man	DEM-SUB	DEM-GEN	flower	slip.through-PRES		continue-FUT

Back-translating from Richert's Guhu-Samane translation, this verse can be read as:

> A man continues to be strong in a test, that is good. (1–2) For that, whoever desires God, God said that he will slip the flower of life through their armbands. (3–5) When the test is over the man will slip his flower through. (6–7)

In the NIV (Anonymous 1978), this verse is rendered as:

> Blessed is the man who perseveres under trial, because when he has stood the test, he will receive the crown of life that God has promised to those who love him.

This suggests that Richert created an underlying message that put the verse in logical, sequential order. God promised man "the crown of life" before anyone actually received it. Therefore, the promise appears before the description of receiving the gift. The underlying message likely mirrored the following organization:

> A man who perseveres under a trial is a good man. God promised this crown of life to those who love him. When he passes the test, then he will receive the crown of life.

"Crown of life" in the Greek and most English versions becomes "flower of life (slipped through an armband)" in Richert's translation, a reference to a flower put in a man's armband as a sign of prestige or victory. Richert was concerned to use the right words and expressions, in the right order, to make the biblical text as comprehensible as possible.

In contrast to Richert's use of what he would call idiomatic English (i.e., a secular, business-oriented, register), the idioms often used in Guhu-Samane biblical texts had idioms coming from the language of the men's house, as, for example, in the name of the New Testament, *Poro Tongo Usaqe*. Richert saw his usage of *poro* terms as part of his project of "judicious selection and blending." However, *poro* talk is a highly specific register form, like much idiom-laced Guhu-Samane language. Far from "idiomatic" (in the sense of "contemporary and casual") idiom-inflected Guhu-Samane, particularly using *poro*-based idioms, are associated with the "heavy" (*hevi* in Tok Pisin [hereafter TP], *bahe* in Guhu-Samane [hereafter GS]) language that big men use when making speeches. In fact, when I asked a group of women what the *Poro Tongo* of *Poro Tongo Usaqe* means, nobody could tell me until a man from the current Guhu-Samane translation project was brought into the conversation to explain the term. These women are devout Bible readers and Christian critics, although they did not, in this case, have the knowledge to affectively experience the sense of heart-language familiarity or critical comparison that Richert was trying to create with this usage. Richert was concerned to constitute the Guhu-Samane language as a vehicle of Christian speech, but he emphasized a politically loaded and gendered register of it coming from the men's house politico-religious system that, for certain terms, remains relatively opaque to (some) women.

Richert's emphasis on constituting Guhu-Samane as a language and culture based on idioms of the men's house seems to have left less room for him to focus on other aspects of the intelligibility and naturalness of the translation. In particular, Richert seems to have paid much less attention to non-idiomatic, textual issues of morpho-syntactic clause chaining. In some cases these are simply due to errors. In the final clause of James 1:12 in Guhu-Samane (line 7 above), note that Richert has not constructed a passive sentence, implying that man himself "slips the flower of life through" the armband, rather than God. Richert intended this to be a passive, however, as seen in his own back-translation of his Guhu-Samane translation (Richert 1965a, 87):

> The man who is unmoved in a test is in a happy condition. For those who love God are the ones into whose armbands he promised to insert the victory flower of life. So then, after the test is over *that man will have the victory flower inserted.* (emphasis in original)

Richert often constructed sentences that lack some reference-tracking and clause-chaining material, which is important for producing the kind of flowing translation that he was aiming for and that he attempted in the English-language version of Romans excerpted above. This is attested by the many Guhu-Samane speakers, who mention that the New Testament translation is sometimes quite difficult to read. For example, in line 3, Richert uses a relative clause, which is a marked form of clause chaining, in contrast to the more common clause linkage device of tail-head constructions that are exemplified and explained below (see lines 7–19). Difficulties in reading are also apparent in recordings that I have of church services where men and women who are relatively fluent readers in Tok Pisin have a hard time reciting from the Guhu-Samane New Testament. In chapter 6, I include a transcript of a recitation of Acts 2:1–13. In that case, the speaker is trying to recite the text faithfully and corrects himself when he makes mistakes, and yet even so, the speaker adds morphological material like switch-reference markers to the text, presumably in an attempt to make the material clearer.

The marked syntactic constructions that Richert uses can be compared with portions of the Old Testament that have been published by native Guhu-Samane speakers, in particular, Timothy's son Mark, who leads the current Old Testament translation work. Mark's translation of Genesis is relatively clear and easy to read, according to local people. Compare Richert's translation in the passage above with the selection below, prepared by the local translators of Genesis 8:8–11, which narrates the end of the flood story, when Noah is testing to see if any dry ground has appeared.

8. Paana naatemi Noa hee,
   clear be-DS Noah QUOT
   Clearing, Noah said

9. "Oba uuromi haba khauratorai mae bamu oke moorako"
   water dry.up-DS place dry-IMP or NEG DEM-OBJ see-FUT
   "[I] will see: has the water receded and the ground dried or not"

10. Hiireqi qusubibi teke paha dzobiremi tuumata.
    say-DS dove one-OBJ again send-DS go-PAST
    Saying, he sent out a dove again and it went

11. Tuuma moomi oba haba pupubire oomi
    go-SER see-DS water place cover.up-SER be-DS
    Going [the dove] saw the water was covering the place/area

12. noi teeta taataquho isaki bamu naatemi
    3SG-SUB one-LOC land-INF-GEN size NEG be-DS
    there was not space to land on

13. paha burisi eete bammi
    again turn do-SER come-DS
    and it turned around and came back

14. Noai boto dzobire qusubibi aima sisimata mootota.
    Noah-SUB hand throw-SER dove take-SER ship-LOC put-PAST
    Noah thrust out [his] hand and took the dove and put it on the ship

15. Mootoqi qaami ete 7 naatemi Noa paha qusubibi dzobiremi tuumata
    Put-SS be-DS day 7 be-DS Noah again dove send-DS go-PAST
    Putting it for a while, seven days passed, and Noah again sent out the dove and it went

16. Tuuma qaami sure mootomi ee oribaho gee teke
    go-SER be-DS evening put-DS tree vine-GEN leaf one-OBJ
    Going for a while, evening fell, [the dove] bit one tree vine's leaf

17. gamaqo aima baami.
    bite-SS take-SER come-DS
    and took it and came back

18. Noa oke mooqi hee,
    Noah DEM-OBJ see-SS QUOT
    Noah saw this and he said,

19. "Oo oba ao uurorai" oke qupadzomata.
    oh! water COMP dry.up-IMP DEM-OBJ think-PAST
    "Oh! The water has dried up." That's what he thought.

Two main construction types typify this selection. First, they consistently have switch reference markers to string together matrix clauses, one after another. There are no relative clauses and few embedded constructions (line 12's "space to land on" is the only one). Serial verbs are used throughout to string together verb phrases performed by the same agent (e.g., lines 14 and 17). Second, every new sentence begins with the common non-Austronesian discourse device of tail-head chaining, where the final verb of the pervious sentence fronts the following sentence, creating sequences such as "Noah thrust out [his] hand and took the dove and *put* it on the ship. *Putting* it for a while, seven days passed, and Noah again sent out the dove. . . . " (lines 14–15). Although this overall consistency of syntactic construction types leads to a certain amount of stylistic homogeneity, it corresponds with local styles of narration.

It is unsurprising that Richert's translation would be less fluent than one done by a native speaker, as any SIL translator would agree. The goal of this brief comparison has been to emphasize that Richert's translation theory put particular stress on the role of idioms, the words and expressions that typified linguistic and cultural locality to him. This process of ethno-linguistic identity formation, and the particular expressions to which Richert attached it, received the bulk of attention, since it was through the construction of "the Guhu-Samane language and people" that the Christian message would be received, understood, and made the medium of radical religious change in cultural denominations. As I will discuss in the following chapters, Richert coordinated his translation work with his evangelistic goals that emphasized critical cultural reflection.

. . .

In this chapter, I have analyzed the ways in which Ernie Richert helped to bring about a local consciousness of a Guhu-Samane ethno-linguistic identity. Through practices and processes familiar largely from studies of Andersonian ethno-nationalism, Richert was able to develop a corpus of materials that objectified Guhu-Samane-ness: a language community organized around shared knowledge with delimited boundaries patrolled by literacy school teachers, a localized space for the collection of material and intellectual traditional property at Richert's Kipu base, a textual corpus of translated materials in Guhu-Samane language and orthography, and a sense of ordered, structured, intensional identity centered on men's house traditions. Beyond just a Bible, dictionary (published posthumously in 2002 as *Noo Supu*), and newspaper, Richert was creating a coherent unit, "the" Guhu-Samane out of the people who had been up to this point the Middle Warias (to the colonial administration), Kipu speakers (to the Lutheran mission), or residents of a given village with a certain set of kinship networks (to local people themselves).

Linguistic anthropology has for a while now found a particular niche in anthropological scholarship with its focus on ethno-linguistic identity. The many analyses and critiques of language-based belonging (e.g., Silverstein 2000; Irvine and Gal 2000; Woolard 1989; Eisenlohr 2006) found that ethno-linguistic identity was not a simple formation: it can combine with other identities, it can be forced from above by colonial scholarship, or it can be invented whole cloth out of a hodge-podge of ethnic differences. But in any of these accounts, the centrality of some kind of perduring identity—partial, conflicted, diasporic, coerced—has remained a constant. Ethno-linguistic identity has also licensed a large corpus of scholarship on linguistic ideologies, with those ideologies often explaining the naturalization or promotion of particular language-based identity formations (e.g., Hill 1998; Blommaert and Verschueren 1998).

In the remaining chapters of this book, I make an argument against the usefulness of a concept of identity in the analysis of Melanesian Christianity. One of the primary aspects of identity is the sense of perduring existence across space and time. As a foundation of ethno-nationalist imagination, identity is supposed to be eternal (as the French textbooks put it, national identity is based on "our ancestors, the Gauls"). It is on this basis that people often fight for a distinct political space or voice. The unique aspect of the nation-forming work in SIL and other mission contexts is that mission-sponsored ethno-linguistic identities contain within them the capacity for self-deconstruction. The Middle Warias had to become the Guhu-Samane *so that they could become Christian*. Ernie Richert needed that complex matrix of understanding provided by the men's house cult of *poro* so that his addressees could move not just from referential puzzlement at the foreign to the affective pleasures of recognition but also from that affective pleasure to a later moment of critical comparison. In that sense, Richert helped to codify an identity that was not meant to last very long, at least not in its totality. That is to say, Christianity is seen in the fracturing of the world through critical work: against culture, against tradition, against other denominations. The story of schism in the remaining chapters of this book is a story of Christianity at its critical height.

PART TWO

Christian Villages

CHAPTER 4

Revival Villages

*Experiments in Christian Social
and Spatial Groups*

In 1975 Ernest and Marjorie Richert distributed copies of the final, published version of their Guhu-Samane translation of the New Testament.
Ernest Richert used the occasion to tell the assembled people to maintain
the metaphorical, spiritual "fireplace" that he had built with them.
According to contemporary accounts of the event, Richert said that he
would soon send a match or a spark to ignite the fireplace, but it would
only light if Guhu-Samane people kept the fireplace ready. This comment
is now largely understood as a prophesy of the Holy Spirit revival (or,
more directly, a promise to send the Holy Spirit). Richert's acolytes, who
were still mostly in residence at the Kipu Academy, were in a state of
heightened expectation for a religious outpouring. At this time, revivals
were sweeping across Melanesia, especially in Solomon Islands and
Papua New Guinea. Yet locally, people today do not recognize their own
revival as having been a part of this larger movement. Rather, the translation itself (or Richert's long-distance summoning of the spirit) is seen to
be the major cause. In 1976 Ernest and Marjorie Richert left the Waria
Valley and returned to the United States. Some of their children remained
in the Waria for a few years, and Richert both returned to the Waria and
flew people to the United States in the early 1980s. However, his sustained presence in the valley ended after the translation was dedicated.

Many of the major players in the contemporary Waria Valley religious scene claim some kind of authorship of the revival, which began in
late 1976. As I will discuss in later chapters, claiming partial authorship

of the revival is one way to claim authority to start a new church. For example, Mark Timothy, who later helped form Reformed Gospel Church, says it began when he and some other men were jailed by the Lutherans for their exuberant (and destructive) church services. Their imprisonment at the Graaina jail led to speaking in tongues and many community members rallying around the young men. Rev. Sabara of Reformed Gospel, who spent much of his life working at the print shop at SIL headquarters and traveling the country as a Billy Graham–funded itinerant preacher, says he started the revival when he traveled home for a visit. But the most common revival narrative involves Ulysses, who had worked with Richert at Kipu in the literacy training program. In late 1976 Ulysses, his wife, and his daughters started to have visions of angels, God, and the Book of Life (written in Guhu-Samane), and they heard Jesus's voice "as if on a radio." Told by a mysterious white man to return to Ulysses's natal village of Au, they traveled across the valley during a major rainstorm and gathered people there to prepare a feast for this unnamed white visitor. On February 2, 1977, just as the feast was ready, the white man disappeared as mysteriously as he originally appeared, but in his place the power of the Holy Spirit descended on the people of Au village. People spoke in tongues, were born again, buried traditional magical items or remaining men's house sacra, and started a movement that eventually led to a split with the Lutheran Church.

It took several years for the split to happen. After the initial court case against some of Richert's exuberant young men, mentioned above, early revival leaders were summoned to defend their practices at a synod conference. Mark, who went as the representative of the revivalists, says that he used his (Spirit-derived) linguistic skills to defend the non-liturgical services and worship practices that people were deploying (loud calls of "Amen" with raised hands, group prayers, dancing during praise songs, etc.). Speaking in Kâte, Tok Pisin, Zia, and English, Mark used the theological training that he had received from Richert to defend himself from his inquisitors. The Lutheran missionaries considered the movement a potential cargo cult, an interpretation given credence by two early scholarly accounts (Burce 1983; Flannery 1983). Some revivalists were calling themselves the *Bilip Grup* (TP, Belief Group), praying on mountain tops, requesting signs (often cargo-based signs) from God, and communicating with heaven via noncanonical media, like flashlight messages in Morse code. It took about five years before the differences with the Lutherans finally seemed insurmountable, and the revivalists decided to start their own church, New Life Bible Church.

In this chapter, I use the contemporary memorializations of the revival to begin to examine how this process of independent Christianity reorganized Guhu-Samane religious groups. During my fieldwork, the revival story was told as a history of emancipatory possibility, when real change was finally going to come to the valley and to Papua New Guinea as a whole. Taking place just two years after the independence of the nation-state of Papua New Guinea, the 1977 revival seemed to be the chance for local people to reinvent themselves, using the power of the Holy Spirit. But this was not just a moment of individuals making covenants with God en masse. In order for Christianity to be localized, the village as a religious place had to be reorganized.

Colonial history provides many examples of administrators demanding the reorganization of space and place (J. Scott 1998; Stasch 2010; in Papua New Guinea, see Barker 1990, 1996; Dundon 2012; B. Schieffelin forthcoming). In order for colonial subjects to be enumerable under the gaze of census-takers, they had to be placed into regular and regulated living situations. People in New Guinea who were used to having houses in far-off garden or forest lands had to maintain residences in government-identified villages, regardless of local settlement patterns and social relationships (see Stasch 2009). Missionaries often tried to create villages that could organize people into congregations, where the panoptic eye of the missionary or lay evangelist could foster local people's sense of being watched and judged by God.

The reorganization of the Guhu-Samane villages as Christian spaces did not require much in the way of actual spatial transformation or outright villagization, as described by Scott or Stasch. As I discussed in chapter 3, post–World War II colonial administrators praised Guhu-Samane villages as already being model spaces of hygiene, order, and civilization. A church had to be constructed as a central node to partially displace the largely desanctified men's houses, but otherwise, the villages looked the same. Instead, the reorganization of the villages was a matter of reimagining the kinds of social relationships that characterize village life.

The relative order of Guhu-Samane villages masked an incredible amount of tension. Many Guhu-Samane people today commonly complain that living in a village is "hard work," requiring people to constantly navigate the endless demands brought on by conditions of such condensed sociality. It was not obvious or easy then to have that mysterious Jesus figure drop Ulysses and his family in Au village and expect them to start a Christian revival there. Figuring out how to make this tension-filled space into a Christian one was a major hurdle that the revivalists had to overcome.

It is important to see that the goal of making the village a Christian space was novel. Neither of the two major missions groups—Lutherans or SIL—emphasized villages as key sites for Christian work. As I argued in the previous chapters, these mission groups focused on contradictory formulations of Christian sociality. The Lutherans were concerned to create an ecumene across the Kâte District, organized according to a bureaucratic hierarchy that placed Christian power either in the circuit seat at Zaka (later Garaina), Lae, Germany, or the United States. The realization of Christian spirit came from not being local. The colonial Lutherans of the Waria Valley were supposed to engage in a far-flung generalized exchange of money and men, achieving Christian unity through the successful overcoming of ethnic and regional difference. The Richerts, as SIL members, focused instead on the ethno-linguistic group as the authorizing context for an authentic Christianity. Ernie Richert established an ethnicity-wide system of literacy schools and Bible instruction, but the focus was rooted in native language as a context for conversion.

The revival, then, was a revelation in the way it brought Christian practice into the village. This is not to say that people had not worshipped in villages before. Lutheran elders often conducted prayer services in villages, for example. It was, however, the first time that Christianity was emanating from a village, rather than from a distant mission station or translator-linguist. The revivalists were starting to experiment with the kinds of social relations and places that a locally centered Christianity might produce.

The revival celebrated ritual moments of individualized responsibility, developing a non-Lutheran tradition of full-immersion adult baptism that signaled a Christian individual reborn. That newly minted individual was responsible to God more than to his or her kin or village mates. But the revivalists developed this emphasis on the individual subject oriented toward God through experiments with the social groups that Christian individuals could form. The Holy Spirit had come down to them because they were speakers of the Guhu-Samane language, and they would have to respond to that call in ways that mirrored this ethno-linguistic form of address through processes of communal transformation. It would require experimentation and cultural critique, but Guhu-Samane revivalist Christianity would embrace the sociality of Christian practice as the way to respond to the Holy Spirit's message.

Mark Mosko (2010) argues that Christianity is not, in fact, a religion of individualism, and he finds in theological and ethnographic texts traces of a relationalism more commonly associated with Maussian gift exchange: God gave his only son so that humans could be incorporated into God's person, an incorporation materialized in the communion meal that has Christians ingest the body and blood of Jesus so as to themselves be absorbed into a Christian body. For Mosko, individualism is really only a fact of market interactions and is not even particularly well evidenced there. Scholars (especially Joel Robbins and John Barker) who purport to find individualist behaviors and ideologies in the global south are, from Mosko's perspective, forcing the rest of the world into a mold that even Westerners do not fit particularly well.

My own emphasis on the sociality of Protestantism could be interpreted as supporting Mosko's position. Certainly I consider it crucial to pay attention to the ways in which lateral relationships among Christians are fundamental aspects of Christian practice. However, my argument is predicated on the fact that there is an importantly individualist component of Christian practice. Social groups and sociality in general are difficult under Christian conditions precisely because of the ways in which Christian individualism demands that people are morally self-responsible. Christian groups like churches or villages are thus problematized as social organizations of critique, helping to constitute shared critical projects that particular communities of sinful humans have to develop.

Much of the relationalism that Mosko finds in Christianity is better thought of in terms of interactional responsiveness. God is nothing but talk, as Robbins (2001) pointed out a while ago, and so much of the concern over the constitution of Christian social groups depends upon getting the details of addressivity and response right. Whom was the Holy Spirit addressing? Who heard the message? How do we respond? With the well-oiled machinery of biblical citation practices that echo between local contexts and the New and Old Testaments, Christian groups form in the critical, quoted afterlife of divine communication. Spadola (2014, 5) argues similarly that embodied practices of Islamic piety and what Mosko might refer to as divine incorporation must also be seen in communicative terms, as responses to God's call to Islam. In this chapter, I examine how Guhu-Samane revivalists worked to remake the village as a space in which it would be possible to respond to the Holy Spirit's urgent moral demands, demands that could only be heard given their enunciation via the Guhu-Samane language New Testament.

THE SPACES OF SOCIALITY IN THE WARIA VALLEY

Before discussing the contemporary (2005–2006) celebrations of the revival, I want to first examine why it is that local people think of villages as spaces of hard work. In particular, I analyze how social formations among Guhu-Samane are understood in terms of locality and movement. Among Guhu-Samane, events of social interaction are based upon two contrasting spatial tropes: namely, clan-based social relations understood in terms of autonomous movement across a nonsocial landscape and village-based social relations understood in terms of conflict-ridden settlement within localized and politicized regions.

This contrast between clan and village is, to a certain extent, predictable, given that Guhu-Samane reckon clans matrilineally and at least stereotypically practice virilocal residence. That is, women establish the primary indexical, genealogical connections of clanship, but since women are on the move, clans are not geographically or even politically unified entities. As described by Victor Turner (1957) in his classic ethnography of Ndembu social life, the matrilineal-virilocal problem creates a situation of regular schism. Politically aspiring Ndembu men would form a new village with as many matrilineally related women and children as they could find, and in creating new villages, they also created new matrilines.

In Turner's account, matrilines and villages undergo schism for the same reason and in the same way. Not so for the Guhu-Samane, who understand their matri-clans to not undergo schism at all in the contemporary era, while they see their villages as doing so with disturbing frequency. That is, there is a marked asymmetry in the ways in which local people perceive the fragmenting potentialities of the two primary social formations that they regularly encounter or ideologize—matri-clans are stable entities in their constant movement across the valley, while villages are highly unstable in their emplacement in the political landscape. Matri-clans are presented as unified and peaceful, but also as being elsewhere (on the road) and elsewhen (in the historical past or in mortuary rituals). Villages, then, are given all the problems of the here-and-now.

This contrast can best be seen in terms of the local histories of Guhu-Samane settlement in the Waria Valley. Migrants from the Morobe coast, Guhu-Samane tell many histories that describe the process of peopling the valley and developing the political and social relations that created the exchange networks that cover the region now. One such subgenre of local history is the story of matri-clan migration, which generally follows this trajectory: "matri-clan Z started from the Morobe coast and traveled in a circuit up through the Waria Valley, over the Bowutu mountains, down to Salamaua, and along the coast to Morobe again. Then they did that same circuit three more times. On the last time, they crossed Z river and so became known as the Z river matri-clan." In these histories of travel, matri-clans are depicted as mobile, autonomous, internally undifferentiated, and alone: they move constantly across a landscape defined by geologic formations (rivers, mountain passes, etc.) rather than by political ones, and they meet no other people until they settle down (see also M. Scott 2007; S. Harrison 1985; and R. Foster 1990 for Melanesian cases of spatialized matri-clan identity). When matri-clans do fission in these stories, it is not a political process of recognizing difference so much as an unintended drifting away: "Some of them were there when a dust storm kicked up, so they became known as the Dust matri-clan." In the idyllic history of matri-clan movement, there never could be a reason to recognize difference.[1]

If clan histories present life as a journey, village histories present life as a destination, and not a very good one. As those spaces where matri-clans settle down and intermarry with other matri-clans after their histories of movement, villages represent the end of the autonomy, harmony, and unity that defined the matri-clan on the road. Histories of village formation and fission focus upon the establishment of the political differences that give social life its definition today. While this process of differentiation created the conditions for the feast exchange networks that interconnect different parts of the valley, it did so through violence, death, and greed. If a dust storm kicks up in one of these *village*-based myth histories, it's because someone is doing the kicking.

This same distinction between harmonious travel and tension-filled settlement can be seen in the difference between two media and means of identifying clanship: *poro ttidza* designs of road-based broadcast identity and clan *pasara*s mediating intra-village difference. A *poro ttidza* is a clan- or lineage-specific design that traditionally was drawn on the bark-cloth capes that people wore on their backs, although *poro ttidza* designs might also be part of the decoration of a men's house or, these days, simply reproduced in notebooks men keep to maintain clan knowledge (sometimes called "culture books" [*kalsa buk*, TP]; see also Besnier 1995; Halvaksz 2005). They are line drawings done in black paint, colored with red, yellow, green, or blue pigment. Some are understood to be highly abstract representations of animals or of features of the landscape. They are, in addition to being clan and lineage identifiers, objects of aesthetic appreciation. The big man of Titio village, in which I lived, for example, found his own clan's *poro ttidza* to be rather ugly.

Regardless of their beauty, *poro ttidza* designs alerted others to the existence of the clan or lineage that it emblematized. In the old days, people would say, one would see a person or a whole group of people from far off walking down a road. One would identify that person or that group solely by the *poro ttidza* design on the back of their bark-cloth cape(s), saying, "oh, there goes (someone of) such-and-such clan." In several cases, people expressed a sense of awe in remembering or imagining the aesthetic beauty of seeing a line of people with identical *poro ttidza* designs on their backs. In this mini-drama of identification, some of the same characteristics of migratory clanship emerge: people are defined only by clanship, because they are on the road. Note too that this form of identification is not a moment of interclan interaction. People are recognized by their clan designs only when others see them from behind. *Poro ttidza* designs are forms of broadcast communication, legible as signs without interpersonal communicative action.

In contrast to the *poro ttidza* emblem of clan movement, homogeneity, and univocality that is prototypically found on the road and away from places of settlement, the clan *pasara* is the emblem most identified with the complexities of interclan interaction that is a necessary part of living in a village. Clan and lineage *pasara*s are ritual, poetic forms of address, two or three lines long, using a form of Guhu-Samane that people recognize as the language of the ancestors (which is to say, people generally do not have the ability to give semantic glosses for *pasara*s except for a word here or there that they may recognize from their contemporary speech). You do not generally say your own *pasara* (although you will say it in the context of certain land claims as proof of your knowledge of clan history); normally, you only hear others saying it to you in greeting. In addition to being differentiated by clan and lineage, *pasara*s are also specific to gender, the *pasara* one says to a male member of a given clan being different from the *pasara* one says to a female member of that clan. Guhu-Samane translate *pasara* into Tok Pisin as *adres* (address). As this translation implies, the *pasara* serves to locate you.

As with *poro ttidza* designs, older Guhu-Samane lament the loss of clan *pasara*s as forms of address, since they see them as a central element of the kind of politeness that makes villages work, when people are given the recognition due to them. Interestingly, however, a number of other *pasara* forms are still in common use, and the ways in which they circulate shed light on the use of clan *pasaras*. Most importantly, the common way of opening a Christian prayer in the Waria is to start with what is referred to as God's *pasara*, "God of Abraham, God of Isaac, God of Jacob," said in either Guhu-Samane *(Abaramuhu Ohonga, Isakiho Ohonga, Jekobho Ohonga)* or Tok Pisin *(God bilong Abraham, God bilong Isak, God bilong Jekob)*. In the sense that God is the persona who people say requires the greatest respect in contemporary life, the fact that a form of the *pasara* ritual address is maintained in prayer, when one addresses God specifically, is an indication of the *pasara*'s primary role as a respectful form of address and recognition.

In contrast to the *poro ttidza* designs, then, *pasaras* are indeed moments of Althusserian hailing, when one is seen by others and confirms that recognition. A *pasara* is the prototypical emblem of the clan as it exists in the village, rather than on the road, for its interactional and addressive nature. No longer seen as a homogeneous and autonomous group engaged in travel and movement, clans and lineages as emblematized by *pasaras* depict individual members in the spaces of virilocal settlement where multiple clans have converged.

In contemporary Guhu-Samane social life, people embrace and expand upon the moral characterizations of space and place that are presented in myth-histories or clan identifiers. Living in a village is "hard work" because it is a space saturated by difference, where every coresident makes unique demands on you. People often express their desire to go live in a "camp" (*kam*, TP) filled only with immediate matrikin, and some do so. Of course, these camps suffer the same fate as any other localization of matri-clans in a largely virilocal system, maintaining coherence and sometimes existence not much beyond the second generation. The impossibility of social unity in a matrilineal but virilocal situation is glossed in everyday terms in the way that mothers address their misbehaving sons as "father." "Fathers are different," said a friend of mine, pointing to their different clan affiliation, need for respectful behavior, and affective distance. Calling your son "father" when he is ignoring your commands indexes this sense that even the immediate family is mediated by these sociopolitical tensions.

Villages are the spaces in which social relations are expanded through marriages, where affinality is posed against matrilineality as two forms of social relating. However, local people understand this as an opposition between *villages* and matri-clans, not *affines* and matri-clans. This is best seen in the ways in which people participate in certain inter-village family conflicts and resolve them. In the examples below, problems of affines are dealt with as problems of villages and are contrasted against clans.

One afternoon in Titio village (like most villages, almost all residents are practicing Christians), a young married man, here called Ono, came back from his garden to see that one of his unmarried sisters had eaten some of the bananas he had brought back earlier in the day. Ono, who is known for his short temper, started yelling at his sister, brandishing the ax that he was carrying, and eventually hitting her on the head with the flat side of the blade. Ono's father had been trying to calm his son down and protect his daughter but was not successful in either goal. The father ran into his house to get his bow and arrow while Ono kept attacking his sister. The father eventually shot Ono in the thigh with an arrow, at which point Ono hobbled off to his mother's brother, who lives in one of the villages of the neighboring Peqira area. Ono stayed with his matrikin until a meeting was called in Titio to settle the matter. Ono came back from Peqira accompanied by several male cousins from his own clan (i.e., parallel cousins), who supported him throughout the meeting.

The meeting was well underway, with both sides given a chance to explain their actions and demand the compensation they felt to be appropriate, when suddenly Ono's mother, Geenoma—the woman who links Ono, his father, and his mother's brother—broke in and took the floor. Seated away from the loose circle in which the principals sat, Geenoma started screaming and crying, stopping all other talk. "Why did Ono go to my brother?" she asked. "This was a small problem, just a village problem, but then Ono made it a big problem when he went to Peqira and his kin there. Had this stayed in the village, everything would be fine. But now it is a very big problem." Geenoma spoke for a relatively long time, crying and wailing as she went, and the compensation that was eventually decided upon reflected her concerns. Ono's father was to give a pig to Ono in compensation for shooting him in the leg. But Ono was also to give a pig to his father in compensation for hitting his sister and for going to his mother's brother and making it "a big problem."

This conflict reflects a common tension in matrilineal societies between fathers and mother's brothers as opposed representatives of two different clans. But note that when Geenoma addresses this, she does so in terms of villages versus matri-clans. It was a small problem, she says, when it was an internal village problem. It became a big problem, requiring whole pigs for compensation, when Ono went to his mother's brother. For Geenoma, something about the *village* (not the family, not the matri-clan) was disrupted when Ono ran away.

Another example, which I heard about on my return to the Waria Valley in 2007, demonstrates that villages as spaces of affinality are seen as being in conflict not with other villages but with matri-clans. A married couple from Au village was having serious marital problems, and the woman, Margaret, took the couple's children and moved to another village. Margaret never went anywhere without a male relative to escort her, because she had been assaulted by her husband on several occasions when he tried to take some of his children out of Margaret's care. On a busy market day, Margaret came without an escort to Garasa Station. Present that day were a number of Margaret's clan-mates who live in Titio, including a Titio village leader, Pati, whom Margaret refers to as "mother's brother." At some point Margaret's husband jumped out from the bushes bordering the Garasa airstrip and tried to grab Margaret's youngest son. Margaret's estranged husband started to hit her so as to loosen her grip on the child. At this point the village leader from Titio—Margaret's classificatory mother's brother, Pati—tried to intervene. So did one of Pati's sister's sons from Titio village (that is, Margaret's classificatory parallel cousin, whom she calls "brother"). However, a leader from Au village spoke to Pati and insisted that he stand down and that he also call off his nephew. "This is Au village's problem," he said. Pati relented and also made his nephew step aside. Margaret's husband left, taking with him the child he had come to reclaim. Margaret was eventually able to get her youngest child back into her care, but soon after, she moved to Lae to live with her sister.

As with the story of Ono's flight to his mother's brother, this story illustrates the ways in which villages are seen as under threat from matri-clan relationships. Margaret's Titio-based matrikin are told to step aside not because it is a private matter, a family matter, or a marital matter, but because it is a village matter. In both cases, women are violently attacked, but these attacks elicit anxieties about the health of villages rather than the health of the abused women. Village-centered and village-centering affinal relations are seen as threatened by extra-local matri-clan relations.

Clans provide a conceptual domain of imagined peace that would be achievable if only people did not have to organize into villages. Even if contemporary experiences of clans never quite reach such utopian heights, they offer a logic of escape from the daily village-based interactions that pull people in different directions. But real relief from the seemingly coerced relationality of villages comes only with death, when mortuary feasts "deconceive" (Mosko 1983) people into having an overarching clan identity. In fact, mortuary rituals are the most common contexts for clan groups to come together, when a clansman's death becomes the context in which the clan is reasserted as the encompassing relationship linking people to the dead person and vice versa. As village-based social life recedes in death, clans can come into primary focus.

There are two main kinds of mortuary rituals. One is actually performed prior to the death of an aging clan-mate and is an event almost exclusively involving the clan of the dying person. These rituals (*sumu biidzano*, GS; literally "holding the stick") are done for both men and women, although I only saw or heard of them being performed for women while I was in the Waria Valley. Especially politically important men are the subjects of a series of rituals *after* death, in which the deceased's wife and children (necessarily of another clan) have to compensate the dead man's clan.

Near the beginning of my fieldwork, a number of people of the Kheruba clan traveled to Garaina village in order to take part in a celebration of an elderly Kheruba woman's life. Kheruba clan members of several different named lineages traveled to Garaina, many carrying adult pigs trussed up on stretchers to be killed and distributed there. All-night singsings were performed after all of the Kheruba people had arrived, and the next morning, the pigs were lined up with stakes. These stakes were treated with magical incantations, described to me as the *strong bilong Kheruba* (TP, the strength of the Kheruba clan). After the pigs were staked and garden foodstuffs (especially taro and yam) were arranged in piles, a grandson and a granddaughter of the feted woman were placed on either end of the line of pigs, representing the reproductive capacity and good care that this woman used in creating a large line of Kheruba clan members. The elderly woman was then brought out from her house and presented with a decorated club or stick, and other Kheruba told her "life history," including her genealogy, her marriage, and the offspring she produced. The reproductive capacity of this life history was visually represented through the line of pigs given by fellow clansmen and capped by two of her grandchildren at either end. After this, raw food was distributed to the guests. Finally, the woman was led back into her house, carrying the stick given to her as well as some of the food. From this moment until her death, she no longer had any social obligations—a retirement from society that precedes the physical process of death itself. She would spend the rest of her days in her house (*i stap long haus tasol*, TP).

This ceremony was meant to forestall any anger her clansmen might feel at her death. Because her death had been announced (the event, people said, was a *tok save* [TP] or *poro kiranoma* [GS], "announcement"]), and Kheruba clansmen had been recognized through food gifts, they could not come and damage the woman's house or injure her immediate family upon her death. Their potential accusations of bad care or sorcery had already been quashed by her family showing their appreciation for her work. The clan was recognizing itself as a collective entity through the recognition of this woman's reproductive and parental capacities.

While the Kheruba celebration was narrated to me as an event involving a single clan, most mortuary rituals are structured through a logic of exchange. Post-death mortuary rituals, particularly for important men, are moments at which both the clan of the dead man and the clan of his wife and children are able briefly to create their clans as corporate bodies at the moment of individual loss. In the instance that I saw, the clan members of the man's wife and children were the sponsors of the event, with cash, pigs, and garden produce flowing in the direction of the dead man's clan.

The deceased man, Bernard, was the first councilor of the area (the local-level government representative) and held the position for two terms. At the time of his death, he was visiting one of his daughters, who lives in Alotau. When news of his death arrived via two-way radio, his wife and children immediately began wailing, doing so for most of the afternoon and into the evening. This initial display of grief was, I was told, a way of showing that the family was not responsible for the death through sorcery or ill treatment, and its intended audience was primarily the dead man's clansmen. People in the village were expected to come witness the family's grief (and innocence) publicly. That first day of mourning was fraught with tension, because everyone was aware that Bernard's clansmen would be questioning Bernard's family's decision to allow him to travel to Alotau—did this show a fatal disregard for their clan-mate? Several of Bernard's clansmen living in adjacent villages who received news of Bernard's death on that afternoon specifically refused to come to his family's house to witness their grief. The mortuary rituals that followed were, perhaps more than usual, aimed at quelling this clan anger through gifts that Bernard's family's clan presented to Bernard's own clan.

As a former council member and member of the army, Bernard was considered such an important figure that, although his daughter's husband's family offered to bury Bernard in Alotau, the daughter and her husband took out a bank loan to cover the K5,000 (roughly $1,800) cost of having his body flown into Garasa on a chartered plane. When the body finally arrived, Bernard's wife and children again took the lead in public displays of grief, crying loudly over both the coffin, along with Bernard's Alotau-based daughter, who had accompanied it. In addition to bringing the body, the Alotau-based daughter brought all of Bernard's belongings, including the K1,000 she had given him earlier in his stay. This money was given to Bernard's clansmen, divided according to a sense of closeness of relationship, although given primarily to male relatives. Much energy was put into proving that Bernard's wife and children had kept none of the money for themselves. (Bernard's material possessions—clothes, blankets, and so forth—were divided among his wife and children in private.)

On the day of the body's arrival, a church service was held, with the distribution of pig and garden food afterward. These pigs were given to Bernard's wife and children by other members of their clan, who also acted as hosts and leaders of the events. The family cooked and distributed the pig meat, particularly to Bernard's clansmen. This pattern continued throughout the next couple of days—when the body was mourned in Bernard's house, when it was buried, and on the day after. In each case, live pigs flowed to Bernard's wife and children from members of their clan, after which Bernard's daughters cooked the meat and gave the major portions of it to members of Bernard's clan. After a week of these events, Bernard's clan announced that they were satisfied with the gifts that they had received and that their anger had been quelled, and they started to go home. It was only upon this announcement that the mortuary rituals were declared over.[2]

The image of the dying Guhu-Samane person is that of someone returning to an encompassing clan identity, similar to the kind imaged in the mythic travels of clans on their migratory paths in the valley. While the church services for Bernard's funeral included speakers who told his life story and elaborated on the many kinds of social relations he had formed throughout his life, the organization of food and gifts that were the central points in the mortuary rituals solidified Bernard as a member of his clan above all else and solidified his clansmen as the people through whom this identification could be made. Unlike the multiplex social relations formed in a village that compromise and complicate one's presupposed clan identity, mortuary rituals describe an arc that brings individuals back to group formations of migratory clan hordes in their constant state of travel. Bernard's grave is on the road too, just outside of the village in which he lived.

Clans and villages are by no means the only forms of social relationship available to people. They are, however, the two most salient ones, the best to think with. Polarizing social life into oppositions of unity and fractiousness, singularity and fragmentation, clans and villages offer culturally specific models of sociality. The problem for the revival Christians who tried to make villages the new home of local and emancipated religious practice is that villages garner mostly negative characteristics in the clan-village opposition. The village institution of the men's house had been the politico-religious center of village life that worked to create unity within the fractious village. But as I discuss below, revivalists ran into problems when they tried to adapt men's house practices of village fortification into village Christianity.

THE REVIVAL: MAKING THE HOLY SPIRIT LOCAL

I want to turn now to the New Life commemoration of the revival that I witnessed in 2006, in which the movement away from Kipu station and the Lutheran church and toward Au village and local Christianity was told in terms of emancipation and real, radical change. New Life memorializes the set of events known as "the revival" in a way that makes a complete break with Lutheran discourse and inserts the revival as the starting point for an entirely new one.

Like the other crusades[3] that happen annually in the valley, the February 2 Crusade is hosted by a different village each year according to a rotating schedule, lasts for about a week, and has at least three church services a day. But unlike the other Christian crusades in the Waria, the February 2 Crusade is a uni-denominational event: only members of New Life are invited, because only they are the proper inheritors of the revival movement. In 2006, a handful of leaders of other churches were asked to come, but this was a new experiment.

All of the worship and cultural practices that are the proximate causes of criticism about New Life (primarily their strong embrace of local cultural practices within specifically Christian contexts) are evident in the February 2 events. Particularly egregious to non–New Life sensibilities are the traditional all-night dances held after the evening church service on at least one night. Coupled with other indices of traditional feasting, members of other churches find much to complain about. For one woman attending in 2006 as a representative of the Old

Testament translation project, the event's mix of the traditional and the Christian could be dismissively summed up as "75 percent material, 25 percent spiritual" (said in English).

That 75 percent of material tradition, coupled with many Guhu-Samane language services, is enough to limit the audience to Guhu-Samane only. Indeed, most of the sermons and speeches I saw during the 2006 crusade, including the one analyzed below, began with the speaker shouting "hello, Guhu-Samane!" *(dzoobe, Guhu-Samane!),* something I had never heard in a sermon or speech before. The loudly broadcast assumption of ethnic homogeneity was another form of social exclusion in comparison to the multiethnic crusades other churches hold in the valley, where neighboring Kunimaipan individuals from the Ono and Bubu Valleys sometimes attend. The traditionalism of the event did have one plus for the few leaders from other churches in attendance: they could finally point out to me many of the elements of traditional culture that they had so far only been able to describe from their childhoods.

As part of New Life's claim on the revival, the February 2 Crusade always includes a formal telling of the revival history so that, as one New Life member put it, the young people can know where the church comes from. This history used to be told by Ulysses, because many of the revival events celebrated in the speech happened to him and his wife, Teresa, which has made him the central figure of the revival church. But in 2006, with Ulysses quite old, a young leader in the church, Simon, recited the history after only a very short introductory speech from Ulysses. Speaking through a bullhorn from a grandstand built for the crusade, Simon read and improvised from a script, titled "The History of How the Holy Spirit Came to the Guhu-Samane." Ulysses stood next to Simon on the grandstand during this recitation, sometimes clasping his hands above his head in victory during particularly important moments of the story. The speech is, in many ways, similar to a sermon in its use of biblical citation and its length (about forty minutes). As part of the experiment in openness with other churches who have some non-Guhu-Samane members—and perhaps for my benefit as well—the speech was performed mostly in Tok Pisin, with regular, but brief, code-switches into Guhu-Samane.[4]

Crucial to this history is the account of the kinds of social groups to whom the Holy Spirit addresses itself. I focus specifically on the problems of becoming local Christians when village locality itself is understood to be the cause of so much unchristian animosity and discord. How did fractious villages become Christian villages in the revival? I begin with the account of how God and the Holy Spirit first identified the Guhu-Samane and, eventually, created real change in their lives. This history of heavenly recognition and change is contrasted with the history of colonization and Lutheran missionization that Simon suggests was completely inconsequential because it could never be local. The colonial era is figured here as a nonevent of history. But as we also see, the colonial era leaves its mark in the ways in which it constructs locality as the negation of Lutheran evangelism or administration governance. In the following excerpt, Simon finishes his prologue and begins to read from the scripted portion of the speech, starting with its title:[5]

1 "Histori bilong Holi Spirit I Kam Daun long Ol Guhu-Samane"

   "The History of How the Holy Spirit Came to the Guhu-Samane"

2 As bilong Holi Spirit i kam daun long Guhu-Samane em i olsem

   The origin of the Holy Spirit coming to the Guhu-Samane

3 mak bilong- mak bilong tanim tok long Buk Baibul i bin stap long hap bilong yumi Guhu-Samane.

   is the point when- point when the Bible translation was happening in our Guhu-Samane land.

4 Em olsem, misin, gavman i kam insait long kantri bilong yumi

   That is, the [Lutheran] mission and government had come inside our country

5 na yumi kamap Kristen manmeri pinis.

   and we were Christian people already.

6 Tasol yumi no gat Holi Spirit long ah- kamapim nupela laip o sindaun.

   But we did not have the Holy Spirit to ah- in order create a new way of life.

7 Olsem na long- olsem na, God i wok long tingting na save bilong ol ah,

   And so in- and so God worked on the thoughts and knowledge of the- um

8 ol save, ol misin na wokman bilong Amerika long kam sindaun long olgeta hap bilong-

   the knowledgeable, the missionaries and workmen of America to come [and] live in all of the parts of-

9 hap bilong Papua New Guinea,

   parts of Papua New Guinea,

10 go long wan- long wanwan ples na tanim tok long- ah,

   in each- in each village and translate- um

11 tanim tok bilong Buk Baibel i go kamap long tokples bilong ol yet

translate the Bible into all their different languages.

12 So taim God i- God i salim ol wokman na misinari i kam sindaun long wanwan hap

And when God- God sent the workmen and missionaries to come live in each village

13 bilong Papua New Guinea

of Papua New Guinea

14 em i salim Dr. Ernie Richert, Rikato

he sent Dr. Ernie Richert, Rikato.

15 No napai hee Rikato hiirorai.

We called him Rikato.

In other words, the colonial government and the colonial church were already there, and had already made (nominal) Christians out of the inhabitants of the country (lines 4–5). They were born into Lutheranism and colonial subjecthood, but this was doing nothing for them. When God saw that the government and Lutheran mission were not creating new ways of life for the people of Papua New Guinea, he called in SIL (6–13). Through SIL's and Ernie Richert's work, the Guhu-Samane translation of the New Testament was able to give the Guhu-Samane access to something that had been denied to them before, the Holy Spirit and its transformative power. The translation and language work was God's response to the mission's and the administration's inept lack of change.

The continuing ineffectiveness of the postcolonial government, in contrast to the highly effective Holy Spirit, is directly confronted when Simon, later in the speech, describes the revival's eruption in Au village, in which everyone renounced their old ways in order to live new lives for God.

1 So taim Holi Spirit i kam daun, inapim ples na manmeri olgeta

So when the Holy Spirit came down [and] filled the village and everyone in it,

2 pasin nogut bilong manmeri i kam ples klia

people's evil ways came out into the open.

3 poisen, marila, olgeta kainkain pasin nogut

Poison, love magic, all kinds of bad things,

4 i kamap ples klia

came out into the open

5 na manmeri i kisim ol samting nogut bilong ol

and people gathered their bad things

6 na kam na beten na planim.

and came and prayed and buried them.

7 (*dzoobe*)

8 Yumi save tok, wet na ol mobails, ol task fos ol i kam

We always say that we should wait for the mobile squads and task forces [of the PNG police] to come

9 nau bai yumi sarenda long ai bilong ol

and that we will surrender to them [lit. in their eyes].

10 Long dispela taim olgeta manmeri bin sarenda long taim Holi Spirit i bin makim

At this time [the revival], everyone surrendered at the time that the Holy Spirit noted

11 o kamapim sin bilong ol insait long haus lotu bilong ol.

or made our sins apparent in their church.

12 Na long dispela taim olgeta manmeri i bin kam, kam, kam antap, na ol i apim han

And at this time, everyone kept coming up and they raised their hands

13 na ol i promis na ol i sarenda long ai bilong God

and they promised and they surrendered under the eyes of God.

14 Yumi- yumi save sarenda long ai bilong ol polisman

We- we always surrender under the eyes of the police

15 yumi- insait long bel polis i no save wokim

we- inside the heart the police don't do anything.

16 Tasol dispela taim Holi Spirit makim bel bilong manmeri na tok

But at this time, the Holy Spirit claimed people's hearts and said,

17 nau yet yu mas sarenda

"right now you must surrender."

18 Na olgeta manmeri sarenda long dispela taim.

And everyone surrendered at this time.

19 Na ol i bin putim aut olgeta samting i save mekim ol i kamap sin manmeri

They brought out everything that had made them become sinners.

20 Ol i putim aut ples klia na ol i apim han
   They brought it out into the open, and they raised their hands,

21 na ol i promis na ol i tok
   and they promised and said,

22 God, mipela lusim ol dispela samting
   "God, we renounce all of these things.

23 Nau mipela laik bihainim laif bilong Holi Spirit nau.
   Now we will follow the life of the Holy Spirit."

24 *(dzoobe)*

Since the onset of colonization, the administration and mission had been trying to rid local populations of various aspects of traditional practice. The administration spent most of its time on homicides; the Lutheran church spent most of its time on polygamy and the premarital or extramarital sex that occurred during the dances and feasts sponsored by men's houses. For Guhu-Samane, these practices are metonymically invoked through the paraphernalia of poison and love magic, respectively (1–5). But it was only "at this time" of the revival (lines 10, 12, 16, 18)—with the sudden formation of a relationship to the Holy Spirit—that the true surrender and burial of these ritual objects could happen.

At one point in the speech, February 2, 1977, is referred to as a "spiritual independence day" (said in English), an implicit contrast with the September 16, 1975, political independence day for the nation-state of Papua New Guinea. However, religious independence, in this case, comes as a form of "surrender" to God and the Holy Spirit (lines 9, 10, 13, 14, 17, 18). This surrender, which creates real change in the form of burial of "sinful" ritual objects, is contrasted with the uselessness of surrendering to the state, in particular, to the national Papua New Guinean police force (8–10, 14–15). "Mobile squads" and "task forces" come through rural areas like the Waria Valley that don't have a regular police presence when word of illicit activities reaches the provincial capital, Lae. A few months before my arrival in 2005, a mobile squad had come to the Waria Valley and, acting only on the word of local residents, shot and killed nine young men accused of various robberies and homicides. One young man from Titio village, where I was based, was chased into the jungle and has not been seen since. His houses and everything in them were burnt down.

In some sense, then, the mobile squads are terribly effective. What the mobile squads and task forces cannot seem to do, however, is create a sustained difference in local lives, if only for the fact that the police can rarely be coaxed out of their urban barracks to come to the more remote parts of the country. Notice how Simon says that "we always say that we should *wait* for the mobile squads and task forces" (8–9), a comment that implies that sins and illegalities are, in general, identified months or even years before the state does anything about them. In contrast to this, the Holy Spirit is a force that can and does come to the more remote parts of the country. New Life Church celebrates the revival—and the church that was born out of it—as the beginning of a sustained local engagement with an effective force for real change. The revival—brought about by SIL—unseats and overcomes both the state and the mission.

In the previous two segments of the speech, Simon constitutes the Guhu-Samane language as the sacred mediator of the Holy Spirit's power, through God's decision to send SIL to the Waria Valley, and he shows how this vernacular-mediated power of the Holy Spirit was far more transformative than the state or mission had ever been. At this point, Simon begins to discuss the specific local origins of the revival. Over the course of the entire speech, Simon concentrates on the character of this new spiritual landscape. In particular, God insists upon the construction of a new village site at Au, where these manifestations of the Holy Spirit were occurring.

1 God i tokim ol Au

 God told the people of Au. . . .

2 i no go yet long Guhu-Samane yet

 It [the revival] hadn't gone to all of the Guhu-Samane people yet

3 God i wok long pulim ol Au nau long dispela taim

 God was pulling the people of Au at this point

4 Spirit bilong God i kamdaun long sekon Febueri

 The spirit of God came down on the second of February.

5 Em wok long tokim ol Au long lusim olpela ples na go painim nupela ples

 It worked on talking to the people of Au about leaving the old village site and finding a new village site.

6 Tasol Holi Spirit i tokim ol olsem

 But the Holy Spirit spoke to them:

7   ples we mi makim yupela mas go tru long en na wokim ples tasol nau long en

"the village site I chose, you [pl] must go there and build the village only there."

8   Em olsem yumi tok pinis

It's like we have already said.

9   Olgeta sarenda pinis na

Everyone had surrendered and

10   em i tokim ol

it [the Holy Spirit] spoke to them:

11   olpela pasin, olpela bel, olpela man i lus pinis

"Old ways, old hearts, old men, are gone now."

12   Olsem na, na em i- em i makim nupela ples olsem nupela laif, nupela sindaun, nupela tingting na-

And so, it- it marked out a new village site for a new life, a new peace, a new way of thinking,

13   planti ol gutpela samting God i laik mekim long ol-

many good things that God wanted to do for them-

14   em olsem, em i mak bilong lusim olpela ples na go long nupela ples

It was the sign of leaving the old village and going to the new village.

15   So God yet i makim ol- makim na- ah- wokim ples long dispela-dispela hap

So God himself marked them- marked it and built the village, in this- this area.

The assumption of an experientially truer Christianity that could make new men was the assumption of village Christianity. While some villages had had Lutheran lay evangelists stationed in them, the power of the mission was always seen to reside at the mission stations, particularly the stations with resident European missionaries. Village Christianity thus refers to the capacity to move the center of Christian power to local villages like Au. But since villages have always been the sites of strife and earthly conflict, a new village was needed to show that a new kind of Christian village was being born, one in which church and village could be coterminous. While this transformation of Au village into an Au village centered on a church is spoken of here as a miraculous one ordained by the Holy Spirit, it is important to see just what the transformation entailed, especially since at later moments, this same transformation was repeated in every village in the Waria region.

RITUAL ELICITATIONS: TAKING THE TEMPERATURE OF THE VILLAGE

Although village residents often speak about them in very negative terms, villages are not just dystopian socioscapes of conflict and difference. Politico-religious leaders have long worked to organize central institutions to mitigate the conflicts of village life. In the past, this institution was the men's house, while today that institution is often the church. I will discuss some aspects of the men's house system in the following chapter, but for the present, I want to primarily draw attention to the ways in which the men's house and its associated practices have been used to elicit village unity in concentrated bursts of coordinated action that temporarily overcome the problems of villages as spaces of discord.

Starting with the ritual that is performed to initially attract potential residents to a new village, village leaders use a kind of powerful magic called *tukuta ma adzaita* to gather people toward a single goal. In these moments of heightened activity and awareness, the village approximates the kind of unity that is otherwise the presupposed norm of elsewhere and elsewhen clan homogeneity. This unifying magic is often used to bring village residents together for large projects of community work.

The efficacy of this form of ritual elicitation of others depends upon a set of conceptual oppositions in which coolness, peacefulness, water, and women are opposed to heat, anger/energy/vitality, fire, and men. Cool women are usually in a state of openness that is most identified with their reproductive capacity to grow and nurture children within them (see also Mosko 1983). Men are fonts of heat and anger that give them power to fight. In the days when initiated men slept and socialized in village men's houses (dominated by two enormous fireplaces), purity taboos restricted male-female interactions so as to minimize the polluting coolness of wives or sex partners for hot men. Men, including Christian men, still bathe upstream from women's bathing areas so they can avoid female coolness (in the form of menstrual blood or other secretions).

However, this hot/cold distinction is not an absolute marker of gender, but a relative and situational one that is the outcome of specific

FIGURE 4. An extremely tall men's house in the Papuan Waria region.

social actions. Women can practice a form of birth control that can make them barren and relatively hot. They eat a bit of a certain kind of vine that had been roasted in their hearth, which makes their wombs likewise hot and brittle. When they want to have children, they can submerge the charred vine in water. A friend of mine suggested that one childless woman in the village must have "cooked" her vine too much, making it impossible to reconstitute a watery environment in which a child could grow.

Likewise, men have to work to maintain themselves in a constant state of heat through their avoidance practices, particularly washing upstream from women and sleeping in a separate space. For special gatherings and events, one or two men can metonymically increase the heat of the village as a whole by engaging in a series of purifying and heating rituals. They avoid water as much as possible, drinking as little as they can, not washing in the river, and eating only food that has been roasted in a fire rather than boiled in a pot.

Tukuta ma adzaita magic requires these water-shunning taboos, since it is magic to "lift and lighten." Just as things that have been desiccated are lighter and easier to lift than when they are in a watery state, certain men desiccate themselves to metonymically make the community's burden easier to lift. Divested of the forms of cooling waters that are used to create people (watery wombs or semen), hot people are put into a same-sex state, in Strathern's (1988) terms, and are able to work as a cohesive unit on major projects. *Tukuta ma adzaita* magic was used to quickly relocate a four-house family camp into Titio village after the people in the camp were assaulted by a gang of youths. It was used to build the Garasa airstrip in a matter of weeks. It is used by host villages preparing for major feast events or dance performances. It is the go-to procedure for helping to create any kind of short, intense, coordinated action.

The burden of success or failure of an event coordinated through *tukuta ma adzaita* is placed largely on the couple of men who take on the water-avoidance taboos. After the completion of the event, the men can finally drink, bathe, and eat the greasy (watery) pig meat that they had been barred from during the festivities themselves. If clan unity is ideologized as an effortless fact of the past and the biographical future (in death), village-based unity is a hard-won, temporary state elicited only through enormous effort and sacrifice on the part of ritual specialists. For Guhu-Samane stuck in the village-based present, it is the best they can do. Or, rather, it was, until the revival of 1977, when Christianity moved into villages and gave people a different way to organize their social lives.

THE FIRST CHRISTIAN VILLAGE: THE FIRES OF THE HOLY SPIRIT

When the Holy Spirit told Ulysses and the other people he was with during the revival to make a new Au village in order to make new people, there was a particular burden of having to transform the site of fractiousness into a space of Christianity. The village had to be reimagined from a space of difference into one of equal brotherhood and sisterhood under God. For the revival leaders, that meant trying to use the kind of social singularity possible under conditions of *tukuta ma adzaita* magic for Christian ends.

In a way, Richert made this equation possible. During his speech at the dedication of the publication of his New Testament in 1975, which I mentioned at the beginning of the chapter, Richert said that he had created a metaphorical fireplace with his translation and evangelization work. He, Richert, would be leaving the Waria Valley, but people should remain alert, because he would soon be sending a spark or a match that would light the fire. In the years after Richert left, his acolytes were in a state of expectant waiting. When Ulysses and his wife and daughters started having visions of angels and hearing the voice of Jesus in their heads, Ulysses knew the spark of the Holy Spirit had finally come. With imagery of tongues of fire in the story of Pentecost and Richert's own prophecy of fiery spiritual renewal, the revival was embraced as a moment of intense "heat" when people were able to perform incredible works, some with precedent (like relocating Au village to a new site nearby) and some unprecedented (like having the courage to throw away all of one's ritual paraphernalia). The association of the revival and heat is perhaps best seen in the way that the later schismatic church, Reformed Gospel, tried to assume the mantel of the real revival church by creating a church logo that prominently featured a fire place.

But instead of lasting for two weeks or until some proximate goal was complete, as with *tukuta ma adzaita* magic, the revivalists had to make this heightened condition of spiritual heat a permanent state of being. In one sense, they did this by simply making revival itself a permanent practice. It was well into my fieldwork and interviews with people about the revival that I realized why I could not get a good answer to the question of when the revival ended: people did not want to admit that it actually had. In an institutional sense, it is true that there was a five-year process of separation from the Lutheran church, even if the history of the revival discussed in the previous section presents it as a definitive moment when the religious center of the valley moved from the Lutheran/SIL headquarters at Kipu down to Au. The separate revival church did not emerge formally until the early 1980s. This entire period is referred to as the revival, a battle for spiritual independence that took years to happen. But at a larger level, the goal was to make revival a permanent state.

The heat of the revival was kindled and kept alive to reorient the Christians of Au through pitched battles between the Holy Spirit and autochthonous spirits of the landscape (*masalai,* TP; *gisi* or *piitu,* GS). Ulysses would lead men on quests to root out local spirits through prayer, what is usually called "spiritual warfare" in Pentecostal circles (see Jorgensen 2005). The daughter of a man from Titio village told the story of one of Ulysses's attempts to root out a local spirit (back in the day when Titio people were members of New Life, likely the early 1990s). There is a hole in the ground in the forest near Titio where a certain kind of being had emerged in the past. Ulysses gathered the adult men of Titio one night to pray over the hole, using the power of the Holy Spirit to combat the local one. Back in the village, women and children were praying in the church. At the hole, the praying men started to hear noises from underground. Ulysses urged them, "keep praying, keep praying, keep praying." They were frightened, but they continued. Finally a spirit jumped out of the hole, and suddenly Ulysses went from urging the men to pray to shouting, "run away!" It was a pitch-black night, and the men scrambled and stumbled in their fright to get away from the hole as fast as they could.

The story is told in Titio for laughs, a way to diffuse the moral qualms over what is currently considered cargo-cultish behavior from the perspective of the church that broke away from New Life and that is now strong in Titio, Reformed Gospel. It is part of a set of stories of New Life members confronting powers of the past with the powers of Christianity, a Christian critique of past forms. But unlike canonical cases of Pentecostal iconoclasm, the ways in which New Life revivalists tried to maintain the heat of the revival as a permanent condition meant that the center of heat from the past—the men's house—could in fact remain as part of a new Christian village.

This too was made possible through Richert's translation work, in particular, his decision to translate "church" as *guhu* in Guhu-Samane. This term refers to the men's house, or *poro guhu,* and it contrasts with the general name for other village structures that take the word for "house," *naga.* For example, a medical aid post is a *heme naga* (sick house) or a trade store is an *oma naga* (money house). As discussed in the previous chapter, Richert was particularly interested in creating comparisons within the translation process between the men's houses and Christianity. Indeed, this only continued a trend that began with the Lutheran missionaries who focused on the *Balumskulten* as the central institutions competing with Lutheran influence.

Au and other New Life strongholds are some of the only villages that still use versions of the old men's houses, although they are much reduced from the fully functioning politico-religious institutions that they were in the past. Nevertheless, these reduced men's houses are supplements to the church, able to help men maintain a sense of heat while women concentrate their heat on their loud vocal performances in church (see chapter 7). The unity of the Christian village comes from the permanent work of revival—of Holy Spirit heat—that even things like the men's house can produce.

FIGURE 5. The Titio village Reformed Gospel Church being used for a men's work meeting.

A NEW CHRISTIAN VILLAGE: THE COOL
WATERS OF CHRIST

The heat of New Life Christianity emanating from both the church and the men's house eventually became a concern for some Christians. Wendy Flannery's (1983) and Amy Burce's (1983) discussions of early revivalist activities as "cargo cultist" were circulating at SIL headquarters. Mark, who was starting to work on an Old Testament translation with SIL and the Bible Translation Association of PNG, received counsel and criticism from people at SIL. Former SIL translators who had started their own mission, Pacific Island Ministries (PIM), and were working near Au at the Garasa airstrip, were also concerned that New Life Church members saw their material investments in the Waria Valley as cargo of sorts. In addition to building up the Garasa airstrip into a PIM mission station, PIM members were building permanent materials churches in villages, seemingly a ratification of the localization of the Holy Spirit. But rumors circulated that the conjunction of the men's house and the church was being taken too far: it was alleged that New Life members made a nighttime visit to a church construction site to pour pig's blood down the holes into which the posts would later be sunk, as is done during men's house construction. PIM members grew increasingly uncomfortable with

FIGURE 6. A New Life Church service in Asama village.

their work in the Waria and left in the mid-1990s. Their extant but boarded-up houses give Garasa the feeling of a ghost town, matching the ghostly presences of missions past that haunt the abandoned buildings of Kipu and Garaina. During this time of outsider and insider critique, a number of men met together to talk about splitting from New Life. In 1994 they decided to break apart, in a perfect example of what Bateson (1958) called *complementary schismogenesis*.

Bateson identified two basic templates for the appearance and solidification of social groups or social attributes with respect to one another. First, groups or individuals can come into a relationship of competitive mutual recognition. *Symmetrical schismogenesis* could describe something as complex as the arms race between the United States and the Soviets during the Cold War or something as simple as the way in which two people can make one another laugh even more just through their own laughter. Maussian agonistic exchange, like the potlatch's ever-increasing gifts, is also an example of a symmetrical, schismogenic emergence of two chiefs in competition. Second, groups or individuals can come into a relationship of mutual recognition through the reification of differences, what Bateson called *complementary schismogenesis*. For example, gender differences that are relatively downplayed during everyday Iatmul life are taken to theatrical extremes in the Naven ritual that Bateson analyzed: women become ever more debased as men are made ever more powerful. An event or event-series can, of course, use both forms of schismogenesis. The final act of the potlatch as Mauss (1954) describes it involves the destruction of a chief who can no longer give away any more goods. Defeated by the gift-giving capacities of his rival, the once-great chief loses social personhood in becoming a debt slave. What starts out as a symmetrical battle ends in a complementary humiliation.

As a communicative system, schismogenesis depends upon differences not being so great that interaction becomes impossible. Even in the cases of complementary schismogenesis, then, a level of parity has to be posited in order for reifications of difference to be seen as such. When people met to consider splitting from New Life, their critiques both created a new form of Christian practice and also solidified New Life as a kind of Christianity. That is to say, even if New Life was taken as a kind of cargo cult locally (and, not so locally, at SIL headquarters), the ways in which people split from the church and the ways in which they tried to claim its hold on the revival establish New Life practices as complementary religious powers. In this sense, the schism within New Life recapitulated that critical comparative project started under missionization, when, for example, the men's house was seen as an inferior rival to Christianity as a religious system.

The people who met to split from New Life were sociologically in a good position to do so. Ulysses had become the major leader of the revival church, and his village of Au had become its main seat of power. Mark and other revival leaders were from villages further upstream, in a region called Muniwa, which borders on Ulysses's Au-Aro region. While Ulysses had the revivalist imprimatur as the first person to experience visions and the one who brought the church to a village, Mark was the son of Richert's main translation helper, Timothy. Both had been literacy teachers stationed at Kipu when Richert's Academy was in operation (although Mark was also the supervisor of the other literacy teachers). As matched adversaries in a new field of prestigious social relations (pastors, literacy teachers), Mark and Ulysses were obvious candidates for competing claims to spiritual authority.

More importantly, however, when Mark and his allies decided to split from New Life and create their critical response of a church, Reformed Gospel, they did so by maintaining the village as a focus of religious sociality. But they flipped the values of villages and local Christianity. New Life ignores outside forms of recognition like pastor training certificates and government registration of their church in favor of direct Holy Spirit authorization. Reformed Gospel insists on having pastors with certificates and was quick to register their church with the government and develop things like a church logo. Where New Life plays drums loudly in church, Reformed Gospel has banned the use of drums altogether (see chapter 7). And where New Life anchors its emancipatory Christianity in the localizable power and heat of the Holy Spirit, Reformed Gospel takes its cues from the cool, peacemaking, and salvational work of Jesus.

Although I have so far focused on the ways in which men make themselves hot for ritual events, there are also men who work to remain cool. The *maripa*, or peacemaker, was a central person in Guhu-Samane men's houses who kept people in order. While typifying the image of masculine aggression and work, men's houses also center on a cross-sex relation between the hot, argument-prone warriors and the cold peacemaking leaders who produce a social space—the village itself—which is able to engage in productive social relations. At the very heart of the village as a political and religious entity is a representation of difference: female characteristics of the cool, peaceful *maripa* encompass the male sphere in those contexts when men's houses threaten to rupture because of the overly aggressive actions of the hot-headed fighters. To put it in the slightly instrumentalist terms that Guhu-Samane sometimes use, villages need men to be hot in order to get work done, but they need their *maripa* to be cold in order for villages to remain unified as villages and avoid schism.

At first blush, there is a surface similarity between the *maripa* and a Reformed Gospel pastor. Both are expected to resolve disputes among coresidents. Both are expected to avoid getting into disputes of their own. Both are meant to lead coresidents in community work. Overall, the most important trait of a pastor, like that of a *maripa*, is that he is cold. The crucial difference between a pastor and a *maripa* is his relationship to his coresidents. If a *maripa* is a cold man surrounded by a bunch of hot-headed warriors, a pastor is a cold man surrounded by a bunch of people—both male and female—who are meant to emulate the pastor's coldness. Villages with churches are villages of cold people unified by their gazes all being turned toward the Jesus. With the men's house initiation system largely defunct and most purity taboos now ignored by Christians, the characteristics of village residents have changed. "We're all cold now," as one Reformed Gospel man said to me.

Formal taboos or informal suggestions have been demanded of Reformed Gospel pastors to help maintain their coldness and keep them as examples for their parishioners. Pastors usually exclude themselves from discussions of land claims, and they are often discouraged from owning pigs, since people use pigs to pay compensation when they get into trouble. If pastors don't have pigs, the thinking goes, they will try to keep out of trouble. Similar taboos are not put on congregants, but that does not mean that lay people are free to get into trouble. Many sermons specifically suggest that Christians should have few pigs and that thinking about pigs and other "things of this world" (*samting bilong graun*, TP) will keep one from thinking about Jesus. Unlike a men's house organization, which balances heat and cold, violent energy and appeasing peacefulness, Reformed Gospel village Christianity recognizes only levels of coldness, in which every person is aiming, however approximately, for the same goal (just as New Life villages aim for a uniform heat of the Holy Spirit that universalizes the role of the ritual water-shunning specialist). Even while differences between men and women remain important, both men and women are supposed to aim for some kind of coldness. The church *guhu* (as opposed to the *poro guhu*) minimizes local, village-level heterogeneity in its moral demand for the peace that is produced when everyone is *belkol* (has a "cold heart" in Tok Pisin). To a large extent, Robbins's discussion of Urapmin pseudo-holism (2004a, 309), a Dumontian term to describe a group that forms a whole only through the sense of all members sharing a characteristic, encapsulates the desire for a cold Christian village.

The new social formation of village Christianity can be seen in another contrast between the qualities of heat and coldness, this time in terms of baptism. As I have shown, coldness is indexically connected to water in much Guhu-Samane imagery. When men try to make themselves ritually hot in *tukuta ma adzaita* magic, one of the biggest taboos for them is the one against ingesting or even being near water. Compare baptisms. The immersion in water is a rebirth into cold peacefulness. But where one or two men can fast and have taboos placed on them in order to make an entire village hot for the purposes of communal work or competitive feasting, immersion baptism was required for each participant in the revival and subsequent formation of village-based churches. Taking Christian authority into their own hands, the latter-day revival leaders of Reformed Gospel brought the church to the village by transforming the basis of the village.

. . .

One of the revival leaders, Rev. Pituro, gave a sermon on the evening of the February 2, 2006, New Life remembrance of the revival (after the speech discussed earlier in this chapter) in which he demanded that his New Life audience members interrogate their personal relationships to God.

> Sumasai- abi sumasanomai ohongaho dzubina.
> *The spirit-filled man is God's marrow*
>
> onita ni paha ohongaho dzubinani, mae bam?
> *And so are you also God's marrow or not?*
>
> Ni paha ohongaho dzubina, mae bam?
> *Are you also God's marrow or not?*
>
> Askim yu yet.
> *Ask yourself.*
>
> Nimae sama nimeke mooro.
> *Look at yourself [lit. look at your own body]*
>
> Ni eto abi temuke mooraino.
> *Do not look at another person*
>
> Ni abi teemuke mooraquko, ni paul eetako.
> *If you look at another person, you will be screwed up*
>
> ni ruume naatako
> *You will be confused*
>
> onihe ni sama nimeke moomi
> *So look at yourself and*
>
> ni ohongaho dzubinani mae bam?
> *Are you God's marrow or not?*

The emphasis on both the interiority of commitment to God as well as the emphasis on moral self-dependence gives this passage the familiar feel of ideological individualism that both Joel Robbins (2004a) and

Webb Keane (2007) discuss as cornerstones of Protestant Christianity. The reverend demands that his audience find a truth hidden in the interior. He also demands that each audience member take individual responsibility for his or her own state of commitment—you will be all screwed up if you think you can answer this question about your moral status by looking at someone else. Like one of Joel Robbins's Papua New Guinean interlocutors, who noted that Christian belief is not transactable (as he put it, "my wife can't break off part of her belief and give it me" [Robbins 2004, 295]), Christianity not only orients people toward God, but it also discourages people from looking to their consociates.

Where Keane and Robbins have been focused on the kinds of selves produced in Christianity, another strand of research looks at the media of religious transmission (Meyer 2006; Engelke 2007; Eisenlohr 2009; Hirschkind 2006). Following this literature, the character of individualism is going to depend upon the ideologized media through which presence with or connection to God can happen. The characterization of one's appropriate relationship to God as being "his bone marrow" establishes a particular form of immediacy premised upon bodily incorporation that some (e.g., Mosko 2010) might argue has an air of Melanesian dividualism about it (in which persons are conceived as bundles of social relations rather than autonomous individuals). Is the reverend's demand for moral accountability just masking standard Papua New Guinean personhood? This short excerpt seems to point in two directions at once. While relationships to other humans are devalued in an individualist demand for moral autonomy ("don't look at another person"), incorporating relationships to God are emphasized in a dividualist demand for divine co-presence ("be God's bone marrow").

The way out of this impasse, I argue, is to move our focus beyond the Papua New Guinean/Christian subject to a consideration of social groups in the Guhu-Samane revival. Roy Wagner famously asked, "are there social groups in the New Guinea highlands?" (1974) and later Marilyn Strathern (1988) elaborated on this in *The Gender of the Gift*, where she noted that Western social theory invented not only the individual but also the social totality into which the individual is coercively pushed: dividualists have neither. I argue that the revival did indeed produce social totalities, an entirely novel one in the ideologization of ethno-linguistic identity and a reformulation of an old one in the creation of specifically Christian villages. Guhu-Samane-speaking Christian villages are supposed to create the context for ideological individuals rather than being characterized by the coercive partibility of village heterogeneity. If there are dividualist moments within Guhu-Samane Christianity, they occur within the context of these hoped-for—if not always realized—social wholes.

Reverend Pituro is problematizing two different issues. First, how can you be a spirit-filled person in close relationship with God? Second, how can you be morally autonomous from other humans in forging this relationship with God? Yet he is asking these questions in the context of a grand, multiday celebration of the founding of a local church, a Christian village, and the linguistic access to God found in the Guhu-Samane New Testament translation. The church may not be the unit of salvation (the individual is), nor the means of sanctification (being God's marrow is), but the church is the crucial context allowing either of these other two issues to exist. The schism that split New Life in the 1990s demonstrates this best insofar as it shows how central the church as an institution is to local projects of Christian practice. As a site of critique and schism, the church constitutes the sociality of Christianity.

This emphasis on social wholes has another advantage in terms of developing a more robust anthropology of Christianity—one that can look beyond the subject—and that is to understand the kinds of social groups Christians work to create, even though they may do so under individualist terms that ultimately make groups unstable and schismatic (see Niebuhr 1929). The heirs to the Protestant Reformation may want to move hierarchy and social organization off the radar when they (for example) denounce Roman Catholic tradition in favor of *sola scriptura* and *sola fide*. However, we do not have to follow suit, nor do we have to fall into the trap of the secularization hypothesis, which demands that social organization be a matter for the political sphere alone.

In this chapter, I have focused on the ways that frictions among clans, villages, and men's houses combined to make the village an unlikely site for church localization. In the next chapter, I look more closely at the ways in which men's houses continue to shape Guhu-Samane engagements with Christianity. Both the Lutherans and Ernie Richert emphasized the ways in which men's houses were competitors of Christian communities. The loss of men's houses as central institutions of village life continues to be a focus for local people when they describe the ways that the revival reshaped their lives. More specifically, I show in chapter 5 how the loss of the men's house complex (or, for those villages that have structures that approximate men's houses of the past, their dramatic reduction in the organization of village affairs) can be understood in terms of the emergence of a powerful, sacred, post-translation form of the Guhu-Samane language. SIL members may work with the assumption that language provides a noninstitutional route to Christian commitment, but in the Guhu-Samane case at least, language has become a powerful institution of its own.

CHAPTER 5

The Surprise of Speech

Disorder, Violence, and Christian Language
after the Men's House

Henry, the head man of Titio village, was in the middle of a long discussion with me about the loss of men's houses for Guhu-Samane people. Extrapolating from his disappointment, Henry made up a story of walking along the main road and seeing a banana tree. "I walked up to the banana tree. 'What's your name?' 'My name is Market.'" The banana tree named Market was a surprise to him. In Henry's story the bananas on the tree had been designated by the tree's owner to be harvested and sold at the semiweekly market held at Garasa station, the site of the nearby airstrip and the abandoned PIM mission compound. Henry was disappointed, because in the old days—prior to markets, mission stations, Christianity, and the dismantling of the men's house system that Christianity brought—bananas, as well as other garden produce, would have been designated for uses through the men's house itself, uses that would strengthen the local community. But women and men no longer think in terms of the community that was metonymically represented by the men's house. Not only does Henry have to walk down a path and jealously eye ripe bananas ready to be eaten, but he has to resign himself to the fact that the only way that the bananas will come into his possession is through a cash payment.

There are many ways to interpret what I have come to call "The Parable of the Bananas." Following economic models, it is possible to see this as Henry's recognition of the ways in which cash economies can delink exchange and social relations. It is also possible to see this as

Henry's unhappy confrontation with the expanded role that women (the main marketers) now have in the final disposition of the produce that they work on. And finally, it is possible to see this as the bitter disappointment of someone who came to power at just the wrong time—someone who is the leader of a village but does not seem to derive much benefit from that fact, at least not as much as he remembers older men doing even in the waning days of the men's house when he was a child.

Henry, at one point or another, touched on all of these interpretations in his well-rehearsed litany of complaints about modern life in rural Papua New Guinea. But The Parable of the Bananas had another interpretation, one that stemmed from something that probably was a surprise to the reader as well: the banana tree could talk. That is, the dissolution of the men's house system has had one particularly salient consequence for Henry: everybody, everywhere, at every moment, seems to have something to say. From every angle, Henry is besieged with surprising voices, from bananas declaring their destination at market to men pressing land claims and to older women claiming garden lands for themselves. Referring on another occasion to the time when the men's house system was in operation, Henry repeated himself in his frustration: "Before there were no meetings. Before there were no meetings. Before there were no meetings. Before there wasn't a lot of talk. Just action. Only one man spoke, and he only said a little." Talk is the opposite of action, and lots of talk just means the delay or disruption of lots of action.

In this chapter, I want to examine why Guhu-Samane history, especially history told from the point of view of the men's house, is silent, and why the present is so surprising for its constant talk. Men of Henry's generation, whether they are devout or only casual Christians (there are no self-identifying non-Christians), remember the men's house system as a perfect machine of social order. Even the fighting and warfare in which men participated was orderly and governed by ritual. In this same history, the arrival of the Good News in the early twentieth century marked the end of the era of fighting and the men's house. And yet it would be very easy to call the contemporary moment in the Waria Valley an era of fighting as well, albeit chatty fighting: fights about land, fights between husbands and wives, fights between villages, and for the last thirty years, fights between Protestant denominations. What is it about contemporary talk in the era of the Good News that makes life so violent? And how does that violence differ from the violence of the silent past?

For anyone who has read Joel Robbins's classic article on language and Christianity in Melanesia, "God Is Nothing but Talk" (2001), the problems of talk that Henry points to should be relatively familiar. In a place where talk is devalued for its unreliability (either epistemologically, in terms of its capacity to represent the world, or pragmatically, in terms of its capacity to produce effects), a religion like Christianity that is focused so much on talk should be unlikely to succeed (see also B. Schieffelin 2008; Robbins and Rumsey 2008). But just as it has in Urapmin communities where Robbins worked, Christianity has become a major focus of contemporary social life in Guhu-Samane areas. Robbins details the ways in which Urapmin acted on their own both to take up Christianity and to improvise a solution to the epistemic uncertainty of talk. Urapmin are able to use the authority they invest in God to characterize him as an omnipotent hearer, one who can judge the accuracy of speech, even if mortal man cannot. Thus, prayers to God become the ritual core of valued Christian speech, in which Urapmin do not talk to one another so much as make one another "ratified overhearers" (Goffman 1981) of their talk to God.

Unlike the auto-evangelized Urapmin, Guhu-Samane communities have had over a century of missionization. The initial destruction of the men's houses and the introduction to Christianity came from the Lutheran Mission New Guinea in the first half of the twentieth century and were followed in the late 1950s with the introduction of SIL translators, who held the men's house up as a contrast with Christianity. In this chapter, I focus on the role of SIL and translation in the construction of linguistic violence to understand why today's talk leads to so much fighting, even though the Word of God is said to have brought the era of fighting to an end.

In characterizing contemporary speech in the Waria Valley as violent and surprising, I point to the ways in which language has emerged as a power that does not seem to be contained by the speaker herself or himself. I do not mean simply the fact that language is necessarily intersubjective and comes from others, although I take that to be the case (Voloshinov 1986). Rather, I want to contrast this ungovernable language with the primary models of linguistic subjectivity described through theories of liberalism. Liberal and even non-liberal models of speech imagine a relationship of language internalized, and it is through processes of internalization that language becomes domesticated.

In liberal, especially Protestant, models like the ones used by SIL translators, language might start as Other (say, a gift from God), but is then made Self through the process of first-language acquisition, in which one comes to be a person through the capacity to be an author of one's own words. When SIL translators spend fifteen or more years of their lives creating vernacular-language New Testaments, it is because this "heart language" is understood to be at the internal core of the self, where Christian conversion should happen (Handman 2007). After taking in a foreign element, like Christianity, the native speaker-convert masters it by becoming an author of the discourse. Like other liberal conventions of effective speech, Protestant models of linguistic conversion depend upon making others' language one's own in order for it to count as affectively real or true. Without this, one is simply parroting, acting as a puppet, mimicking, or otherwise not living up to one's human agentive potential.

Under liberal assumptions, if language is not internalized, it is dangerous. In the wake of 9/11, for example, pundits frequently tried to link pedagogical practices at Islamic schools, characterized in the media by rote repetition of Koranic verses, with the willingness of young men to become suicide bombers. Richard Dawkins's *The God Delusion* provides a particularly inflammatory example of this connection:

> Suicide bombers do what they do because they really believe what they were taught in their religious schools: that duty to God exceeds all other priorities, and that martyrdom in his service will be rewarded in the gardens of Paradise. And they were taught *that* lesson not necessarily by extremist fanatics but by decent, gentle mainstream religious instructors, who lined them up in their madrasas, sitting in rows, rhythmically nodding their innocent little heads up and down while they learned every word of the holy book like demented parrots. (Dawkins 2008, 348, emphasis in original)

Here the problem is imagined to be that young men were denied subjective existence because they were forced to say others' words rather than be authors of their own, and others could then use these robot-like men for violent ends. That is to say, language was internalized and governed by some, but not all, and that left open a space for the devaluation of human life.[1]

Scholars working in religious traditions outside of the confines of liberal models of the self have taken issue with this characterization of linguistic and religious agency. Mahmoud (2001) and Hirschkind (2006), for example, discuss the ways in which Muslims in Egypt find a form of agency in the difficult process of coming to understand oneself as subject to (or as a subject through) God. Whether it is slowly beginning to feel comfortable wearing a hijab or learning to listen to sermon oratory, the end goal is not autonomous self-mastery but selfhood through constant attention to God. Likewise, Fader's (2009) analysis of language use among Hasidic Jews in Brooklyn, NY, demonstrates the ways in which Orthodox Judaism is practiced as a form of subordination to the sacred texts (in Hebrew for the men and the traces of the sacred discernible in Yiddish for the women). What is dangerous in these instances is being set loose without a subject-making relationship of subordination to God through carefully honed linguistic or bodily practice.

In either of these traditions of understanding linguistic personhood, the emphasis has been on the processes of mastery and governance, the cultivation of a self either "alone," as in liberal imaginaries, or through an external other, as in the non-liberal ones. But as I argue below, the incorporation of SIL's liberal tradition of linguistic selfhood has created a situation in which the Guhu-Samane language has become a force incapable of mastery. That is, the problem seems to be that language now has a power that people cannot control, and for that reason, it has become a violent force. Guhu-Samane Christians now work with a language that has been structured and defined through SIL translation by scientific, linguistic analysis and biblical use, something that people value. De-linked from older norms of communicative practice, however, the sacred Guhu-Samane language licenses speakers and speaking in order for people to practice their Christian commitment. But the power that this has invested in the language does not seem to be containable from within the individualizing model of personhood that Christianity offers. Guhu-Samane Christians thus do considerable work to create a Christianity in and of the social, which has meant a marked focus on denominational groups that both constrain and yet also increase the dramatic powers of sacred speech.

Guhu-Samane Christian men, in particular, experience the universalization of Christian speaking subjects within their communities as disruptive and disorderly, a cause of the recent intra-ethnic denominational conflicts that sometimes rise to the level of outright violence. More broadly, I use this as an opportunity to engage with debates about the seemingly inherent violence of neoliberal processes of desubjectification. In recent anthropological accounts, instances of violence are often seen as places where people stop being subjects (Biehl 2005; Biehl and Moran-Thomas 2009). These physical and psychic violations of selves become analytic entrances to different ontological and epistemic worlds. But in making such desubjectivizing violence the site of possibility, we run the risk of nevertheless privileging pain as a kind of salutary, embodied authenticity existing outside of cultural histories. In this Guhu-Samane case, the possibilities of violence come not from the eradication of subjectivities but from the profusion of them in the local revivalist responses to waves of colonial missionization. In this chapter, then, I want to examine the ways in which Guhu-Samane Christians keep surprising—and upsetting—themselves with their own possibilities of violence and speech, developed through a century of missionization and Christian subjectification. That is to say, for Guhu-Samane men, too many speaking subjects can be just as disruptive and even as violent as too few.

Much of this history stems from the missiological equation of Christianity and the men's house. As a form of cultural translation, the Lutheran Mission equation of the church and the men's house was simultaneously an assertion and a denial of equality between the two institutions—an assertion of equality in that missionaries saw the men's house as a rival to the church, a denial of equality in that the church was seen as superior. (The simultaneous assertion and denial of the same proposition is a characteristic sign of a fetish; see Pietz 1985, 1987, 1988; Latour 1999.) Given the power to approximate Christianity's world-making force, only to be denied that power for its apparent excesses of violence or idolatry, the men's house has become a central component of male nostalgia for order. The power of reinvention, of possibility, that has become part of local understandings of Christian revival has also meant that the power of the men's house system of the past is equated with social order rather than social invention.

Below I trace out this argument in greater depth. I first discuss contemporary memorializations of the men's house system of silent order and ordered violence. I then discuss SIL's role in shaping the Guhu-Samane language and the unintended ways in which language became not a site for self-mastery but a torrent of power stemming from the excess of speaking subjects. I then show how language is used and discussed in contemporary Guhu-Samane communities as a semiautonomous power, sometimes for good, but often to the detriment of community coherence. I conclude with a brief discussion of linguistic violence and social order.

MEN'S HOUSES AND THE MEMORY OF SOCIAL ORDER

While there are still some extant men's houses, no male initiations have been performed since the 1950s. I was able to meet and briefly interview only one man who had been initiated, a very old man in a village far downstream from my home in Titio village. The remembrances of the men's houses I discuss here are from older men who lived as children in villages with men's houses that were already in decline. As such, the stories they tell of men's house practices present a world in perfect order, uncluttered by the kinds of daily disturbances that any central institution has to bear. If the following description reads like an older structural-functionalist anthropology, it is at least in part due to the ways in which people described the institution to me.

As I discussed in the previous chapter, the *poro guhu* (GS, men's house, lit. the "house of the poro spirit") was the focal point of male life and a central institution in maintaining villages as coherent social units. The *poro guhu* partially mitigated the schismatic tendencies of villages in this largely matrilineal but virilocal culture. Symbolically, victory leaf bushes (*tanget,* TP) planted around the *poro guhu* were supposed to maintain the village as a coherent unit. If the *tanget* died or was pulled out, people saw that as the end of the village's power. There were also more complex ways in which the *poro guhu* established order, which I describe below, after providing some initial background.

Guhu-Samane male social roles conform roughly to the norm of the "great man society" identified by Godelier (1986). In the more well-known big man systems of the highlands of Papua New Guinea (Sahlins 1963), a single, almost entrepreneurial man can lead villages and organize massive generalized exchanges of women and pigs. But in great man societies, there are a number of different roles for male leadership, and men tend to engage in restricted exchanges that require a wife taken for every wife given in marriage, a life taken for every life lost in warfare.

More than one older man compared the *poro guhu* leadership system to a parliamentary one. There was an overall leader or *ohonga abi* (GS, *ohonga,* lord, *abi,* man; *ohonga* is also used now to refer to God), today compared to a prime minister. There was a peacemaker (*maripa,* GS, also referred to in English as "lawyer man"), who could also be seen as a prime minister if there was no *ohonga abi.* Then there were various ministers with different portfolios, described to me as the Minister of Gardening, Minister of Magic, Minister of Hunting, and so forth. Members without a portfolio, so to speak, were the *qaa abi* (fighters).

There was a single initiation of young men. During their ritual seclusion, boys would be guided by a mother's brother, and ritual homosexuality, in the form of ingestion of semen, occurred. Boys who violated taboos while in seclusion could be killed by the *poro* fathers, and the rest of the village was subject to equally strict rules emanating from the *poro guhu*. Encircled by a high fence, activities within the *poro guhu* were hidden from women and young children, and contemporary people had a strange delight in imagining their grandmothers' or mothers' fright at hearing the bull roarer (*poro ungapa*, GS, or male poro) that would call out for food or to gather people together. Paired flutes (*poro atapa*, GS, female poro) played tunes that people remember with incredible fondness as some of the most beautiful sounds in the valley.

Taking off from previous analyses (e.g., Strathern 1988), I want to focus for a moment on the gendered imagery of the *poro guhu*. As is true of other men's houses in Melanesia, both female and male elements are present in this supposedly single-sex domain. Female elements are apparent, for example, in the *poro* flutes, which have an overall female gender (although one flute is female and the other male) in contrast to the male bullroarer. A male version (semen) of female substance (milk) was fed to young initiates to make them grow. Most importantly for this discussion, Henry, who told me the Parable of the Bananas, calls himself a *maripa*, a role that is especially noteworthy for its female characteristics (see chapter 4). He is a cool (*keba*, GS) man, like women, whereas the fighters and the Minister of Magic are particularly hot (*mutu*, GS). He sits in his house or the men's house, within the domesticated confines of the village, while hunters and other men roam in the bush.

It is this capacity to be a sedentary but female-like persona that makes the *maripa* such an important position to *poro,* and thus village, stability. In a matrilineal but virilocal situation, women are constantly on the move. Men who need to follow ancestral marriage patterns in order to access clan land must "follow the footsteps of the ancestors" (*bihainim lekmak bilong tumbuna,* TP) or "open a road" (*tete geema,* GS) that has not been used in a while. That is, they must try to follow where linking women went for marriage in order to establish subsequent marriages that will bring women "back" from previous generations. So the *maripa*'s tendency to sit in the village (functionally explained as necessary to welcome visitors) makes him the best of all possible women: a foundational woman-like character who stays in place and maintains continuity in a situation where rupturing female movement is the norm.[2]

At the same time, the men's house leadership could create patrilineal linkages to counter the matrilineal clan reckoning that causes such movement and schism. I was not able to gather enough genealogical information about leadership to know if patrilineal inheritance of leadership was the norm (sister's sons, sons, and men of no immediate relation could take over leadership roles), but several current village leaders in the area had ascended into the roles their fathers or fathers' fathers had held previously. As I will discuss more below, the local leaders of the ongoing Bible translation projects form a patriline: Timothy, the original man who worked with the SIL translators, and his son Mark and grandson Sean, who currently are translating the Old Testament.

As an institution to counterbalance the dislocations of women's movement, the men's house was important, but it, of course, did much more than this. Various leaders in the *poro guhu* were able to plan communal gardens, prepare as much as five years in advance for major feast gatherings (*masere*s, GS), regulate marriages, and engage in inter-village warfare. For the present purposes, it is particularly revealing that this varied and complex work is seen by contemporary older men to have been accomplished by largely silent men. Men told me stories of absolute order, an organically solidary society of such all-encompassing awareness on the part of individuals of the roles and rules of social life that no talk was needed. Durkheim himself might find it all a little farfetched.

So, for example, Mark told me a complicated story of how to ambush a potential enemy, likely a story he repeats in many contexts to highlight the differences between the Christian present and pagan past. If there was a man from another village with whom people had fought, that man would be invited to the local men's house for peace negotiations (an unfortunate moment requiring talk). If the negotiations broke down, there was no need to carry on with them, as people are forced to do today. Rather, a leader of the men's house would discreetly tap the toe of a young man. This was the young man's signal to get up, gather some able-bodied men, and wait in ambush for the enemy on the road back to his village. Then they would kill him.

Or, as Henry told me, if one was an *ohonga abi* or *maripa,* there was no need to ask your wife for food to entertain even unexpected guests (having unexpected guests is a hazard of duty of the head man). The *maripa* simply banged a bit on his lime pot, which he used for chewing betel nut. This was a signal to his always-alert wife to prepare food. His wife had anticipated this possibility and had previously harvested extra food from her garden that day, so there was no need to ask for anyone's help.

Of course, every village had its screwups. These, Henry said with a bit of relish, were dispatched with a discreet nod in the direction of the

Minister of Magic, who would poison the ne'er-do-well soon enough. Parcel sorcery, in which an object that had been in contact with the victim is bespelled (e.g., the victim's hair or excrement, or the small butt of a tobacco cigarette), required talk. However, this was regulated and ritually scripted speech, incantations that were used via the heat and energy of the Minister of Magic himself.

This heyday of silent social order was not, therefore, a particularly peaceful one. People were poisoned, initiates could be killed for breaking taboos, and inter-village fighting could result in deaths as well. Yet, these forms of violence, like inter-village fights, had their ordered resolution. If one side had suffered a fatality, the other side had to offer up a sacrificial lamb of sorts to the other. Called the *hoo dzoba* (GS, roast pig), a young man from the village that had caused the previous death would be dressed in finery, and a mock battle would take place in which the young man and only the young man would be killed.[3] With the score of fatalities evened up, fighting could cease.

But even if precolonial life is remembered as ordered, that does not necessarily explain why it needed to be silent. In order to understand this silence, I want to return to Joel Robbins's analysis of Urapmin language ideologies. Robbins's (2001) piece on language and Christianity argues that, unlike speaker-focal Western models of communication, Melanesian communicative practice is ideologized as listener-focal in the sense that people understand meaning to be made only in speech's aftereffects. As he puts it, Melanesian semiotic practice follows a "run-it-up-the-flagpole-and-see-who-salutes" model, in which the truth or efficacy of speech is found in the kinds of reactions it elicits from others, a model of semiotic agency that aligns well with what is called Melanesian "dividuality" (Strathern 1988; see also Wagner 1975). The tight connection between listening and acting can be illustrated in one Guhu-Samane woman's way of telling her brother to pay no attention to the ridiculous demands an in-law was making on them. "Just hear it with your ears," she said, "don't act on it."

In a somewhat paradoxical manner, this attention to the value of listeners explains the remembered silence of the men's house. That is, people did, in fact, speak in the men's house, but the real success of it as an institution, from the contemporary perspective, was that everyone else listened and followed a single speaker's instructions and that this speaker embodied the totality of the *poro*. As Rosaldo (1982) argues in her classic article on Ilongot speech acts, commands must be understood in terms of "Ilongot views of the cooperative activities that a directive act evoked" (223). In Guhu-Samane terms, the *poro* came into being through the coordinated responses to the idealized singular speaker.

In contemporary terms, the single-speaker model of the men's house is carried over in the leadership position in the local government called the "committee" (*komiti,* TP), which, contrary to expectations—given the English meaning of the term—is actually just a single person. The *komiti* is a man who acts as something like a town crier, shouting out to bring people to meetings or get them ready for communal work for the day. He is the spokesman for the village headman. Even if he is not the author of the words being spoken (in Henry's village, the assumed author would generally be Henry), his role is incredibly important for inciting people (*kirapim bel,* TP) to action. While Henry, as *maripa,* is a female-like cold man capable of maintaining peace, the *komiti* has to be hot and, in particular, to have a "hot mouth" (*too mutu,* GS) in order to bring people together under the banner of community work. The silence of the men's house is probably better characterized as the cooperative social world organized by the single voice of the *poro.*

So if the era of the men's house was silent and violent, this was violence in the service of social order. Put otherwise, social life worked because there was only one speaking subject who elicited the cooperative power of the men's house through the active forms of listening that other members of the men's house engaged in. Even though people feel that they are now "free" (*fri,* TP) because there are no more Ministers of Magic governed by the men's house to poison them, they also realize that it is this same freedom that has led to the rise of *raskolism,* gang-based violence from young men who are disconnected from gerontocratic forms of power. Absent the power of the men's house, people are constrained now only by the Word of God.

THE END OF FIGHTING AND THE WORD OF GOD

Henry's namesake, his father's father, was also the *maripa* of the Muniwa area in which Henry now resides. Using the Tok Pisin word for "ancestor," I will call this person *tumbuna* Henry. People in Muniwa attribute the Christianization of the Guhu-Samane people to *tumbuna* Henry, given his role in ending the *taim bilong pait* (TP, era of fighting; see B. Schieffelin 2002 for Kaluli forms of marking time in Christian contexts). According to local histories, *tumbuna* Henry gathered *poro guhu* leaders from across the valley to orchestrate a valley-wide peace.

Tumbuna Henry capped off the peace ceremony by breaking a spear in half. It was only after this that the Lutheran Missionary Johannes Flierl made his first appearance in the valley to survey the area for mission work. In some versions of the story, *tumbuna* Henry distributed heaps of food to the assembled village leaders (as would be appropriate for an inter-village gathering of this sort) and topped each pile with Bibles that he had seemingly magically produced. Regardless of the details, the coming of the first missionaries and the end of the era of fighting are indelibly linked in local historical traditions. The Lutheran strategy of dismantling the men's house solidified the connection between Christianity and peace, or at least the connection between Christianity and the decline of certain forms of male sociality and power iconically indexed by fighting.

Ernie Richert, perhaps familiar with this story of *tumbuna* Henry, also tried to emphasize the ways in which his work was aimed at producing peace in the valley. As I discussed in chapter 3, Richert founded the Kipu Academy, a school based at the Lutheran Kipu mission station where local people could be trained in carpentry, hygiene and home economics, literacy teaching, pastoral leadership, and any number of seemingly random skills that friends of the Richerts would drop by to teach. People today remember the upside-down club that hung on the door of the main building at Richert's Kipu compound, signifying that the translation project was to unify and harmonize local people. Translation work was done literally under the sign of the end of warfare.

As I note in chapter 3, Ernie Richert worked to codify and consolidate the Guhu-Samane language. Richert brought together older speakers from across the valley to his Kipu compound to learn the language and culture. He developed a corpus of ancestral knowledge and conducted surveys of subregional Guhu-Samane dialects. Much of this was used in the posthumously published Guhu-Samane lexicon, called *Noo Supu* (Talk Repository). Local people held a major celebration at the time of its publication in 2002 to laud the material artifacts of cultural continuity that the dictionary project promised. Ernest Richert, then, was something of a one-man purveyor of Andersonian print capitalism, constructing a Guhu-Samane ethno-linguistic identity.

While it is impossible to get a sense of precolonial language ideologies, it is unlikely that something approaching German Romantic ethnolinguistic identity was a particularly important component of social life in the past. As immigrants from the coast near Morobe Station, Guhu-Samane speakers seem to have had an adaptive sense of social practices and norms. Guhu-Samane attended *masere* feasts in Kunimaipan communities to the south and west or hosted people from these communities at their own feasts. *Masere* is, in fact, derived from a Kunimaipan word *(matere)*, and there is evidence that even the *poro guhu* itself was originally an import from the Biaru and Biangai groups to the west. Marriages across ethnic lines were not common, but not especially remarkable. Farther downstream from the Muniwa-based village in which I lived, Guhu-Samane speakers told me about a moribund trade jargon used for interactions with Goilalan neighbors. That is to say, Guhu-Samane communities were likely multiethnic and multilingual, with fluid boundaries and overlapping cultural traditions, what Simon Harrison (1993) would call a Melanesian "borrowing culture."

Richert's creation of "the Guhu-Samane language" was an act of unification that was largely seen in terms of the solidification of these previously fluid boundaries. Moreover, the codification of a Guhu-Samane identity seems to have implied for local people a turn inward and away from the multiethnic interactions of the past so as to focus on the moral discourses about tradition that Richert was promulgating. But importantly for the argument I am making here, the turn inward was signaled as a turn toward peace within the Waria Valley. Even people who came to dislike Richert's role in destroying the Lutheran monopoly in the Waria Valley praise Richert for "unifying the language." So, regardless of the causation—linguistic unity producing peace, or peace producing linguistic unity—a Christian ethno-linguistic group and peacefulness have become fused together.

At the same time, however, Richert seemed to local people to tap into a reserve of power and "heat" that has, in some ways, been transmitted to the language itself. As I noted in the previous chapter, when the Richerts distributed copies of the completed Guhu-Samane New Testament and got ready to leave, Richert gave a speech asking Guhu-Samane speakers to "tend the fireplace" that he had built and promising that he would soon send a "spark" to light the fire. However Richert phrased his farewell speech, people at least remember it as a statement of his power and capacity to send a divine message to Guhu-Samane Christians from his home in Southern California.[4] The man who spent over fifteen years organizing, learning, speaking, publishing, and teaching literacy in the Guhu-Samane language seemed to have a connection to God and the Holy Spirit. The connection between language and divine power only got stronger in the years following the revival. How did this project of linguistic sacralization become the origin of a new form of power and a new era of sometimes violent disorder?

DISORDER AND THE POWER OF LANGUAGE

In the Guhu-Samane lexicon, there are numerous lists of cultural items that are celebrated as print-artifactualized collections of tradition: plants, clan names, rivers, villages, and others. I sat with Henry one day trying to go over the dictionary list of "spirits" associated with the men's house. The conversation went nowhere. Henry, certainly the most knowledgeable person about traditional and men's house culture, did not know how to talk about the list. After some frustrating false starts, Henry finally said that the list was uninterpretable. "If people had signed their names [to their contributions to this dictionary listing], I could talk to you about it." But language without pragmatic information about the events of speaking makes no sense.

Here is the problem, then. Through translation work, the language was made into a codified structure of grammatical and semantic norms, but in that process, it lost the quotation marks that originally linked speech to positioned moments of listening/acting. Now, it seems, language has been made into a sacred force of religious power delinked from norms of communicative order. Voloshinov (1986) calls the language produced from structural, linguistic analysis an alien, other language produced by priests, a language conceived as an autonomous, structured system. Henry is, in part, voicing a sense of dislocation from the language in terms familiar from Voloshinov's analysis, but there is more to the uninterpretability of the dictionary listings and autonomy of the sacralized Guhu-Samane language. The problem is that this language can now be spoken by everyone and, in fact, needs to be. I want to return to the revival for a moment to explore this problem.

The revival began as a series of events of listening—both in private, where the revival leader's daughter heard the voice of Jesus in her head "as if on a radio," but also in public, where the Holy Spirit commanded the revivalists in Au village to complete a series of tasks. These tasks largely revolved around constructing the proper social groups for Pentecostal worship, including a new village and a new church. Acting like the *komiti* of the cosmic men's house, the Holy Spirit spoke to the revivalists as the ultimate *too mutu* (hot mouth) capable of inciting people to extraordinary acts of reinvention.

This was not simply a moment of syncretistic mapping from the men's house to the church, though the history of missiological commensuration of these two institutions might suggest that to be the case. Because in addition to establishing the church as a sacred group, the revival also licensed—

demanded, even—that everyone become a speaker in addition to a lis-
tener/actor. In particular, everyone started to pray, the linguistic correlate
to the individualizing baptisms that they were also doing at this time.

Delinked from men's house norms of minimal talk, the sacred Guhu-
Samane language that had enabled communication with the Holy Spirit
during the revival continues to license speakers. This has led to a surfeit
of people who (disparagingly, I admit) I call the "ambulance-chasing pastors." Like the shady lawyer who follows in the wake of disaster to trawl
for clients, there are a number of men who—officially or unofficially—
try to be spiritual leaders in times of need. One day a young woman who
was almost delirious with an illness poured a kettle of boiling water on
her head. Her screams reached every corner of the village, and people
came rushing in to see what had happened. Soon a pastor pushed to the
front to begin praying over her. Everyone agreed that prayers were necessary and also that her apparently irrational act of pouring the hot water
on herself was caused, in some sense, by the fact that she was known to
sin. But in speaking with people later on, I gathered that there was a
sense that the praying pastor was a bit too eager to jump in, a bit too
ready to help his own reputation (*apim nem,* TP) for healing.[5]

Prayer more generally is something that most people work on; different styles are tried out, and people judge prayer styles for their affective
power and ability to produce results (e.g., of healing or dispute resolution). Because confession is considered a kind of prayer, everyone has to
pray on their own to work at their own salvation. Whenever I slept in the
same house or room as other women (like most other women, I did not
sleep in the same room as men), I saw that it was standard practice to flip
on a flashlight to look at a Bible verse for a moment, and then engage in
whispered prayers just before going to bed. Many women start their days
in a similar way. In that sense, one's waking life is bookended by moments
of Christian reading and the prayerful speech that Bible reading elicits.

In delinking speech from the men's house norms of communicative
efficacy indexed by the attentive listener/actor, the codified, structured,
and print-artifactualized language established through the Guhu-Samane
translation projects made it possible for everyone to become a speaker at
least theoretically capable of the kind of Truth (with a capital *T*) that the
New Testament contains. Nor is this sense of speaker-focal language limited to the Christian contexts that initially inspired the translation work,
as is seen in the following brief example of the power of secular talk.

While I was living in Titio village (where Henry is the *maripa*), a
major land dispute flared up after someone's pigs rooted up gardens

FIGURE 7. A man argues his point during a meeting to discuss land ownership.

belonging to people in an adjacent village. The technical issues of pig governance and land tenure that were debated are not immediately relevant here, but eventually a series of back-and-forth accusations of negligence turned into more serious and fundamental questions about land ownership. The owner of the foraging pigs, Isaac, made a novel claim that the gardens had been made on his clan's land.[6] Henry and the leaders of the other village scheduled many meetings to try to sort this out, and Isaac had a few weeks to prepare and hone his argument. He and I spoke several times during this period. I asked at one point if he was going to try to throw the people from the other village off the land (in Tok Pisin, *yu bai rausim ol?*). "*I* wont throw them off the land," Isaac said, "*the stories* will!" (Mi *no bai rausim,* stori tasol *bai rausim.*)

Aiming for a kind of nomic truth, Isaac saw his clan histories—bought with payments of cash, tea, and meat to his mother's brother over the course of his adult life—as capable of enacting a major social upheaval on their own. Partially revealing elements of his secret stories in conjunction with the use of powerful magic, Isaac was sure that his stories spoke a powerful truth. He spoke with bravado about the attempts on his life that would be made after (partially) speaking his stories. "But it won't help. I wrote the stories in my book, so my children have them." Given that Isaac's male children were between roughly seven and fifteen years old, they were completely incapable of commanding authority in a land claim, much less turning the text in Isaac's notebook into an interactionally successful performance of knowledge. Nevertheless, Isaac believed he could harness the power of his talk into a reversal of what was then the conventional wisdom regarding the ownership of the disputed piece of land.

As if inspired by the revolution caused by sacred talk in the moments of the Holy Spirit revival, everyone now seems to want to talk their way to a revolution of their own. Undoubtedly, such talking revolutions happened in the days before missionaries or the downfall of the men's house, but without the governance of the men's house—at least as it is remembered now—talk seems to have no resolution. Even banana trees, in Henry's story that began this chapter, can try to talk themselves into new kinds of action. Land disputes are the most common and upsetting forms of talk, where men like Isaac try (from the perspective of competitors) to rewrite the history of Guhu-Samane clan migrations and genealogical alliances. But domestic disruptions ring out in the village regularly, with women confidently shouting at their husbands or brothers even as they dodge their blows.

In a sense, women's talk—while upsetting—is excusable, given gendered stereotypes of female lack of control. Relegated to the edges of village meetings, women often carry on their own side-conversations that act as commentary on the center-stage debates of the men. The only way in which women can break into a village meeting is to do so through a display of affect—to be moved to anger or tears and then explode with commentary. The story I related in chapter 4 about Ono's mother's outbursts in the middle of the compensation negotiations for Ono's actions is an example of this. Women's public speech, you might say, has always been ungovernable and disordered, in contrast to the order of male authority. Men's ungoverned speech in the Christian era seems to present yet another way in which men and women are converging in a Christian social space that makes no room for gendered distinctions.

Men's ungoverned speech, like the endless land-dispute meetings that took place in the wake of Isaac's pig problems, often fall under a genre I call "unjoined stories." People speak of the need to bring verbal material from several sources together, such as the histories of migration, matri-clan genealogies, and the secret names of land that Isaac was trying to hide-while-telling (cf. Weiner 1985 on keeping-while-giving).

FIGURE 8. Preparing for a meeting to discuss land ownership in Titio village.

Isaac's stories could not be "joined" (*dzoinim*, TP) with versions that other members of his matri-clan were telling or that people from other matri-clans were telling. Early in my fieldwork, my husband witnessed a moment of un-joinable stories being told. We had requested to hear some stories about forest spirits (*masalais*, TP; *gisi* or *piitu*, GS), and prior to coming to our house, my husband listened as some older men were conferring about the versions of the story they had decided to tell. This was a rather low-stakes operation in contrast to something like a land dispute. But even here, the stories could not be "joined." One man would speak for a while, and then someone would say *"bamu!"* (no! GS). The second man would then speak, and after a while, the first speaker would say *"bamu!"* It went on like that for about twenty minutes, and when they could not come to a resolution, they decided to come up and tell us a different story altogether, a fairy tale of sorts usually told to children that had a standard and well-known version.

My presence as a researcher "of language and culture" quickly became an opportunity to try to govern and join speech together. Several men involved in Bible translation work suggested that the methodology for this project should to follow the SIL translation procedure. In any translation, the first draft would be composed, edited, and then brought to village elders for an oral recitation, what SIL manuals call "the village check." I was told to collect stories with names attached to them, print them up, and then assemble them for a set of older men, who could then join them all together. This would produce a correct and truthful history of the Guhu-Samane. Even though everyone knew that village leaders—and, in the past, men's house leaders—altered stories for politically strategic goals, there was still a hope that a final truth could be revealed. Indeed, this is what cross-cultural comparison was supposed to show.[7]

The attempts to turn my research into a project of developing the Guhu-Samane Master Narrative failed, and not just because I was hesitant to participate. People simply did not want to talk to us if they thought that everything they said would be put up to a kind of public scrutiny akin to the "village check," Either because they were afraid to find that their versions of stories could not be joined or because they were unwilling to reveal the secret knowledge in their stories that they had paid for. And yet they still desired the production of a Master Narrative and hoped that their versions could be joined, could be made official like the New Testament text or the Guhu-Samane dictionary. That is to say, the contemporary problems with licensed, universal speakerhood could potentially be abated if everyone could agree to speak from the same script in a way that would mimic the singular voice of the men's house as it is remembered today.

The SIL translation project continues to be a powerful force in contemporary Guhu-Samane life. There was a grand celebration when the Guhu-Samane/Tok Pisin/English triglot lexicon *Noo Supu* was published in 2002. Richert's original language consultant, Timothy, died several decades ago; however, his son Mark and grandson Sean continue the translation work. Mark and Sean partner with SIL's sister organization for Papua New Guinean translators, the Bible Translation Association. Mark has been working on a Guhu-Samane translation of the Old Testament since the 1980s, and Sean joined him in this work in the late 1990s. Genesis and Exodus have been published as test books to gauge the continuing interest in and support for the translation project. When the Old Testament is finally done, there are plans for New Testament revisions and adaptations for downstream and upstream dialects.[8] Mark hopes to publish exegetical interpretations of various books of the Bible after that. In other words, there is no end in sight to the translation work.

The biblical Guhu-Samane language is indelibly linked to Richert and his primary helper and language consultant, Timothy. I joked with one Guhu-Samane friend that we could call it the "Timothy Memorial Language," and he agreed that it was a good name, since it really was Timothy's language in the Bible. This refers not only to the fact that the New Testament translation is modeled on Timothy's dialect but also to the fact that Timothy is seen as an ancillary author of the translation. The tight family connection within the translation work (besides Timothy, Mark, and Sean, two of Timothy's other sons have been involved at various points) gives an added sense of kin-defined authority and ownership over the translation that seems to recall the patrilineal leadership governing the men's house. That is to say, the translation work is sometimes set up as a contemporary analogue to politico-religious control of village life by the men's house.

While SIL models of evangelism would expect every native speaker of Guhu-Samane to have a sense of ownership over and deep connection to the translation in their own language, few do. People who now sit on the multi-village and multidenominational translation committee that officially oversees the Old Testament work lament the fact that Richert did not pass along his translation skills very well. Timothy and, to an extent, Mark received some knowledge of how translation is done, but none of the other Guhu-Samane elders who were involved with Richert at Kipu feel like they have that same sense of ownership. A few men have gone to SIL/Bible Translation Association headquarters in the Eastern Highlands Province for training, but the general lack of training among the rest of the committee members is seen as an important cause of the slow pace of work. People may feel licensed to talk, but they do not have a sense of their talk contributing to a unifying, larger project. Translation fails to be a replacement for the order of the men's house. Absent the men's house, absent the anthropologist's ordering of culture, was there any way to contain the power of talk unleashed by translation?

GOD'S WORD AND GROUP PRAYER: LISTENING AND SPEAKING IN DENOMINATIONAL FORMS

During a series of sermons titled "What Is Sin?" at the revival-inspired Reformed Gospel Church in Titio village, the two sins that different pastors emphasized as the most grievous were *apim nem* (TP, increase your own reputation; that is, vanity) and *sakim tok* (TP, ignore talk; that is, disobedience). Ungoverned talk is something of an epidemic. Yet if it was the power of constituting the Body of Christ in a church that initially licensed Christian speakerhood during the revival, people also hope that the power of the church can bring them back into a position of being cooperative listeners. In other sermons at Reformed Gospel services, people were constantly told to listen for God's word. As one sermonizer put it, being a good Christian is like trying to talk to someone using a two-way radio (as people in the Waria Valley and many other rural communities in Papua New Guinea do). If you want to communicate with someone using this medium, you have to do a lot of work: travel to where the radio is, be by the radio at all times, and then turn up the volume and concentrate when you hear your interlocutor's voice. As this same man said on another occasion, God's word should be your bridle. One metric for church strength, in fact, was the length of the sermon. If sermons were too short (a short sermon was about twenty minutes; a long one could last over an hour), people would complain. Even if everyone looked terribly bored in church, listening is an important part of Christian practice. Like the men's house of the remembered past, listening is a mode of action, although in this case, a mode of active self-discipline (Robbins 2004a, 266; see also Knauft 2002b on the "passive agency" of listening in church). Listening is also heavily emphasized in other contexts, like village meetings (for adults) and schools (for children).

Christian linguistic subjectivity, in which one must speak one's self to be Christian, for many people means that there are too many speakers and not enough listeners. Moreover, attempts to discipline Christians through listening (for example, having them listen to sermon oratory) are often foiled by the endless problems of the sins of speaking that happen in village life. When it seems like people are getting completely out of control, one recent response had been to start a new church. When the original revival church, New Life, started to do things that people equated too much with a cargo cult, a number of men called a meeting with like-minded people to see if they could schism and start a new church. Henry was at this meeting and has a particularly men's house–inspired take on the events. Henry argued to break off from New Life but said they should do so by going under the umbrella of a new international denomination (something like the Lutherans). Henry wanted to have an overarching power that could be used to curtail the ritual and linguistic experimentation that New Life was engaging in. He saw nothing but ineffective action in trying to do things *yumi yet* (TP, ourselves). But Henry was out-voted. Even the men who were most outraged by the quasi-traditionalistic practices that they had heard of or had seen New Life perform were too committed to the possibilities for powerful speech to cede that territory to another institution again.

Instead, people decided to create a church on their own again, to contain the power of speech through the recreation of the Body of Christ. Living as they do in the era between Christ's time on earth and the final judgment, the primary way in which Guhu-Samane Christians can overcome this dislocation from God is through the church itself. As the Body of Christ, the church is meant to be the earthly shadow of the kind of immediacy that will be possible in heaven. Under the evangelical and Pentecostal norms that Richert taught to his students at the Kipu Academy, people had to do a great deal of linguistic work to create the Body of Christ. A crucial practice for achieving this is what is known as *bung beten* (TP, group prayer), in which everyone in church prays individually, but at the same time. Timothy's grandson Sean, who works with SIL and is familiar with American evangelical worship styles, specifically pointed out to me the importance of the *bung beten* for Papua New Guinean churches. "We do *bung beten*s here. I know you Americans don't, but you are in PNG now," he said early on in my fieldwork. Group prayer is, in fact, a worldwide Pentecostal phenomenon, addressed in a Zambian context by Haynes (2013).

In the revival churches, *bung beten*s are a standard part of a worship service. Without a liturgy, the prayers that each person says during a *bung beten* are all different, producing a cacophony of voices that together produce a powerful moment of communication with God. But this is not simply individuals each calling out to God on their own, since the prayers are given added strength in the ways that they call into being a church unit, working together for a specific prayer or praise point. In New Life Church, the first church to emerge from the revival, *bung beten*s are incredibly and joyfully noisy. The worship leader will give the congregation a topic for their prayer and then shout *"Emo!"* (GS, go!). Then the congregation—especially the women—launch into loud and quick prayers that normally last around three or four minutes. During special prayer sessions, *bung beten*s can last for an hour. While everyone prays, guitarists will strum their guitars on a single chord, and drummers will beat their drums at a steady pace, contributing to the general sonic chaos. One by one people will slow their prayers and lower their voices, until the worship leader's voice can clearly be heard above all the others. At this point, people in the congregation will stop, allowing the worship leader to, in essence, summarize and package the cacophonous prayers into a monologic voice that can be singularly addressed to God.

Women are particularly powerful participants in *bung beten*s. In contrast to the men's house (where their voices were almost entirely excluded) or contemporary village meetings (where women sit at the outskirts of the meeting area and contribute only in emotional bursts), *bung beten*s are the prime times for women's voices to be heard. Not only are a lot of women talking, but they are talking a lot: part of the aesthetic of the *bung beten* is for each person to constantly produce talk for the entire length of the prayer, so that it is both strong and sustained. These moments of petition are powerful resources that not only create individual Christians but create the church as such.

As an example of a *bung beten,* I provide a few seconds from the beginning of a prayer that was said for my husband and me one night. Five men (most of whom were known as the village "missionaries," or Christian spiritual leaders) had asked to come up to our house to pray for a problem we were then encountering. The pastor for the village church (marked as "S" in the transcript below) led the events. He asked my husband and me to explain our problem, which I did. Then he gave us a Bible text to guide our prayer (*Samting i no inap long man i mekim, God i bai mekim,* TP; "With man this is impossible, but with God all things are possible"; he cited this as Matthew 10:27, although it is actually Mark 10:27), and he summarized the topics ("prayer points") that people should focus on. He then started the prayer, speaking loudly while everyone else slowly warmed up with whispered prayers. As is usual, the prayers began with statements in praise of God.[9]

In the transcript below, I have tried to represent the overlapping talk using side-by-side columns, spacing lines in an approximation of the order in which they were spoken. In this early part of the prayer, people are offering verbal ready-mades, pat phrases that punctuate their own particular prayer style (e.g., *God yu Bikpela,* "You are Lord, God"; *God yu gat blessing,* "God you give blessings"; or simply "Hallelujah"). Later on, the men moved into more substantive prayers, although they remained flecked with their own particular phrases that they used to keep the flow of talk constant and insistent. At a certain point, I simply had to stop transcribing as the prayers—even with just five speakers—became a wall of sound that no longer allowed for distinct voices. The transcript covers about thirty-five seconds of what was a nine-minute *bung beten,* during which these men kept up a constant stream of prayer. The first transcript below is untranslated, with speakers using both Tok Pisin and English. The second is an English translation of the first. In both transcripts, utterances originally spoken in English by the speaker marker here as "E" (the most formally educated man in this group and who was raised in town) are underlined.

S [prayer leader]	E	O	Po	Pi
		Hallelujah		
God bilong	tsk[a]			
Abraham na		God yu gat		
God bilong Isaac		blessing		
na God bilong				
Jakob, yu				
God i gat olgeta	tsk			
strong		God mipela		
		liptimapim yu		
	Praise God			
Na yu God	tsk			
			tsk	
Jehovah				
		Hallelujah		
yu save				
provaidim		God yu gat		
olgeta samting		blessing	tsk	
long laik bilong				
mipela wanwan				
laif bilong	tsk		God	
mipela, taim				God yu
God yu bin				Bikpela
mekim				
yu bin i gat		namba wan	mi beten long	
spesol,		Papa God	dispela	
yu bin I gat	yu gat pawa		nait	
function				
na yu bin mekim	it's more than	wok na masta		
mipela model	enough	bilong mipela		
Na olgeta	God olsem		Papa God	
laif bilong			tok bilong yu	
mipela			na	yu bikpela na
i gat purpose			sios bilong yu	
			long dispela	
			nait,	
			mipela stap	
			ananit long	
			han bilong yu	
olsem na God	powerful God	Hallelujah	Papa God	
long dispela nait			mi beten long	
mipela kam bipo			dispela nait	
long- ah presens				
bilong yu				
long dispela nait			God mi beten	Ol i stap
na			long dispela	wantaim yu
mipela sindaun	Yu Bikpela even		nait	
wantaim tupela	before			
brata na susa				
James na				
Courtney				

[a] I could not actually tell who was making the (ingressive, plosive) 'tsk' sounds, but I attribute them here to the men who used that vocal tick frequently in their prayers.

English translation:

S [prayer leader]	E	O	Po	Pi
		Hallelujah		
	tsk			
God of Abraham and God of Isaac		God you have blessings		
and God of Jakob, you				
God the mightiest	tsk	God we praise you		
	Praise God			
And you God	tsk			
			tsk	
Jehovah you always		Hallelujah		
provide everything		God you have blessings	tsk	
that each one of us asks for				
our lives, when	tsk		God	
you created our lives				God you are Lord
you had a special...		the greatest Father God	I pray on this night	
	you are powerful			
you had a function				
and you made us with that	it's more than enough	and Lord of us all		
And all	God is		Father God your word and your church tonight we remain under your guiding hand	you are Lord and
of our lives have purpose				
and so on this night we come into your presence	powerful God	Hallelujah	Father God tonight I pray	
tonight and we sit here with			God, tonight I pray	Everyone is with you
our brother and sister	You were the Lord even before			
James and Courtney				

After the initial moments, transcribed above, when S was speaking the loudest, the men modulated their own voices so that they were all speaking at roughly the same, and eventually quite loud, volume. From then on, only small bits were intelligible above the steady thrum of noise. The intensity waxed and waned over the course of the prayer, but the unity of the indistinct voices remained. Finally, the men started to pray more slowly and lower their volume, waiting for S to come back into focus and bring the prayer to a close. The speaker here marked "O," however, took the floor and tried to close the prayer himself, possibly part of his own push to become a more highly regarded spiritual leader, after a major sin had left him sidelined from church for a few months. There was an awkward pause after O finished, and eventually S, the official prayer leader for the night, and then the pastor of the Titio Reformed Gospel Church, re-performed the ritual closing of the group prayer. Whether or not O's attempt to become the group's leader for this prayer was successful (given S's repetition of the closing, I would say it was not), both prayer closings tried to summarize and unify the prior eight minutes of powerful, individual speech.

The *bung beten* thus organizes the cacophonous sounds of communal prayer, bracketing them at each end with a singular voice. S provides the other speakers with their topic at the beginning and provides God with a summary of these prayers at the end. In that sense, speakers start and end the prayer with moments of attentive listening, finding the right moment for their own voices to emerge. Talk is now open to all—a plague of language, from the perspective of someone like Henry. And yet churches still try to find a way to contain this power in the ritualized and controlled explosions of speech that pastors lead. Individual talk is a necessary part of a Christian life, but rituals like the *bung beten* help to give it institutional form, to rein in the outpouring of language with bridled listening at beginning and end.

As much as the *bung beten* seems to be the denial of men's house models of communication, I argue that the revival churches continued the simultaneous affirmation and denial of the equivalence between the men's house and the church. On the one hand, the revival church became important as a group formation through which community—in this case a sacred community—could be formed. Importantly, this community initially came together through moments of listening to and acting upon the words of the Holy Spirit during the revival. On the other hand, the revivalist—and, more generally, Christian—sense of communication also required that the sacred community be formed through the speech of all people involved. In a kind of Christian linguistic individualism, the participants in the revival became morally responsible for themselves through individual speech and a linguistic subjectivity based on speaking, echoing the other rituals (like individual, immersion baptism of adults) that also developed at this time. The proliferation of denominations that has continued to this day in the Waria Valley can be seen as the product of this oscillating relationship between speaking and listening that constitutes Christian practice today.

For over a century now, missionaries, translators, and Guhu-Samane speakers themselves have asserted and denied the equivalence between the *poro guhu* and the church as the central institution of the local community. The ongoing translation projects have added three other elements into this mix: first, the codification of a sacred Guhu-Samane language in translation projects, which allowed for access to and communication with the divine in the post-translation revival; second, the delinking of the codified, sacred Guhu-Samane language with the listener/actor-focal communicative norms of the men's house; and third, the incorporation of evangelical and Pentecostal worship styles that emphasized the ways in which the Church becomes the Body of Christ through communal talk like the *bung beten*. This has lead to the licensing of universal adult speakerhood and the disorderly proliferation of disruptive talk that this licensing engenders. But it has also lead to the reassertion of the importance of the church as an institution similar to the men's house in that it can control the speech of others. And yet, even these calls to return to listenerhood have been made in the context of trying to create a new church, that is, a new position from which to powerfully speak.

. . .

I want to conclude by taking a step back from this discussion of speakerhood and powerful language to talk about something that does not get much air time in contemporary anthropology: social organization. While not trying to recuperate the structural-functionalism of Radcliffe-Brown, sometimes a move away from the strict focus on the subject can be helpful. To do this, I want to briefly bring in a contentious article from the Melanesianist archives, Ron Brunton's "Misconstrued Order in Melanesian Religion" (1980). In this article, Brunton suggests that Melanesianists may have been wrong to assume that religion and religious practice is universally a matter of coming to final answers about the major culturally defined problems of life. Echoed later in Talal

Asad's (1993) critique of Geertz's (1973) definition of religion as crypto-Protestant, Brunton suggests that while some highly structured societies may, in fact, work toward resolutions of major cultural contradictions, other groups (groups that do not value large-scale cultural divisions of society into, for example, gender, class, and age-grades) may simply find contradictions to be a fact of life. As evidence for the latter kind of society, Brunton cites work by McArthur (1971) and Hallpike (1977) on Guhu-Samane's neighboring communities of Kunimaipan and Goilalan speakers. McArthur's article, in which she admits to finding no resolution to discrepant stories—and even more, suggests that Kunimaipans themselves are not bothered by the discrepancies between different versions of stories—had largely been ignored by her colleagues working in Melanesia. This was because, Brunton surmised, people had assumed that this was simply a product of unsuccessful fieldwork.

Without pretending to be able to access precolonial social order and evaluate it along a single dimension of contrast, I still find something useful in Brunton's acceptance of contradiction and emphasis on social organization. The Guhu-Samane have likely had a long history of "unjoined stories" similar to McArthur's Kunimaipan informants. And while Guhu-Samane society—having to confront the dislocations of matrilineality and virilocality—likely would count as more "structured" on Brunton's continuum, it seems to have long been a place in which the contradictions of social groups have seemed inevitable. Christianity has both been a revelation and a continuation in that sense.

Christianity has been a revelation in the sense that it has offered up a competing perspective that licenses autonomous action: everyone is responsible for their own salvation as equal children of God. With shame or great admiration, men remember the men's house now as a perfect system of social order, organized and organically solidary in every way that Christianity is sociologically flat. Today, with each person a prime minister of his or her own salvation and licensed to be a speaker of his or her own voice, the contemporary Christian world—from the perspective of current memorializations of the men's house—is a world of disorderly and ungovernable speech.

Christianity has been a continuation in the sense that it has nevertheless left open a corner for the disjoined stories of salvational practice to coexist in the form of denominations. In the post-revival era, when more and more denominations have taken root in the valley, denominational disputes would seem to be the sociological recognition of the need to contain the multiplying speakers in a way that is similar to how men's houses could at least partially contain the disputes, land claims, and everyday arguments that come up in any community.

I find the focus on the sociality of Christian life important not only for the Guhu-Samane and their very particular history of Christian encounter, but also for a larger anthropology of Christianity. Even though Protestantism is considered the religion of individualism, one cannot ignore the fact that Christians do not worship alone. (In this sense, left-liberal Americans who see something stale in "organized religion" would really be the practitioners of a religion of individualism.) Christians in many places work hard to find the right balance between an individualizing orientation to one's own salvation and a desire to gain a better sense of that salvation through becoming a part of the collective work of the Body of Christ. The Guhu-Samane use proliferating denominations to help keep the tensions between revolutionary speakerhood and bridled listening to God in some kind of check. Different ways of maintaining these conflicting aspects of Christian practice undoubtedly exist in other contexts.

And while broad questions of governance and sovereignty seem to be increasingly important in contemporary anthropology, works in this vein also seem to focus on the limits of subjectivity. Biehl's (2005) discussion of the deplorable conditions of the mentally ill in Brazil, with his focus on the ways in which one patient existed almost outside of subjectivity, could be called a discussion of disordered language. I have argued here for a kind of linguistic disorder very much at the heart of Guhu-Samane social life, precariously balanced between subjects and memories of social order. The profusion of subjects, not the lack of them, is, for the older men of these communities, the cause of so much recent violence.

PART THREE

Denominations

CHAPTER 6

Events of Translation

Intertextuality and Denominationalist
Change

In the decades since the revival's ecstatic anticipation of a Christian heaven on earth, the Guhu-Samane have had a hard time keeping hold of the sense of transformation that they experienced in 1977. The acrimonious schisms within the Christian community and broken promises from the national government about "development" contribute to the deep skepticism about change that Guhu-Samane Christians now grapple with. It is in light of this skepticism that the attention to Guhu-Samane engagements with the text that, for them, constituted change in the first place—the translated New Testament—deserves particular attention. With New Life and Reformed Gospel, the two revivalist churches, battling for dominance in the area, the differences in their engagements with the translation can be seen, as I argue below, as central ritual enactments of models of change: is change something that happened in the past (in 1977) and that people today have to orient themselves to, as New Life members suggest through their strict adherence to the original translation? Or, as Reformed Gospel Church members say, is change something that, given the continuing failures of development, has to be ritually reenacted each Sunday by retranslating the New Testament?

Translation has long been a part of anthropological data and practice, and recently analysts have focused on the politics, poetics, and ethics of translations that account for so much of the global flow of discourses around the world (e.g., Asad 1986; Gal 2003; Merry 2006;

Meyer 1999; Rafael 1993; B. Schieffelin 2002, 2007; see also Venuti 1998). Much of this literature can be thought of as histories of how translators forge denotational links between source and target texts and how communities engage with the texts that result from this process. I discuss some of these accounts more at the end of this chapter. Before that, however, I want to highlight how connections between source and target texts can become models of transformation for the communities that engage with them. I argue that, in fact, a community can enact transformations in ritual moments that foreground the relationships between translated texts. As I discuss below, this perspective offers a particularly compelling way to investigate Christian models of temporality.

I examine translation as a species of intertextuality, by which I mean the ways in which one text can point to, or index, another text for people in particular moments of interaction (Agha 2007; Bauman and Briggs 1990; Silverstein and Urban 1996; see also Bakhtin 1981). For example, if I directly quote someone else's speech, ("The blind man said, 'I am healed!'") then my text points back to some other text (i.e., the blind man's).[1] In discussing the role of intertextuality in interaction, Briggs and Bauman (1992, 149) note that speakers employ different strategies for minimizing or maximizing the differences between texts related in this way, differences that they refer to as producing an unavoidable "gap." The gap may be minimized, as in the direct quotation above, or it can be maximized, as in the kinds of characterizations produced through indirect quotation ("The blind man exclaimed with joy about his suffering being over!").

One can use this model of intertextuality in an account of translation, and to a certain extent, people already have. For example, when analysts discuss histories of translations, they often describe the process that translators go through to produce a target text that can intertextually index a source text for himself or herself (the "hermeneutic motion" in Steiner 1975 could be thought of in this sense). However, actors do not stop forming and reforming the intertextual linkages after the work of equivalence-building is developed through grammars, ethnographies, or any of the other texts that translators use. That is, *engagements with* translations can also be intertextually related to finished (or published) translations, where the fact of the history of translation itself is ritually forefronted. Like Benjamin's (1968a) and Venuti's (1998) calls for a foreignizing translation that brings attention to a text as having been translated, communities can ritually engage with translations in ways that highlight this transformational process. This can happen whether the translator intended the translation to be foreignizing or domesticating. As Rutherford (2006) notes, translations may be important to a community only if their foreignness is highlighted. However, this does not mean that, as in Rutherford's Biak example, a community could not also incorporate the translated text into local discourses. In the Guhu-Samane example I present below, it is instead the denominationally specific schematizations of the movement via translation of a text from a foreign there-and-then to a local here-and-now that is ritually foregrounded.

If a community has access to a translated text, then different recitations or performances can have larger or smaller "gaps" between the translated text and the event of its use. Speakers can paraphrase the translation, reengage in the process of translation itself, read from the translation word-for-word, or some mixture of these or other options. In the materials presented below, we will see two radically different approaches to translation (which can be glossed for now as word-for-word recitation versus performative retranslation) in New Life and Reformed Gospel, two denominations using the exact same translation of the New Testament. These different formations of intertextual linkages are indexically connected to the initial translation events—when the New Testament was originally produced by the Richerts. The formations of intertextual linkages made in contemporary performances are then further events of translation. In these linkages, the Guhu-Samane grasp for models of transformation that can anchor their understanding of their place on a Christian timeline that has moments of "real" change as opposed to the false changes of (post)colonial governments, those failures that weigh heavily on local people's shoulders.

The formations of equivalences central to many other anthropological accounts of translation have focused special attention on the structural history of linguistic and cultural transposition. That is, they focus on what word was used to translate or, more often, mistranslate a particular key concept. In what follows, I give an event-based, or "evenemential," approach center stage. I take the term "evenemential" from Sahlins (2004, but see also 1985, 1991), who uses it to discuss the ways in which cultural structures are transformed in practice. In contrast to Annales school historians who vilified "event history" in favor of a structural history of the longue durée (as described in Sahlins 1991), Sahlins argues that events transform structures, given contingent alignments of people and contexts. In discussing the role of such dramatic events, Sahlins writes, "It is from this revolutionary denouement, work-ing backward, that we discover and rhetorically motivate the tempos, turning points, and agents of our history. The structural reversal in the story is the determining principle of historical value and relevance, a telos that rules the organization of the account" (Sahlins 2004, 130–31, citations omitted).

While Sahlins discusses evenemential histories as kinds of texts pro-duced by historians and anthropologists, I want to borrow this notion to describe the ways in which local Christians in Guhu-Samane com-munities are trying to provide a meta-commentary on the kinds of transformations they have experienced. Events of translation are places where people can imagine themselves from a desired telos, moments where ritual performances produce an effect that could be glossed as "our world has transformed, and we need to keep orienting ourselves to that moment of change" or "we have only experienced partial change—we need to keep transforming." Even if these sentiments will not, under their Christian logic, be proved true or false until Judgment Day, events of translation provide local people with the ritual means to comment upon and enact their hoped-for place within a Christian model of con-version and salvation.

Because these events of translation can tropically model and enact the kinds of transformations that local people experience, this form of intertextual linkage between a translation and its subsequent perform-ance is particularly important in the context of Christian missionization and global Christianity. This emphasis, in turn, can help to refocus a recent debate in the anthropology of Christianity about the temporal models found in this religion. As voiced most pointedly by Fenella Can-nell (2006) but also Comaroff and Comaroff (1991), Gow (2006), and Kipp (1995), it has been suggested that anthropologists need to be wary of the discourse of radical personal and social change most evident in the evangelical and Pentecostal forms of Christianity popular in the glo-bal south. Anthropologists of Christianity often argue that transforma-tions rarely, if ever, take on the kind of Saul-on-the-road-to-Damascus temporality in which sudden change is possible. For them, Christian communities need to be understood in the same terms as any other com-munities, where social and personal change is at best a long-term, grad-ual phenomenon.

Joel Robbins (2007), however, has argued that attention to Christi-anity's model of change can open new ground for anthropological theo-rizing of local social transformation. Robbins shows that anthropology is predicated upon a notion of temporality fundamentally at odds with the Christian one. In particular, he argues that anthropology is committed to the secular notion of "homogeneous, empty time," whereas Christianity requires the bumps and breaks of Benjamin's messianic time in which radical change is possible (Benjamin 1968b). Robbins focuses on the ways in which discontinuity comes to be high on the cultural agenda for Christians. In other words, either Christianity's model of change is a myth (as Cannell argues) or it is central to the creation of Christianity itself (as Robbins argues). I suggest that by looking at performative rituals like events of translation, we can examine the ethnographically particular models of transformation used by local people in particular contexts of global Christianity.

While narratives of conversion have been studied from this perspective of creating the temporality of *personal* rupture (e.g., Harding 2000), in this chapter, I explore the ways in which translations can create contrasting temporalities of rupture through which Christian social forms like denominations define both themselves and the denominations with which they compete. The evenemential account of translation can then be used to examine conversion as a locally and denominationally variable kind of event through which Christian adherents of different groups organize.

DENOMINATIONAL CONVERSIONS IN GUHU-SAMANE CHRISTIANITY

In the course of collecting life histories from older adult members of Reformed Gospel, I found that it was extremely rare that they would acknowledge the ten or more years that they had spent in New Life. Kitore, a man who spoke frequently with me about Christianity's role in his life, only discussed his pastorship in New Life several months into our acquaintance. He omitted it completely when, late in my field research, I asked him for a history of his spiritual life. That is, he skipped from his years as a Lutheran directly to his years with Reformed Gospel. While not shy about disclosing what are now considered shameful traditional practices in describing their pre-conversion moments within the genre of the conversion narrative, these Reformed Gospel members nevertheless erase the history of their involvement with New Life, whose practices they now deride. Why is this one church erased from local narratives of conversion, even when other denominations and transformations are included?

One answer can be found in the events of translation and conversion that members of Reformed Gospel practice. New Life has created a denominational organization that authoritatively links to the 1977 Holy Spirit revival through ritual performances paying allegiance to the 1975 event of translation—the official distribution of the Guhu-Samane translation of the New Testament—as the ultimate moment of spiritual transformation. Contrastively, Reformed Gospel's events of translation constitute a denomination organized by an ongoing rupture that its members experience, while also wresting away from New Life the exclusive authority over the temporality of the 1977 Holy Spirit revival. By making Reformed Gospel the church of continuous change and attempting to establish exclusive authority over the revival, they can, in effect, say they have been Reformed Gospel for as long as they have been experiencing change—thus negating their New Life affiliations. These translation practices have been important resources in creating New Life and Reformed Gospel as schismatically divergent denominations.

Taken from a perspective that primarily examines the contexts of production of translations, the differences between these denominations are mysterious. They use the same translation of the New Testament, *Poro Tongo Usaqe* (Anonymous 1975), and they confront the same semantic mismatches between local and Christian meanings. Likewise, the leaders of both denominations were part of the original translation project led by Ernie Richert in which these decisions about denotational equivalences across languages were made, and they were part of the classroom experiences where Richert taught Western sermon forms. It is only from the perspective of translation as an event of intertextual linkage that different temporal organizations of Christian denominational sociality come into focus. Translation in the Waria Valley is most interesting because translation is figured by local people as the process that calls into existence and characterizes the very distinction between the traditional and the Christian, the local and the foreign, that defines denominational difference for Guhu-Samane Christians. These denominations vary precisely on the figuration of change—as a job well done or one that never ends.

RETURNING TO THE EVENT: NEW LIFE CHURCH AND THE POLITICS OF LOCALIZATION

In the two years between the official distribution of the Guhu-Samane New Testament in 1975 and the the Holy Spirit revival in 1977, young

Christians used *Poro Tongo Usaqe* in Bible study, dreamed of it and other Christian texts at night, and had it with them during mountain-top prayer retreats, where angels visited them. New Life Church founds its institutional and theological identity on the New Testament transla-tion. For New Life, the 1975 SIL translation is as authoritative as the events of the revival were transformative.

The role of the translation in their local history of transformation can be seen first in terms of language policy in New Life Church. As I discussed in chapter 1, prior to the translation and the revival, Guhu-Samane Lutherans spoke or, more often, only partially understood Kâte, the mission's lingua franca, which had been imported from the Huon Peninsula. Although the Lutheran Mission started to develop liturgical materials in Tok Pisin in the 1950s, older New Life and Reformed Gospel members remember the colonial Lutheran church as being an exclusively Kâte-language institution. During one translation-workshop presentation to the community that I attended, local transla-tors asked older community members to come up and sing some old Kâte-language Lutheran songs. The performance produced nervous, embarrassed guffaws from both the singers and the audience, with eve-ryone laughing at both the singers' failing memories and the oddity of this foreign language being used as a language of local spiritual prac-tice. In the post SIL-translation era, it seemed absurd to use Kâte.

After the translation and the revival, New Life members put in place a Guhu-Samane-language-only policy in church services, marking the now sacred status of their local language. During my fieldwork, there was a greater emphasis on monolingualism in New Life Church con-texts than anywhere else in Guhu-Samane social life. For example, in a sermon recorded during New Life's annual celebration on February 2, 2006, 682 lines of text were in Guhu-Samane while only eleven were in Tok Pisin. The speaker's borrowings from Tok Pisin and English were minimal, mostly biblical and colonial terminology. In addition to this monolingual emphasis on a sacralized local language, New Life mem-bers do not spontaneously retranslate the New Testament (from, for example, Tok Pisin or English language versions) into Guhu-Samane. The Guhu-Samane translation's authority is demonstrated by the extent to which people faithfully reproduce it in ritual performances. Kâte, Tok Pisin, and English are all maintained as external and extraneous to the translated Guhu-Samane Bible text and the translated Guhu-Samane Christianity implied therein.

Excerpts from church services demonstrate this clearly. In the sermon mentioned above, the speaker, Reverend Pituro,[2] introduces the Bible text that will be his main focus: the beginning of the story of Pentecost as found in Acts 2:1–13. He had been speaking about the Holy Spirit revival of 1977, and he tells the audience that they should read about it too (i.e., read about the biblical precursor to which he is aligning local events). Speaking entirely in Guhu-Samane, he cites the verses he will read, uses the local quotative framing device (*oi hee,* "it says"), and then reads straight from *Poro Tongo Usaqe* the subsection heading and the thirteen verses, closing the quotative frame with a series of "thank you's" to God. In the transcript below I include only the beginning of this ritual recitation. Starting at line 4, when Pituro begins reading, I include the published version of *Poro Tongo Usaqe* for comparison beneath each transcript line. The slight differences between Pituro's recitation and the published text are in bold (at lines 7 and 9).

1 Oho quba napa noo oke isaitako
   let's read about this thing

2 Oi Aposoro hu tu bisa wan ma tertin
   it's [Acts of the] Apostles two, line one through thirteen

3 oi hee
   it says

[reading the Bible subsection heading]

4 Sumasai Qaru Abike noonomaiteta
   [Sumasai Qaru Abike noonomaiteta]
   The Spirit made the apostles talk

5 Sumasai Qaru Abike noonomaiteta
   The Spirit made the apostles talk
   [verse one]

6 Qate Ingonaho dzuma ao kharata tuumami
   [Qate Ingonaho dzuma ao kharata tuumami]
   Then the sacred day had at last come and

7 bodza pipiti naatemi patta ponabetaquho **bodza** dzuma naate oomi
   [bodza pipiti naatemi patta ponabetaquho dzuma naate oomi]
   the time was xxx and the Pentecost day arrived

8 Peetoro ma kara nokoi gama susupu ttutturateqi

[Peetoro ma kara nokoi gama susupu ttutturateqi]

and Peter and his set, they gathered together

9 tupu teenate oota.

[tupu teenata oota.]

as a single group.

As can be seen from this excerpt, the differences between the Bible quotation spoken by Pituro in the first lines and the Bible quotation printed in the Guhu-Samane New Testament in the second lines are extremely minimal. Many of the alterations seen here and in the rest of his recitation involve his addition of material for greater clarity: temporal lexemes, directional lexemes, reference-tracking morphology, morphological case marking, and so forth. Other differences (such as the vowel in line 9) may simply be performance or transcription errors.

Like many other Guhu-Samane speakers, Reverend Pituro finds the SIL translation to be unclear in places. Speakers complain that the circumlocutions used to explain foreign concepts make the text long and ponderous. One young church leader has developed an aesthetic of verse length and complements the English version for its succinct brevity, tolerates the Tok Pisin version, and finds the Guhu-Samane version overly long and ungainly. Pituro has quietly annotated his personal copy of the New Testament where he believes it is unclear, making small corrections to syntactically awkward clauses by adding material (like the temporal marker *bodza,* "time," in line 7). However, Pituro is not interested in the official project of wholesale revision and republication that the members of Reformed Gospel are engaged in with SIL. That is, he has an allegiance to this version of the New Testament that contrasts with the other church's interest in creating the text anew, a point I return to in the following section.

The fidelity with which the reverend orally reproduces the text as written suggests an ideology of intertextual linkage in which successful ritual performances depend less on referential clarity than on proper procedure. Other forms of ritual language that Guhu-Samane speakers use, such as incantations, magical spells, or clan-based forms of ritual address, are generally performed with a version of the language that contemporary speakers consider an "older" form (*tok bilong tumbuna,* TP) that is "heavy" (*bahe,* GS) and buried several layers "below" (*ananit, tok i dip,* TP) the kind of language used in everyday speaking. In general, these ritual couplets or incantations are semantically opaque to speakers. A similar sense of ritual language use is at work in Pituro's delivery of the New Testament text. He aims primarily for correct delivery as a performance of fidelity to the revival that the translation brought about.

Based on the clear, quotative framing of the biblical text—the speaker's halting recitation in contrast to his free-flowing speech in nonreading moments, as well as the fidelity with which he reproduces the quotation— the Bible text appears as a bracketed, separate textual object ("entextualized" and only minimally "recontextualized"; see Bauman and Briggs 1990; Silverstein and Urban 1996). To use Briggs and Bauman's (1992) intertextual framework cited in the introduction, Pituro reproduces the Bible translation with minimal "gaps" between his and the published versions. As a ritual event of intertextual linkage, this performance is constructed to achieve maximal identity with the prior events of translation, that is, the 1975 event of translation that produced the 1977 revival.

In the annual weeklong gathering that brings together members of New Life who are spread across Papua New Guinea, both scheduled and impromptu speakers make frequent reference to the 1975 New Testament translation and to the SIL translators. After a New Life leader read the official history of the church during festivities on February 2, 2006, including a lengthy section on God's plan in bringing SIL to the Guhu-Samane, an impassioned audience member momentarily took control of the proceedings to reiterate the crucial role that the translation played in bringing the Holy Spirit to the Waria Valley in a way that the Lutheran missionaries had not been able to do.

For many, including the speakers at the February 2 celebrations, the power of the SIL translation is understood as God's valuation of the local language, and from the contemporary perspective, it contrasts with the powerlessness of the Lutherans' lingua franca to create "real" Christian conversions, as noted in the February 2 speech discussed in chapter 4. The revival thus marked a moment of independence and a localization of religious power and authority, a localization made possible through and also indexed by the New Testament translation into the Guhu-Samane language. The translation was the local route to the power of the Holy Spirit, outside of the colonial hierarchies of the Lutheran mission. In the February 2 celebrations, New Life members figure themselves as the perduring social formation produced through the revival, a figure that is created through the intertextual allegiance to the 1975 New Testament translation that forms minimal "gaps" between contemporary performances and what is for New Life members the original moment of linguistic and spiritual transformation. Likewise, New Life members remain committed to other ritual practices that act as emblems of their localization of power. For example, the full-body-immersion baptisms performed during the Holy Spirit revival happened outside of Lutheran authority and certainly went against Lutheran traditions of infant baptismal sprinkling.

Local material culture is used in New Life services to help members create the vibrant, electric feeling of their Sunday services that are themselves ritual returns to both the 1977 revival and the original moment of Pentecost described in Acts 2. New Life members use traditional drums and song styles in church services in conjunction with their loud calls of *oi mee* ("amen," "it is true") (as I discuss more in the next chapter). Like their pastors and reverends, New Life members also have a policy of Guhu-Samane-language-only when they participate in call-and-response routines. They take pride in the ecstatic expressions of devotion coming from what they now see as the humble frame of bush-materials churches.

This spiritual-linguistic emphasis on localization is reflected also in the church's attitudes toward government and economic institutions. The daughter of the original founder of New Life told me that, while her church's members and leaders do not have the money or access to education that other churches do, their direct access to the Holy Spirit makes this lack unimportant. New Life members do not send their pastors to tertiary Bible colleges for external recognition or certification as other churches do.[3] They also refuse to register their church as a government-recognized organization. Economically, they struggle to rid themselves of external dependencies beyond just the refusal of external education. For example, some New Life churches engage in rice-growing collectives, substituting their spirit-inspired agricultural work for the one-kilo store-bought bags that cost upward of three kina (roughly the amount a woman makes in two trips to the local market to sell garden produce).

Finally, New Life members also localize the divine future, imagining a heaven on earth centered at the Garasa airstrip. Not only will this heaven accommodate the total population of Papua New Guinea, but all seven million will be speaking Guhu-Samane. It is this allegiance to indexing the event of localization of church authority that provokes members of other churches to see them as having cargo-cult characteristics.

In order to create this alignment of revivalist conversion, translation, and Christian social change, Reverend Pituro is doing his best to *not* create a new translation, and the extent to which that is successful can be established through the slight differences and overwhelming similarities that mark his performance of the text. Demonstrating the church's localization of the power of the Holy Spirit involves the construction of intertextual linkages to the primary event at which the transformation from foreign to local forms of language and power created those distinctions. New Life takes on the authority of the revival by positioning itself as the social formation that embodies these distinctions. By aligning with the translation and the revival, they can make the contrast between an earlier moment, characterized by the foreign, Kâte-speaking Lutherans who did not create spiritual change, and a later moment, characterized by the local, Guhu-Samane-speaking revivalists who did create spiritual change and local power. It is not simply that Pituro recites word-for-word from a text, but that he does so from a translation that marked the moment of radical rupture in the order of the world, when the Holy Spirit went from being foreign to being local.

REITERATED EVENTS: TRANSLATION AND TRANSFORMATION IN REFORMED GOSPEL CHURCH

Where New Life Church pegs their institutional and theological authority to the singular transformation of the mid-1970s, the schismatic Reformed Gospel Church has developed a theology and ritual practice that emphasizes constant change and constant movement of objects and agencies into the Waria Valley. The main leaders of this church tell a history of revival in which they take credit for the 1977 event as well as two revivals in the 1980s, two in the 1990s, and one in the 2000s. Unlike the February 2 events that New Life hosts, the annual gatherings that Reformed Gospel hosts (along with other local churches) do not refer back to the revival of 1977. Instead, their annual Body of Christ gatherings are understood as novel (yet scheduled) opportunities for new outbreaks of fervor through which to reincorporate Christianity.[4]

Like their sensibility that revivalist (re)conversion is replicable on a consistent schedule, church leaders' sense of translation is iterative. Reformed Gospel leaders, especially Mark and Sean, have long worked with SIL and its partner organizations to produce Old Testament texts (they now include a few New Life and Lutheran members in this practice). They also plan to create a new version of the New Testament, add dialect-specific versions for communities at the upstream and downstream borders of the language community, and eventually have a series of biblical commentaries in the local language. In contrast to Reverend Pituro's private and unannounced corrections of slight syntactic and lexical problems with the 1975 translation, Reformed Gospel leaders publically want to claim the authority over translation as a project of ongoing Christian practice.

In addition to these long-term goals of text production, Reformed Gospel preachers give weekly sermons that produce new events of translation and events of transformation, in which their congregations participate. Unlike the Guhu-Samane- only language policy of New Life, Reformed Gospel pastors in their sermons track constantly between English, Tok Pisin, and Guhu-Samane, producing spontaneous translations between these languages in doing so. This practice of spontaneous sermonic translation is such a central characteristic of Reformed Gospel preaching that local people use it to distinguish Reformed Gospel preachers from New Life ones. For one female New Life member, "they [Reformed Gospel] use English and Tok Pisin; we [New Life] use Guhu-Samane." So while it is the Reformed Gospel leadership who are most involved with official events of translated text-artifact production, they are nevertheless the least likely to use these translated text artifacts in their services. Instead, they use texts in Tok Pisin or English, maintaining a regular schedule of translation events that reiterate what Reformed Gospel members think of as the historical moment in which the New Testament (and Christianity) was transformed from an English there-and-then to a Guhu-Samane here-and-now.

Take, for example, the following excerpt from a sermon delivered by a talented and charismatic pastor of Reformed Gospel. Pastor Bosepo bases most of his sermon (a mix of English, Tok Pisin, and Guhu-Samane, which I analyze below) on a quotation from Romans. The main point that Pastor Bosepo will take from this verse is the idea of one's body being a sacrifice. The NIV translation of this verse is:

> I appeal to you therefore, brethren, by the mercies of God, *to present your bodies as a living sacrifice,* holy and acceptable to God, which is your spiritual worship. (Romans 12:1, emphasis added)

First, it is important to give a standard denotational account of how Guhu-Samane speakers have created equivalences between English, Tok Pisin, and Guhu-Samane versions of "sacrifice." "Sacrifice" is rendered as *ofa* in the Tok Pisin Bible (Anonymous 1989) and as *kiridza* in the

Guhu-Samane New Testament. The Tok Pisin *ofa* is cognate with English "offer" and generally refers to weekly tithes or Old Testament events of animal sacrifice. A back translation from the Tok Pisin version of Romans 12:1 reads, in part, "You must give your bodies to God as an offering *(ofa)*." The Guhu-Samane *kiridza* refers to rewards for work or awards given in school or sports competitions, but it also referred to offerings made by religious officials in men's houses. Several expressions in the New Testament use *kiridza* in this secondary sense, and it is used in this verse from Romans (see table below).

Dzairamane	Ohongaho	.baruna heena.	erana	gama	hiirorai
dear-PL	God-GEN	mercy	here-LOC	all	say-PROG

Dear ones, in all God's mercy I am saying

oho	ipike	nike	ma	napai	isanate
DEM-GEN	return-OBJ	you-PL	and	1.INCL-SUBJ	fit-PRES

for this you and we are fit

.qupa ma sama.	ma	.oora ma qaara.	napame
bodies	and	lives	1.INCL-EMPH

to shoulder our own bodies and lives

gama	qeeremi	qaite	noho	kiridza	naatorare
all	shoulder-DS	burn.SER	3.SG-GEN	offering	AUX-PROG-FUT

and they shall burn as his [God's] offering.

Oi	tuhotuho	oho	isaki	naate	oomake
DEM-SUBJ	worker	DEM-GEN	fit	AUX.SER	AUX.SER-OBJ

So acting like a servant,

Ohongahota	bagenomanipamu	naatakoi
God-GEN-LOC	good-ADJ-EMPH	AUX-FUT

[it] will be in God's goodness.

The translation expands upon the notion of "bodies" being offered, in that the Guhu-Samane includes *qupa ma sama* (heart and body) but also *oora ma qaara* (an idiom that means something like "lifestyle" [literally, "existing and being"]). The sense of *kiridza* as an offering akin to *ofa* and *sacrifice* is relatively clear, although the Guhu-Samane specifies that it will be a burnt offering, something neither of the other translations do.

While these forms of equivalence exist in the 1975 New Testament and the Guhu-Samane–English–Tok Pisin dictionary *Noo Supu* (2002), Pastor Bosepo works to recreate them in his sermon, ritually producing the linkages between the different translations. Unlike Reverend Pituro's reading of the Bible text, Pastor Bosepo interweaves the quotation from Romans 12:1 into his sermon to the extent that it is more appropriate to speak of the multiple authoritative voices that he uses—his own and a biblical one—rather than a strict quotation of the text as such. Pastor Bosepo also has multiple authoritative voices through his deft code-switches between Tok Pisin, Guhu-Samane, and English. He maximizes the gap between the 1975 New Testament translation and his own text in such a way that the Bible texts become recontextualized to his sermon and the English, Tok Pisin, and Guhu-Samane texts are recontextualized with respect to one another.

In the following transcript, Pastor Bosepo's translation practice is a trope of the directionality of Christian discourse: text segments begin in the national language, Tok Pisin, and then move into the local, Guhu-Samane. English-language paragraph markers punctuate his entire sermon (calls of "amen" and "praise the Lord"). Since all adult church members under fifty years old are fluent in both Tok Pisin and Guhu-Samane (and most have copies of both the Tok Pisin and Guhu-Samane New Testaments), this translation practice is not a matter of clarifying referentially confusing sections of the Guhu-Samane text. Rather, it is a ritual practice of intertextual linkage that characterizes the nature of linguistic and spiritual transformations organized through Reformed Gospel as a church.[5]

1 Olsem na long Roman sapta twelf na ves wan Paul i tok olsem[6]
   And in Romans chapter twelve verse one Paul says

2 long marimari bilong God mi tokaut strong long yupela em i olsem
   through the mercy of God I say sternly to you that it's like this:

3 yupela i mas givim bodi bilong yupela i go long God olsem . . .
   you [PL] must give your bodies to God as . . .

Pastor Bosepo pauses to let someone in the congregation supply the final word he is emphasizing:

4 [Congregation member: ofa]

5 ofa.
an offering

6 <u>Amen</u>?

7 [Congregation: <u>Amen</u>.]

8 Brata na susa bilong mi
my brothers and sisters

9 taim yu no dai yet,
before you die,

10 yu stap laip,
and you are still alive,

11 em gutpela taim bilong yu
that is a good time for you

12 yu mas kisim Jisas long laip bilong yu.
you must take Jesus into your life.

13 Amen?

14 [Congregation: Amen.]

15 Na Baibel i tok olsem
And the Bible says

16 yu mas givim yu yet i go long God olsem ofa.
you must give yourself to God as an offering.

17 Dispela em i no minim olsem
This doesn't mean that

18 yu brukim yu yet olsem tupela hap
you should break yourself in half

19 na yu givim hap i go long God na yu givim hap i go long graun
and you give half to God and give half to this world

20 Em i no tok long dispela.
That's not what it says.

21 Taim yu kam long Jisas, pikinini bilong God,
When you come to Jesus, Son of God,

22 yu givim <u>full</u> yu yet i go long God olsem ofa.
you give your whole self to God as an offering.

23 <u>Bodza ni ona Jesu Kristuke nooka hisi eetorai.</u>

   When you believe in Jesus Christ.

24 <u>Bodza ota ni oko ma boto ma sama minara oke gama Ohonga moitemi,</u>

   When you give your leg and hand and whole body to God,

25 <u>oi quba ape?</u>

   what is that?

26 <u>Ohongaho naatare. Ohongaho kiridza naatare.</u>

   [You] become God's. [You] become God's offering.

27 <u>Amen</u>?

28 [Congregation: <u>Amen</u>.]

29 <u>Praise the Lord</u>.

This excerpt is structured around a ritual, performative event of translation co-constructed by pastor and congregation that creates intertextual linkages between different versions of the Bible through the focus on *sacrifice/ofa/kiridza*. This not only establishes a denotational equivalence between these terms but also establishes the weekly, repetitive nature of transformations.

In lines 1–7 Pastor Bosepo reads the verse, leaving the key term, *ofa*, to be supplied by a congregation member (line 4). In lines 8–14 Pastor Bosepo gives a short commentary on the verse. In line 15 he quotes the key phrase of the verse again and begins a more elaborate commentary. In lines 17–20 Pastor Bosepo offers a hypothetical biblical quotation that he negates (the Bible does not say . . .). In line 21 he then begins a series of statements composed of when-then clauses: "when you . . ." (come to Jesus), "then you . . ." (become an *ofa*, line 22). Originally in Tok Pisin, this when-clause form is repeated in Guhu-Samane language in lines 23–24. But instead of providing the answer right away, Pastor Bosepo asks "what is that?" (line 25), which is finally answered with the Guhu-Samane *kiridza* (sacrifice) in line 26. The textual parallelisms focus on a question of translation posed to the congregation, who are asked to supply the key term, *ofa,* in the first iteration of the verse (line 4) and who are asked to identify its translation, *kiridza,* in 25–26. Pastor Bosepo provides a formal, parallelistic connection across the text that is otherwise divided by the moment of code-switching and the interrogative transformation of the repeated text. More schematically:

Tok Pisin	when you do × (21)	. . .	then you are an offering (22)
Guhu-Samane	when you do × (23)		
Guhu-Samane	when you do × (24)	. . .	then what is it? (25)
Guhu-Samane			then you are an offering (26)

Through a number of different techniques, Pastor Bosepo is able to both incorporate biblical language into his own voice and re-situate the different translations with respect to one another. What begins as a Tok Pisin excerpt from the Bible distinct from Pastor Bosepo's sermonic voice ends as a Guhu-Samane text that incorporates biblical phrasing. The equivalence between *ofa* and *kiridza* (well known for most Guhu-Samane speakers) is emphasized as part of a ritual practice that connects one translated text to a prior text. Pastor Bosepo and other speakers from Reformed Gospel present an ongoing, multilingual process of translation that enacts a constant transformation of Christianity into the local language and a constant transformation of people into Christians.

Like the translations produced by Reformed Gospel, other elements of Christianity have to carry with them their pedigree of a foreign origin. That is, Reformed Gospel Church emphasizes a maximal intertextual gap that has to be stitched together through the weekly transformation of an external religion into the local context. In contrast to the local forms of self-authorization that are integral to New Life, Reformed Gospel leaders proudly note that their church is a government-registered organization. They also insist that they bestow the "pastor" designation only on those men who have gone to one of Papua New Guinea's major Bible colleges[7] and have certificates to show for it. Pastor Bosepo's sermon was performed in a church that was renovated in 2010 with a tin roof to mark its "modern" members inside and, like all Reformed Gospel sermons, it was bookended by songs sung to Western melodies and accompanied by guitars and tambourines. Traditional drums of the kind New Life uses extensively are explicitly excluded as signs of the local that do not carry with them any marks of having gone through a Christian transformation.

As opposed to New Life's celebration of the power of local Christianity rooted in the singular 1970s moment of emancipation from the colonial church, Reformed Gospel pastors re-create Guhu-Samane as a sacred language of the Bible on a weekly basis and in the iterative revivals that they claim credit for during the 1970s, 1980s, 1990s, and 2000s. Reformed Gospel Christians and their translations are in a constant state of transformation. Rather than highlighting the localization of religious power as New Life does, Reformed Gospel Christians celebrate the distance traveled for Christianity to come to them.

To return to a question posed at the beginning of this chapter, if Reformed Gospel members are so committed to the reiteration of the moments of conversion and of translation, why do they consistently erase their own conversions from New Life church, even as they incorporate their conversions from Lutheranism or other denominations that have entered the valley? I suggest that even though Reformed Gospel is engaged with an ongoing process of reformation, their continuing reforms still require an originary moment of change against which other events can be seen as iterations. For them, this is still the 1975 translation of the New Testament and the 1977 revival, the conjoined events that created Guhu-Samane as a sacred language of Christianity. However, the translation and the revival have for decades been identified with New Life Church. By erasing New Life from their histories of conversion and by exclusively claiming the revival as the root of their own church, they maintain the evenemential origin of transformation, even though their own practices are rooted in the continuous reinvention and reformation of that original event. By making their denominational practice at the macro level one of constant transformation, members can argue that they were always part of Reformed Gospel, even when they were officially part of the older New Life. By making their sermonic practice one of constant translation into Guhu-Samane at the micro level of text segments, members can see the New Testament translation and subsequent Holy Spirit revival as the origin of "true" but impermanent transformation. Nevertheless, they take symbolic ownership of that moment in their constant re-creations of that transformation. They reenact the sacred character of the local language established in the revival through their continuous incorporation of what they perceive as the origins of Christian discourse, indexed by Tok Pisin and English. At the same time, they explicitly critique what they perceive as the over-localization (cargo cult-ism) of New Life.

THE DENOMINATIONALISM OF TRANSLATION

Translation and conversion for these different churches model and enact a number of different transformations—linguistic, temporal, and religious—that overlap and implicate one another. Linguistically, both churches are dealing with religious texts whose ongoing histories of scriptural translation have produced a hierarchy of postcolonial locality that emphasizes English as the most powerful and remote, Tok Pisin as a supra-local form, and Guhu-Samane as the sacred language most intimately associated with the coming of the Holy Spirit to the Waria Valley. At the same time, contemporary Guhu-Samane Christians see themselves as products of a generational process of Christian growth that encompasses the ethno-linguistic group as a whole. According to current members of both of these churches, while older generations were only minimally Christian at the point of initial conversion, parents or grandparents were more-than-nominal Christians but incapable of taking over the church for themselves. Only the current generation sees itself as fully Christian and independently so after the Guhu-Samane language had been baptized as a religious language through the translation and Holy Spirit revival of 1977. The moment of localization of Holy Spirit revivalism in Guhu-Samane language (together with the formation of independent Christian churches) has become the zero-point of conversion and translation—the most important moment of transformation, even if it wasn't the first, because it was the moment at which groups that were both Guhu-Samane and Christian emerged.

Frustratingly, for Guhu-Samane Christians, there are still more changes that both churches hope for, but these are imagined as also following the logic of spatial and temporal transformations modeled in the denominational disputes discussed already. New Life members imagine the final and sudden transformation of the world when the Waria Valley becomes the center of a new heaven on earth. Reformed Gospel members imagine a gradual change as God recognizes their hard work more and more, eventually leading to the end of rural labor that roots them to their local land. Thus, translation governs the models of millennial salvation, when Guhu-Samane Christians will anchor other Christians' transformations or when Guhu-Samane Christians will themselves be translated out of the valley altogether.[8]

While both churches are dealing ostensibly with the same translated text-artifact and the same problems of transduction (Silverstein 2003) that anthropologists of translation often analyze, these two denominations have developed temporal models of transformation that can best be appreciated from the intertextual, event-based model of translation that ethnographically examines how local people create linkages between and temporal framings of moments of transformation. The temporal frame of rupture that governs members' accounts of personal transformation also creates denominationally specific forms of enfolding members within contrasting versions of Christianity.

In church sermons, pastors from New Life and Reformed Gospel use the New Testament translation to implicate the Guhu-Samane language community as a whole. By linking weekly sermons to the revival and the SIL translation, pastors point back to the moment when the Guhu-Samane as a community was addressed by the Holy Spirit and was able to address God in return. Moreover, the contrasting ways in which pastors align their congregations to the translation create denominational unities as the (con)temporary stand-ins for the now fractured language community. Each church may feel other churches are not on the right track, but each church sees itself as coming after an initial moment of critique (of the Lutherans, traditional culture, or the colonial government).

SIL translators working in the second half of the twentieth century, like Ernie Richert, largely depended upon Eugene Nida's domesticating model of dynamic equivalence translation. The words and reference points in the translated text should, as much as possible, come from the local context. But as I argue in chapters 2 and 3, this moment of domestication should be followed by a moment of critical distance from the local context, of foreignization. This is most obviously true for Reformed Gospel, which emerged as an institution when people came together to critique New Life. However, I argue that critique and foreignization is also operative in New Life practices. Although I have said that New Life members work to localize the Holy Spirit, they do so under the critical project of coming after the false transformations of the Lutherans or Australian administration. As much as Reformed Gospel or Lutheran members try to paint New Life as little more than a nativist cargo cult, the church constructs a critical perspective on the local, trying to determine which aspects of traditional practice can best save their chances of realizing the promises of the revival (see also Gifford 2004). In that sense, foreignizing processes of critique can coexist with localized Christianity.

. . .

My evenemential analysis of intertexuality differs subtly but importantly from approaches where translation is primarily an activity of the translator or the analyst, but not necessarily of the target community itself. Birgit Meyer's (1999) historical account of Pietist translations of the Bible into Ewe, with their focus on the "diabolization" of local Ewe culture, is an excellent account of translation (or "transduction") in this sense (see also Browden 2003; Comaroff and Comaroff 1991; Durston 2004). For Meyer, the Pietist translators' denotational linkages between a German folk definition of the devil and different Ewe divinities are crucial to understanding the responses the Ewe had to missionization. However, the Ewe do not (at least according to Meyer's publications) ritually focus on the process of translation itself, that is of the movement from German to Ewe. Translation is an important process in the spread of Christianity to Ewe communities, but it is not something that Pentecostal Ewe focus on or thematize in their ritual practice today.

In a series of important articles, Bambi Schieffelin (2002, 2007) discusses a number of linguistic and ideological differences between Kaluli and Western/ Christian modes of speaking that actually are so divergent as to prevent the production of stable equivalences or traditions of translation. For Schieffelin, this lack of translation indexes a lack of (or at least qualification of) Christian ideology among Kaluli speakers, even those most intimately involved in Christianity. Schieffelin's case would suggest that both the ideologies and the intertextual relations indicative of Christianity are absent.

Vicente Rafael's (1993) account of Tagalog responses to Spanish conversion and colonization focuses on the ways in which Tagalog speakers did not grasp the semantic meanings and intentions of the Spanish priests. Instead, Tagalog people "fished" words out of context (Rafael 1993, 4). In this sense, "the priest's message was not internalized. . . . Instead, the native listeners moved to appropriate fragments of the priest's discourse and so to deflect the force of his intensions" (Rafael 1993, 7–8). While Rafael remains focused on a word-based, semantic sense of translation dependent upon a structural transposition of equivalent meanings, at times he comes close to the kind of event-based account I discuss here, particularly when he notes that this lack of referential clarity can also produce "an alternative history of submission" (Rafael 1993, 8) thematized by local people.

This chapter also argues for a synthesis of different approaches to Christian temporality. Although recent scholars working on the anthropology of Christianity (Cannell 2006; also Comaroff and Comaroff 1991) suggest that analyses need to avoid the Christian myth of radical transformation implied by the notion of conversion, or they suggest taking seriously this theological model of transformation (Robbins 2007), I have argued here for an analysis that makes the ritual practices of temporality in Christianity its object. By paying attention to the evenemential models of Christian churches, we are able to gain insights into the models of transformation that they construct.

Both New Life and Reformed Gospel are committed to a notion of afterness, in which the linguistically defined community tracks the changes that differentiate the pre-colonial and colonial moments from the contemporary one. However, the evenemential processes through which these church members connect themselves to trajectories of change differ. New Life ends up looking traditionalist as a church because of the ways in which members (re-)create historical connections to singular, non-repeatable events of transformation in the 1970s aimed at the negation of colonial orders and Guhu-Samane peripherality through the revaluation of localism under the sign of Christianity. Reformed Gospel looks more engaged in an overt process of transformation in its commitment to create ever newer moments of conversion, even though its members too are dependent upon the authorizing events of the 1970s that in many ways produced the linguistic community that forms the baseline of Christian transformation.

Guhu-Samane Christians sometimes view these asymmetric approaches to afterness as a symmetric question of identity-bearing codes: New Life is the church that uses Guhu-Samane language; Reformed Gospel is the church that uses Tok Pisin and English. In these moments of denominational comparison and conflict, the church looks more like an institution of enforced uniformity rather than an agent of change. In the next chapter, I analyze the relationship between afterness and identity, which seems to pit religious transformation against political difference. For the moment, it is important to see how these contrasting views can exist within the same discursive sphere of evenemential translation.

While other models of translation would argue that Christian conversion depends upon the formation of a Christian subjectivity created by the translation of linguistic and cultural materials—for instance, based on which words are used to translate "soul" or "sin"—the evenemential model of translation gives us a way to talk about conversion as an issue of intertextual interactions between Christians in different social formations. The potential for transformation lies neither in a single text nor in the semanticized subjectivities of the readers. Instead, the experience of transformation takes place through the experience of intertextuality in rituals of translation and conversion, from weekly sermons to annual commemorations to unique events that fundamentally transform history not merely by their happening but also in their intertextual afterlife.

Translations are not, then, inert textual objects. They are constituted through the events in which they are deployed. In this case, they are also constituted through the comparative work that members of the different churches do as they fight for the sacred authority of the initial 1977 revival. The Guhu-Samane translations of the Bible are a product of denominational conflict. The reverse is also true: denominations come to be formed through the media of church worship practices. In the next chapter, I examine how denominations find their own voices, and how they find themselves in the music and noise that they produce.

CHAPTER 7

Mediating Denominational Disputes

Land Claims and the Sound of Christian Critique

In *The Social Sources of Denominationalism* (1929) H. Richard Nie-buhr describes the endless, cyclic movements between sects and churches that mark the history of American Protestantism. His model of denomi-nationalism has been particularly influential for people working in the sociology of religion (see Johnson 1963; Swatos 1998 and references there). In this model, a group of Christians becomes dissatisfied with a church's organizational form because of the ways the church has come to exclude certain social categories of people or because of the ways it has come to be simply a bureaucratic organization that has lost its "spirit." This group of dissatisfied Christians then breaks off from the church to form their own group, what Niebuhr calls a "sect." Voluntar-istically formed, the members of the sect see their organization as a utilitarian aid to maintaining the spirit. It is an organization in name only, since the point of the sect is to deny institutionality and instead merely meet the minimal conditions for people to worship together.

Reducing the social to its barest existence, Niebuhr then describes the Sisyphean tasks these sect-makers perform to keep the social—the bureaucratic, the institutional, the mundane, the constricting, the arbi-trary—as far from their sect as possible. Life gets in the way, though. Sect-formers have children, and the voluntaristic spirit that guided the first generation gives way to the weight of social reproduction and the need to create systems of education to teach the second generation the stories of the sect's founding. Niebuhr's story then becomes a tale of the slippery slope, as institutions of education beget institutions of role inhabitance (a priestly class is formed, a "normal" member is sociologically identifiable). The sect has become a church and can only wait until a segment of the second or later generations becomes dissatisfied enough to break off and form a new sect themselves.[1]

Greatly inspired by Ernst Troeltsch's *The Social Teaching of the Christian Churches* and Max Weber's work more generally, Niebuhr depicts a version of American Protestantism that seems to have taken individualism to an extraordinary extreme, but one that, for Troeltsch, was expressed in the original gospel ethic. For Troeltsch, "[i]t is clear that individualism of this kind is entirely radical, and that it transcends all natural barriers and differences" (1931, 55). In his conclusion, Niebuhr cries out to Christians to form a meta-church, a church that people can congregate in even as they are really members of other churches, a church that can end the cyclic movement between institutionality and individualist freedom of worship that for him defines the church-sect division. As he makes clear in this call to arms, Niebuhr sees real Christianity existing only when the social world can be excluded, when the sects that allow for Troeltsch's radical individualism can take hold (in this meta-church form). Everything else—every church—is a reduction of the universality of Christianity into the arbitrary particularity of purely human affairs.

Taking off from a number of recent analyses of Christianity (Keane 2007; Engelke 2007; Robbins 2007; see also Latour 1993), it is possible to view Niebuhr's story of schismatic sect formation as following the contours of many different struggles within modernity to create the context for an individual free from any constraints, with the sense of "constraint" itself being fashioned as the domain of the social. Following Niebuhr, anything social would count as "politics," a diminution of Christianity's capacity to bring the individual into God's universalism. This distinction between the universal and the particular holds even if one reverses the origin of the liberating universalism of individual choice. For example, the recurring laments about the "return of the religious" within secularist discourses (see de Vries 2001, 3–10) are versions of this process of "purification" (Latour 1993), in this case, an attempted purification of the supposedly secular and universal realm of politics from what is, for the secularist, the poisonously arbitrary authority of religion.

What Latour and, following him, Keane speak of in terms of "purification," I would like to talk about in this chapter as a process of critique (see also Robbins 2004b). The change in terminology is in part an attempt to use a vocabulary that is more ethnographically focused. Guhu-Samane Christians see their denominational disputes as processes through which they are able to criticize the forms of worship that have emerged since their initial introduction to Christianity in the 1910s. Here I examine Guhu-Samane denominational disputes from two different perspectives. First, I look at a land dispute at the Garasa airstrip and adjoining station, where two denominations fought over control of the area via proxy village forms, as examples of local versions of Niebuhr's sense that "politics" forces a reduction of Christian universalism. By, in fact, being embarrassed by their engagement in the this-worldly domain of land tenure, Guhu-Samane Christians seemed to recognize that "real" Christians would not be concerned with the social in these ways.

But does finding Niebuhr's critical (or purificatory) Christianity in Papua New Guinea mean that we are forced to simply see the tensions of denominationalism as coming from the same source in all cases? Does Niebuhr's explanation suffice? And how can we explain the many moments within denominationalism when Christians seem to be celebrating the sociality of their Christian organization? Here I want to engage with the emerging literature on religion and media or mediation (Engelke 2007; Eisenlohr 2009; Hirschkind 2006; Meyer 2006; de Vries 2001; and also Keane 2007). Rather than focusing on the idea of the individual versus the social, this literature engages with the problems of making immediate a transcendent God. As Engelke in particular notes, however, the problems of immediacy and the problems of sociality are similar in his African case. Those things that make immediacy impossible for Engelke's Masowe Christians are those things that are ideologically understood as "social," such as clocks, books (including the Bible), or fashion. Here then is a way to see the variations in Niebuhr's problem: how do local Christians perceive different media of the social? Where do they see the possibility of immediacy? This will help to construct my second perspective on Guhu-Samane denominationalism. Central to much of the discourse of denominational fighting are local analyses of music and sound: Can drums be played in church services, or are Western guitars and tambourines the only appropriate instruments through which to create a connection to the divine? How do the moments when drums (or guitars) are celebrated fit into a larger "semiotic ideology" in which forms of sociality are supposed to be excluded? That is, when is politics not merely "politics"?

Where the first Niebuhrian perspective suggests a distinct parallelism between the denominations as two groups equally fighting for control of a piece of land, the second perspective—on sound media—suggests a sharp asymmetry between the churches in terms of their differing sense of the origins of Christian authority and histories of critical engagement with them. The sounds of Christianity actually transduce (Silverstein 2003; Helmreich 2007) the location and locatability of Christianity into an aural medium of worship. In both cases, we are dealing with "the political" in the sense that both engage with questions of authority and control in this world, even if the goal is to transform or otherwise alter one's relationship to this world. Finally, the question is, how are local Christians able to be embarrassed by the mediating sociality of their Christian forms even as they celebrate these media as the sources of a connection to God?

As I argue in at the end of this chapter, it is important to see these denominational disputes as producing "remnant" churches, by which I mean churches that claim both the universality of the Christian message and a recognition of the partiality of its realization on earth. Remnant churches are, therefore, ones that proliferate difference but do so in ways that do not align with common senses of politics as the negotiation of differences and powers. I reiterate the conclusions from the previous chapter by suggesting that denominational disputes have to be understood in terms of different projects of historical memorializations of critical debates.

SCENE I: GARASA AND THE POLITICS OF LAND

Garasa airstrip was opened in the early 1980s, and as is often the case in Papua New Guinean land disputes, it has several different origin stories. The Council (a local government representative) petitioned for money from the state to build the airstrip to serve the Middle Waria Valley, which at that point was served only by the Garaina Station strip, roughly a four-hour walk upstream from the Garasa site. Compared to other areas of Papua New Guinea, a four-hour walk is not terribly long to reach a major transportation node. However, the people of the Waria Valley had long been promised a road into their area—a road that still does not exist but is annually promised anew by politicians jockeying for support—and the airstrip seemed a consolation prize. With then high hopes for local coffee production, money for the airstrip was found.

At the same time, New Life Church started to actually do the work of building the airstrip. According to Ulysses, the leader of New Life, he had been told by God (rather than the Council) to build it. He had his church members from his base at Au village move to the airstrip for several weeks and work on its construction. According to Ulysses, everybody laughed at them—"just like with Noah"—with the naysayers taunting them that no plane would ever come to the airstrip.[2] Working at a fast clip over several weeks and using the *tukuta ma adzaita* magic of making people work cooperatively in a "hot" state of excitement, the airstrip was completed, consecrated with prayer, and became the miraculous landing site of a plane the very next morning. According to many New Life members who told this story, a befuddled white pilot exited his plane, map in hand, and exclaimed that he didn't know there was an airstrip there. From that point on, all the regional airlines serving this part of Papua New Guinea—including TalAir, North Coast Aviation, and MAF—had flights in and out of Garasa (and some still use the strip). For Ulysses, this was the beginning of a millennial City on a Hill that would transform Guhu-Samane communities and Papua New Guinea as a whole.

With the airstrip in place, other ventures soon followed. J.B. Martin, a Lae-based businessman, opened a trade store and attempted to get another of his unsuccessful cattle projects going on land next to the airstrip. In the early 1990s, Pacific Island Ministries (PIM), a mission organized by two former SIL translators began an education project at Garasa as well.[3] As with the airstrip itself, the Garasa Bible College (as it was later known) has both a local and a more extended origin. Mark, Ulysses's main rival for leadership in the post-Lutheran revivalist movement started to collect money at the semi-weekly markets held at Garasa for a Bible college. Mark had, as he tells the history, already bought books and pencils when Neal Kooyers and the PIM organization arrived with Christian educational plans of their own. For Mark, the Bible college would be an organizing space from which the Guhu-Samane and other Papua New Guineans would be able to engage with a wider theological world.

Already, then, Garasa was crowded, if only with aspirations. With plans that ranged from the millennial to the capitalist to the pastoral, Garasa was pushed in a number of directions from several sources (Ulysses, Mark, PIM, and Mr. Martin). With so many claims to use of the land, a land dispute was almost inevitable. Before getting to that dispute, though, I want to lay out two other aspects of local land politics and their relationship to the authority of the churches organized around Ulysses and Mark.

First, Garasa is a border zone between two different regions of traditional political importance. As I discussed in the introduction, Guhu-Samane villages along the Waria Valley can be thought of as having a hub-and-spoke organization centering on men's houses that were built in the distant past for major feasts. Given the tensions inherent in a matrilineal but patrilocal system, villages are prone to schism, and each of the major feast sites is surrounded by villages that previously broke off from it. The boundaries of each such hub-and-spoke grouping are, of course, fluid, and people often speak of a region as having several boundaries. Henry, the leader of Titio village, where I lived, spoke of the Muniwa region as having a first (*namba wan,* TP) boundary, a second (*namba tu,* TP), a third (*namba tri,* TP), and so forth. Each ordered boundary reflects the changing shape of Muniwa (or any other region) as new schismatic villages are formed. Garasa is on one of these later boundaries, forming a dividing line between the Muniwa and the Au-Aro regions. The last undisputed Muniwa village from this direction is Wakaia, and in an attempt to display a Muniwa origin for the village directly above Garasa, it came to be known as Wakaia #2 (the earlier Wakaia became Wakaia #1).

However, there is also a large contingent of people living at Wakaia #2 who come from the Au-Aro region. They maintain their allegiance to their place of origin by referring to themselves with a "tribe" (*traib,* TP) name that comes from the primary Au-Aro men's house. Tribe names refer to organizations of men in men's houses. A single men's house could have different tribe names affiliated with it, and these would sometimes be spatialized into different segments of a men's house. So, each "door" (*tete sirasira,* GS) of the men's house would be named for a different tribe.[4] Given the almost total destruction of men's houses, many contemporary Guhu-Samane do not know what their tribe is. Nevertheless, partisans vying for Wakaia #2 to be claimed as a part of the Au-Aro region held that they were members of (or descendants of) the Au tribe that was paired with the Neepo tribe at the main Au men's house.

Thus, two different modes of claiming land were at work in the emerging dispute over Garasa, one based upon a historical connection to Muniwa territories and another based upon the tribal affiliations that anchored the former men's house at Au. These larger framing histories, which are both—interestingly—organized along patrilineal lines, then

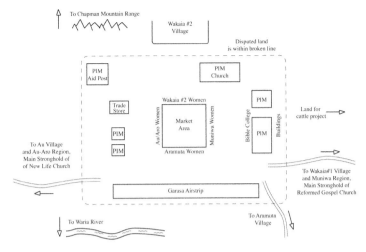

MAP 2. The Garasa area, not to scale. Map produced by Kevin Henner.

organized the matrilineal genealogies told during the actual land dispute meetings. The success or failure of any such claim depends upon
having such a patrilineal framing narrative and upon having the particular knowledge of a matrilineal clan history—that is, women's names
in lengthy, eight-generation genealogies, as well as clan identifiers of
various sorts. So, in addition to the opposition of Au versus Muniwa,
this dispute was also played out as competing claims from Sakidza and
Enepa matrilineal clans.

This organization of land and regions is played out not only in the
realms of primarily male land politics but also in the everyday practices
of women using the Garasa station during market days. The central
Garasa market is formed as a square around which women sit and display their garden produce and sometimes store-bought goods for resale.
Women sit in groups according to their region of residence, so Muniwa
women sit along one side, Au-Aro women sit opposite them, Wakaia #2
women sit perpendicular to these two, and women from Arumuta and
other villages near the Waria River sit along the final side (see map 2).
Wakaia #2 women thus are positioned between the two competing sides
of Muniwa and Au-Aro.

In addition to this organization of traditional land politics, there was
also a new organization of local church authority stemming from the
1994 schism in which Reformed Gospel Church split from New Life. As
I discussed in chapter 4, for Mark and several other men, New Life

seemed to be bending the Gospel too much to their own particular desires for wealth, release from work, and the creation of a New Heaven and New Earth at Garasa. New Life was too local, both in aspirations and in ritual forms that seemed to verge on the syncretistic. As Niebuhr would have guessed, Mark's new sect saw itself as constituting a proper church, unencumbered by the "social" goals and aspirations of the older church.

Ulysses, the leader of New Life, is from Au-Aro, and Mark, leader of Reformed Gospel, is from Muniwa. Overdetermined by regional differences, New Life and Reformed Gospel were soon at odds. Each was perfectly poised to have their competing claims to Garasa become a part of the land dispute, since each saw an opportunity for their projects to succeed if "their" side could gain control of the land (again, see map 2). As a parochial problem of land tenure, the two churches fit into an already-existing structure of opposed political regions of land control.

However, there is another, more specifically Christian, aspect of this story. Because the 1977 revival was experienced as a specifically languaged encounter with the Holy Spirit—that is, made possible through God's revelation *in the Guhu-Samane language*—the churches that formed out of the revival have likewise worked to maintain an intimate association with the Guhu-Samane language (see chapters 5 and 6). One such manifestation of this linguistic legacy is that both New Life and Reformed Gospel churches see the universe of their influence as minimally determined by the boundaries of the Guhu-Samane linguistic community (and as maximally including Papua New Guinea and the rest of the world). So even while the Au-Aro region is the stronghold of New Life, it is by no means the only area in which they operate. Reformed Gospel is mainly focused in Muniwa, but it too stretches into other regions, including Au-Aro. In contrast to a simple local politics of land, where Muniwa and Au-Aro partisans were fighting to extend the boundaries of their respective regions to include Wakaia #2 and the Garasa station, New Life and Reformed Gospel focused on Garasa as a central node through which a larger Christian world would be constructed for the ethno-linguistic Guhu-Samane community as a whole.

There were at least two ways for these church leaders to engage in the Garasa land dispute. On the one hand, the Garasa station was a central position from which Ulysses's and Mark's visions for Guhu-Samane Christianity were to be played out, either in forming a millennial City on a Hill or in being the passage point for external Christian knowledge to be disseminated through the Bible college. They could have acted as churches in the fight for this land, presenting themselves as religious groups capable of effecting social transformation. On the other hand, Ulysses and Mark and their respective sects could contest the Garasa station as two opposing sides in a land dispute that was framed largely in terms of questions about the origins of Wakaia #2 villagers and their histories of land tenure over the adjacent Garasa land. In fact, both Ulysses and Mark engaged in the land dispute through this latter option. As one man, Daro, put it to me during my field research, both Ulysses and Mark acted through village proxies, and the entire question of church control over Garasa was played out in terms of a village-based politics-of-land-as-usual.

Mark had the institutional upper hand in this fight, since one of his parishioners was Henry, who, in addition to being the head of Titio village, was also the local land mediator assigned by the state who has the authority to make rulings about local land issues. But in Daro's and others' accounts, the Au-based people aligning themselves with the Au tribe had longer matrilineal genealogies. As Daro has said at other occasions, land claims should not even be attempted unless one has knowledge of eight generations of women connected to a particular piece of land. The Au tribe disputants had the requisite eight generations and displayed enough information and clan identifiers to make this knowledge authoritative. The Muniwa-based villagers of Wakaia #2 only had five generations. But partly because Henry was invested in the Bible college and in Mark's continued presence in Muniwa, he determined that the land should go to the Muniwa-based Wakaia #2 people.

Daro and others were well aware of the bias involved in this. Henry and the rest of the Wakaia #2 disputants were acting on behalf of Mark, while Ulysses was the motivating force behind the Au tribe claims. Although Ulysses had little connection to the state at that time, one of his daughters has since married a Guhu-Samane man who was the deputy governor of Morobe Province until 2008. Ulysses has been able to work through his son-in-law (a move common in matrilineal systems) to try to regain control of Garasa through a plan to move the provincial government's district headquarters from Garaina station to Garasa. However, on the very day when this plan was to start being implemented—by having Morobe governor Luther Wenge officially declare Garasa a "basecamp" (a bureaucratic first step toward making it a district HQ)—some town-based residents of Wakaia #2 who aligned with Muniwa had a cease-and-desist order put in place. The plane that was supposed to bring the governor, alas, came with the court order instead. As of 2008, the case was at the land claims courts in Lae.

People from both churches expressed to me a certain discomfort with having had to play out this claim in terms of village and matriclan politics. With both Mark and Ulysses setting their sights on higher goals, neither was particularly satisfied that they had to be shadowy players behind the seemingly village-based dispute. Mark, in particular, prides himself on abstaining from land claims in most cases. For Mark, the necessary multiplicity of stories about land should in no way be confused with the singular truth of the Bible. That is, for Mark, stories about land mutate over time and are understood as partisan. Pastors and church leaders should refuse to take part in them lest the Bible come to be seen as a partisan, partial depiction of man's relationship to God.

Forced into a village-based land claim for the Garasa station, both Ulysses and Mark ended up looking exactly like partisan players—an image that Mark, in particular, had hoped to avoid. Without a local authorizing structure for churches to take part in land claims, they were required to be background movers of the village-based parties. Here, then, was the point at which Niebuhr's sense of denominational sociality comes into play. In seeing any sense of the social as necessarily diminishing the universality of Christianity (although note that it is at the most local level an ethno-linguistic universality), the "political" machinations of Ulysses and Mark were an embarrassment, both to them and to many of the outside observers, like Daro, who consistently complained that these church leaders were not acting like church leaders at all. Pushed into the realm of the political, both churches seemed definable by their equal lack of engagement in the realm of the spiritual, a distinction locally discussed as the "body side" of life (*sait bilong bodi*, TP; *samaho neta*, GS) in contrast to the "spirit side" (*sait bilong spirit*, TP; *gisiho neta*, GS). If one of the legacies of the SIL translation-inspired revival is that local, vernacular Christianity can provide change where (post)colonial states and missions did not, the revivalist Christian churches have much at stake in entering into the realm most obviously connected with land politics and development.

In acting through village proxies, Ulysses and Mark approach a Niebuhrian perspective on the illegitimacy of the this-worldly in Christian communal life. Both churches look like the kinds of institutional failures of spirit that would make them ripe for new sectarian schism. Indeed, new churches are constantly appearing in the Waria Valley, although often through the importation of national and international denominations rather than through schisms of local forms. But it is not enough to simply characterize these two churches by their worldly, "body-side" engagements with land. They were trying to create Christian spaces at Garasa that would lead to novel forms of development. And they do still sometimes revel in the institutions and practices of their worship. How then does this happen? Why are they sometimes embarrassed by the social and sometimes ready to celebrate it? In the next section, I will examine one such domain—the soundscapes of worship—in which sociality is trumpeted.

SCENE II: DRUMS, GUITARS, AND THE SOUNDS OF CHRISTIANITY

Sunday mornings and some weekday evenings in the Waria Valley are filled with the sounds of Christian worship. But depending upon which Guhu-Samane village you are in and which denomination is present, those sounds might be radically different. Danielle, the wife of Daro, whose comments were featured in the previous section, tells a story of drastically misunderstanding the different denominational music traditions of Christianity. Several years ago Danielle was traveling with a group of women to a village farther upstream from her normal sphere of social relations. Left on their own in the house that they would be sleeping in, the women were excited to suddenly hear loud drumming coming from further down the village line of houses. After some discussion, the women got up to go check out the *singsing* (TP, dance) practice that was going on, since dances and their practice sessions are exciting social events around which everyone congregates. Following the sound of the drums, the women drew closer to the commotion. But instead of coming upon a men's house where performers would be practicing, Danielle and her friends landed in the middle of a New Life church service. Embarrassed for themselves and for the New Life members who were making so much noise as to be mistaken for a *singsing*, they quickly rushed back to their house. Years later, during my fieldwork, this was still an important story for Danielle to tell when she spoke out against New Life Church. Unlike New Life's inappropriate use of many drums, Danielle said proudly, her Lutheran church only used a few—and used them to greater effect. (I return to the New Life and Lutheran uses of drums below.)

Rather than seeing this as the kind of narcissistic minor difference of which Freud spoke, or the kind of social difference that Niebuhr tends to condemn, I want to look at the different kinds of soundscapes produced by a number of churches in the Waria Valley as moments when denominations come to social formation through multiple media that transduce different histories of critique into everyday practice. In contrast to the previous section, where the engagement with the social was a point of politics-as-usual and Christianity-in-decline, I want to examine churches during those moments when they are celebrating the very forms of sociality (e.g., the use of a more appropriate "few" drums to New Life's "many") that are supposed to be anathema to Protestantism.

Keane argues that there is a specific Protestant "semiotic ideology" that downplays codified social forms because they are seen by Christians as the locus of constraint for morally autonomous individuals. When Sumbanese Calvinists note that their eyes remain closed during prayer, they want this to point to the ways in which their prayers come from an authentic, personal "inside" rather than the disparaged, external, and therefore inauthentic prayer books of the Catholics (Keane 2007, 2). Engelke's (2007) Christians "who don't read the Bible" have taken the desire to remove the social to such an extreme that they do not even authorize the written canon of Christianity as capable of producing a relation with God.

Guhu-Samane Christians sometimes make comments similar to those provided by Keane and Engelke, and one could locate them through these comments within Keane's semiotic ideology that puts authenticity, personal freedom, and Christian commitment within the individual self rather than in the external (read: social) world. Indeed, the story of Mark's and Ulysses's discomfort with their behavior in the Garasa land dispute—as well as Niebuhr's entire cyclic story of sect-church formation—should be read in these terms. Mark, for instance, once expressed his desire for Guhu-Samane Christians to practice their religion the way that Americans do. In his understanding, in any American family the father, mother, and each of the children can go to a different church, and nobody pushes them to be a family in their Christianity. They are all perfect individuals, worshipping and practicing on their own, outside of any other mediating form, even the nuclear household.

However, as much as Guhu-Samane Christians work to exclude the social world from their worship practice and thus employ the Protestant semiotic ideology that Keane identifies, they also celebrate moments of the social as the very capacity for right Christian practice. Coming to see such moments in relation to the more socially excluding ones is the larger goal of this chapter. I want to focus in this section on how sounds and soundscapes constitute the medium through which these celebrations happen. In particular, I want to focus on the ways in which soundscapes offer Guhu-Samane Christians a way to critically engage with the history of their connections to global Christianity and thus to what they think of as "correct" Christian practice. These connections are, I am arguing, transformed into the medium of sound ("transduced"; see Silverstein 2003; Helmreich 2007) and thus made available for use in events such as Sunday services.

Silverstein's use of the metaphor of energy transduction importantly insists upon the "inefficiencies" of translation across languages or, in this case, media. "By [tranduction] I mean a process of reorganizing the source semiotic organization ... by target expressions-in-co(n)text of another language presented through perhaps semiotically diverse modalities differently organized" (Silverstein 2003, 83). It is a metaphor that nicely points to the ways in which translations across media will orient people to certain aspects that may not necessarily be present in the original medium. In this case, critical histories of denominational disputes transduced into the medium of sound will take on new foci, like heat or coolness, that are not necessarily central in the medium of the original debate, which might have been more focused on issues of localization as such. As Harkness (2014) argues, music and sound can be central domains for the production of Christian selves. Before getting to this transductive critical process, I want to provide a brief discussion of sound and songs in the Waria Valley.

As was hinted at in Danielle's story, drums emit a powerfully affect-laden sound for many people in the Waria Valley, capable of calling up memories that can lead listeners into trance-like states (see Feld 1991; Gell 1995 on similar reactions to birdsongs and sounds of the forest in other parts of Papua New Guinea). This was made clear to me when I went to a major dance event in 2005. Bathsheeba, whose long-dead, politically important husband had been the owner of several dances (dance ownership is discussed below), was almost unrecognizable as she circled the dance ground after one of her sons revived her husband's prized dance. Usually slowed by arthritic joints and usually very disagreeable, Bathsheeba was suddenly dancing like a spry young woman, a look of intense concentration on her face. As I came up to the parade ground where the dance was happening, everyone in the audience pointed Bathsheeba out to me, noting the total change that had taken her over. As her friends and kin said, the spirit of the drums had taken over her (*spirit bilong kundu i kisim em*, TP), the drums seemingly transporting her to memories of her deceased husband and his dances.

Like Feld's (1990) discussion of bird songs that can evoke memories of particular people among Kaluli, drums are deeply evocative of specific social relations for Guhu-Samane.

This emotional connection to sound is not limited to the instruments of traditional dance. Guhu-Samane speakers often use songs of different kinds to mark ritual moments, whether they are happening under the banner of Christianity, traditionalism, or state-sponsored celebrations (e.g., Independence Day festivities). Particularly for adults who wish to look back fondly on their youth, the major festivals that they have attended in their lives—from the traditional feasts that ended in the 1970s to the brief heyday of string-band dance parties in the 1980s to the current era of yearly church tent-revivals—are the musical backgrounds to stories of flirtations and other semi-taboo activities. Music not only evokes these memories, but it is thought of as an aphrodisiac (in addition to love magic) that feeds the small intrigues of major multi-village events.

Departures are marked through song as well. Farewell events for people off to town, or for anthropologists heading back home, tend to include renditions of the leaving person's favorite songs. Likewise, the dead are celebrated with all-night pre-burial wakes at which songs are used to evoke the life of the deceased. In their more combative moods, several of my Guhu-Samane friends also enjoyed relating their participation in a cultural dance competition in Port Moresby, where their own intricate dance moves and songs won out over what were, in their eyes, the boring and repetitive performances of the much-hated "Chimbus," the local term for all Highland New Guineans. Most importantly in the Christian context, the strength of a congregation as a whole is often judged based upon the quality and power of its singing (see also Robbins 2004a, 262). When songs are sung well, and when many people participate in the singing, the church has spirit. Christians all seem to have their own favorite songs, which they request during especially moving services.

This litany of moments at which songs are central to Guhu-Samane memory and social practice could go on. With this background in mind, then, I want to look at the three different Guhu-Samane denominations that have most consistently been in critical dialogue with the others. New Lifers, Lutherans, and Reformed Gospel members each participate in different Christian soundscapes that index historical engagements with Christian others or with Christian entities that once were other. In this history of engagement transduced through sound, we can see a different aspect of the Protestant "semiotic ideology" that Keane, Engelke, and, with different terminology, Robbins (2001) use so productively.

New Life's Noisy Christianity

In the later years of the SIL New Testament project, Ernie Richert produced a booklet of Guhu-Samane songs whose words had been given Christian meanings. Part of this Christianizing project involved transforming these songs from being objects of personal ownership into being objects for universal Guhu-Samane ethno-linguistic use. "Traditional" songs are always owned by specific individuals (men like Bathsheeba's husband), who may come to own them through a number of routes. They can come to a man during a dream, they can be composed during one's waking life, they can be songs that are purchased from one's mother's brother or similar kinsman, or they can be purchased from other groups. The middle of the twentieth century saw a great influx of new songs into the Guhu-Samane repertoire as many young men went down to the coast on labor contracts and lived with a wide variety of coastal ethnic groups whose songs they learned and paid for (Handman 2010b, chap. 3; see also S. Harrison 1993). Returning to their villages, these new owners of songs would teach them to other men for major ritual events. Some of the most commonly performed songs today came from this history of labor contracts. Because male matrilineal kin are often spatially far away from each other, men can also become the local owners of songs that are more often performed farther away by the song's true or main owner. Each region (in the sense used in the previous section to distinguish Au-Aro from Muniwa) might have a different owner of a given song.

During the early 1970s, Ernie Richert assembled a large number of male song owners at his base on the Kipu Lutheran mission station and arranged to have these songs "translated" into Christian terms (although still in the Guhu-Samane language). Given the particular histories of song ownership and inheritance that Richert was dealing with, there are several different versions of particular songs that were "translated" a few times. Richert identified these by village as well as by individual owner. Each song—in either Christian or traditional form—was often as short as four lines long, with the song repeated many times during a single performance of it. A Lutheran couple who had worked as domestic servants for the Richerts kept a copy of a booklet of these songs. An example of one song is given below, using the formatting that Richert employed followed by my loose translation. This song appears in the middle of a section that includes several versions of the Madzame song: versions from Aramuta and Kapiso villages, as well as versions listed as originating from neighboring Kunimaipan groups (referred to in the booklet as Gazili, Gaziri, and Gunimaipa), but with local Guhu-Samane male owners.

MADZAME GUNIMAIPA (BAPUBA KAPISO)

1. Sumasai aimami gama qoridzo: Aimami qoridzo: oo ee

2. Qoridze qara qara: nakuta dzuubo: oo ee

3. Dzuubami Ohonga beedzae nana mooito nana mooito: oo ee

1. *The spirit takes us, and we all get up, it takes us and we get up,*
   oo ee

2. *Get up and life is born inside us, oo ee*

3. *Born and God gives us power gives us power, oo ee*

Richert was trying to create a local corpus of songs with new Christian lyrics that retained Guhu-Samane singing styles and melodies; each of these songs was to be accompanied by traditional *kundu* drums that were otherwise used during *singsings*.[5] Richert here distanced himself from the Lutheran practice to have Christians sing (often a cappella) from published hymnbooks. Although Lutherans had experimented with local instruments in other places (see Zahn 1996 on the development of a Jâbem conch-shell band), the songs were still renditions of primarily German hymns. Richert's emphasis on local song styles was a marked contrast with the Lutheran norm. Note that as this was prior to the 1977 Holy Spirit revival, the Lutherans still had a denominational monopoly on Guhu-Samane Christianity. Richert had a coterie of young men to whom he was teaching new, more evangelical Christian worship practices (in addition to the older men with whom he was translating the New Testament), but these men were all officially still Lutherans.

After Richert's departure in 1975, and after the Holy Spirit revival began in 1977, these young men started leading church services that were—in contrast to the Lutheran services—extremely noisy. Not only did they perform the new Guhu-Samane-style songs with loud *kundu* drum accompaniment, but people were shouting prayers and "amen" at an incredible volume. Kurudza, Mark's wife, remembers that when the revival first started she sided with the Lutheran hierarchy in thinking that holding your hands up and shouting "amen" was a sin. It was only later, she said, that she learned that shouting "amen" was just another way to praise God. As Kurudza's comment indicates, the increase in volume coming from both the participants' mouths and their drums struck many people as contrary to proper Christian practice.

As Danielle's story from the beginning of this section suggests, New Lifers are still very noisy, and they still use *kundu* drums as central elements of their church practice, so much so that Danielle and her friends thought they were hearing the first rumblings of a *singsing* practice rather than a church service.

At every New Life service that I attended, several men and women held drums and used them to keep time for the songs and would also beat them when the congregation applauded. The Western courtesy of applause (and for that matter, handshakes, see Robbins 2004a[6]) has taken Papua New Guinea by storm. Not only do people applaud after a speaker has finished a sermon, prayer, or even an announcement, but the service leader will frequently just tell people between songs or other moments to "clap your hands for Jesus" (*paitim han long Jisas,* TP). Although the applause tends to be loudest at New Life events, given the drum accompaniment and New Life parishioners' particularly loud cries of "amen," applause is a major sonic feature of Christianity across all of the denominations whose services I attended.

New Life members are well aware that the volume of their worship has become a point about which other Christians criticize them (see Danielle's comments above), but they insist that this is part of the revival tradition, marking the moment when the Holy Spirit came to Guhu-Samane people through their own language and their own church leaders. Ernie Richert prepared the way for the Holy Spirit to come with his translations of both the New Testament and the local songs. The revival that followed soon after Richert's departure was a moment where Christianity appeared in local terms and was the moment when Guhu-Samane Christians went from being missionized to being missionizers themselves. The noise that their Christianity produces celebrates the fact that they were finally hearing God's voice just as God was finally hearing them, after too many years of tepid (or no) communication via the Lutheran church and its liturgy. New Life members index this history of audibility in their loud worship practices, allowing the unconstrained voice of the Holy Spirit to be transductively revealed through drums, local songs, and loud shouts.

FIGURE 9. A New Life Church service with a man playing a drum.

Lutherans and the Gendering of Drums

Returning one last time to Danielle's story that began this section, it is clear that New Life is not the only church to use *kundu* drums in services. But as Danielle and many other women from her church frequently stressed, Lutherans use only "a few" drums, in contrast to New Life's booming choruses of many loud drums. Whenever I attended any New Life events, however, I found that only two or three people were holding drums, while at Lutheran services, there might be as many as seven or eight drummers. Rather than a difference in numbers or in volume, I soon realized that the bright-line test to distinguish New Life from Lutheranism was the gender of the drummers. At New Life services, drummers are both male and female; at Lutheran services, drummers are female. How did gender come to be understood as a matter of volume?

When Ernie Richert started to "translate" local songs into Christian hymns to be accompanied by *kundu* drums, a new question emerged for local practitioners: could drums be used in a Christian context? At first, the Lutherans defended a drum-free worship service against the revivalists, but eventually drums came to be incorporated into the liturgy as part of a national transformation of Lutheran practice. The Evangelical Lutheran Church of PNG (ELC-PNG) wanted to more fully localize both the pastorate and the liturgy in the 1980s, and allowing local instruments was one way to do this. But given the local history of animosity between New Life and the Lutherans, some distinctive characteristic had to be found to distinguish these two denominations at the local level. At first, people thought that Christians could have two different drums: one for church services and another for *singsings,* a distinction of the body side *(sait bilong bodi)* and spirit side *(sait bilong spirit)* put into a musical idiom, where these two terms are used to gloss secular versus gospel music, respectively. Eventually, though, Lutherans made drumming in church a specifically female task. Men might have other instruments—for example, guitars are prominent in Lutheran services and are exclusively played by men—but now only women use drums in Lutheran services.

The distinction between the "loud" male drumming of New Life and the "quieter" female drumming of the Lutherans can be understood in terms of the characteristics of traditional dances. In almost every dance that I witnessed, men held and beat drums, while women carried decorative elements in their hands and sometimes moved them around in time to the music. Also, men danced in circles or rows toward the center of the dance space, while women danced at the peripheries, either circling the men (often moving in the opposite direction of the men) or at the ends of the rows in which the men danced.

This male:center::female:periphery structure also held in the ownership and teaching of dances. For example, when Bathsheeba's husband brought a new dance to the Waria Valley after his labor contract on the coast, he taught the dance to other men in a men's house. Until the dance was officially unveiled at a performance, the men would be hidden, learning the precise lyrics, melody, drum beats, and dance steps inside the walls of the men's house. In the past, when men's houses would be encircled by high fences, this secrecy was an even more pointed aspect of the practice sessions. Men describe these practice sessions as intense projects of trying to achieve highly precise, technical performances of intricate coastal dances requiring great bodily control and ritual "heat." The Guhu-Samane sense of superiority over the "Chimbus" mentioned above partly stems from the intensity of these practices and the exacting bodily movements demanded by dance owners. (What are the Chimbus doing during practice, Guhu-Samane ask, if their dancing just consists of bouncing up and down?) In addition to male dancing practices, the owner of the dance would deputize his wife to teach certain peripheral parts of the dance to a group of women, often the wives of the owner's cosponsors of the performance. These women would also practice, but—obviously—would do so outside of the men's house, often standing directly outside the men's house to practice their steps in public, listening to the drum beats of the men practicing within the house itself.

As I noted in chapter 4, men's houses and the men living in them were considered "hot" in contrast to women and uninitiated children, who were "cold." The heat of a traditional men's house was an index of a group's capacity for fighting, for power, and for the forms of bodily control required by things like dances. Given the post-conversion dissolution of men's houses as the primary centers of politico-religious importance, many men in the Waria Valley take it as axiomatic that, as Christians, they are now cold. Coolness is, indeed, seen as a key Christian virtue, and one of the very first converts to Christianity, around 1930 (the man I referred to as *tumbuna* Henry in chapter 5), took the name "Kebaita" (GS, made cool; *keba-* cool *i-* causative, *ta-* past tense) during baptism as a sign of this transformation.[7] The only time I heard someone suggest that Titio village was not a cold place was just after a nighttime dance practice. Sitting outside by a fire, a friend jokingly chastised a younger man for making a ruckus. He explained himself by saying, "the village is hot tonight" (*ples i hat,* TP).

How the Lutherans read New Life's male drumming as "loud" or as using too many drums now makes more sense. When Lutherans started to use drums in their services, and when those drums were taken over by women, New Life's male drumming, by contrast, started to look like traditional drumming. It also started to take on, at least for the Lutheran critics of the practice, the power and force—that is, the heat—of men's house–based drumming. Female drumming is then capable of being read as a sonic critique of New Life practice, of how it is possible to both be localizing and yet still maintain the coolness that is a requisite virtue of Christianity. With female drummers, Lutherans can both adopt the localizing practices that have been instituted by the national ELC-PNG organization and also take a position in the denominational disputes that are so important in the Waria Valley. Female drumming is then read as "quieter" than the masculine New Life drumming that evokes the heat and power of a traditional men's house. As with all churches in the Waria Valley, women and men sit separately, so it is usually very easy to see and hear which side of the church drumming is emanating from. Thus the critique of locality and images of heat and coolness are transduced into questions of volume, reflecting the earlier Lutheran antipathy to the "noisy" revivalists.

The vocal unison of liturgical prayers is also a central component of Lutheran formation, contrasted with the tumult of the *bung beten* (TP, group prayer) that is specific to the Pentecostal churches of Papua New Guinea like New Life and Reformed Gospel (see chapter 5). Vocal unity indexes not only a tradition of Christian practice and access to the published hymnal but also a form of communication with God that is audible in ways quite different from the audibility described for New Life. Rather than an audibility based on local language and local forms, the liturgy (now in Tok Pisin rather than Kâte) and its regular prayers provide Lutherans with what seems to be a field-tested, internationally accepted route to God. Indeed, Lutherans often scoff at the noise produced by a *bung beten* as too irregular to be heard by God. (Pentecostals, on the other hand, retort that God is powerful enough to hear each prayer within the cacophony of voices.)

The Lutheran soundscape is also importantly constituted by the local brass band that plays at all major Lutheran events (e.g., Easter, Christmas, ELC-PNG Day), depicted in figure 10. As noted parenthetically above, the early Lutheran mission experimented with different kinds of musical groups, including the conch-shell band in the Jâbem area (Zahn 1996). Although the conch-shell band was not exported to all of the different Lutheran areas, the brass-band form has come to be an important part of many Lutheran congregations. Young men and women travel to the Trumpet School in Raipinka, outside of Kainantu, to learn to play, and they are given instruments for use back in their home areas.

The brass band plays European/Western songs, most often hymns from the German Lutheran tradition, but their songbook also includes "God Save the Queen." As a youth-oriented group, the brass band is not only able to provide a set of linkages to national Lutheran institutions like the school at Raipinka, but it is also able to avoid some of the critical discourse that surrounds drumming in church. Like guitars (about which, more below), the brass instruments are marked as foreign, but unlike guitars, the brass instruments are signs specifically of the kinds of connections that Lutherans have made and that are possible given the sorts of institutional affiliations that only national and international denominations are capable of. With male guitarists, female drummers, and young trumpeters, the Lutherans have carved out a unique soundscape of Christian connection.

FIGURE 10. The Lutheran Brass Band during ELC-PNG Day.

The Remediations of Reformed Gospel

The Reformed Gospel Church emerged from a split with New Life after some members felt that the latter had become overly local in its concerns. As Niebuhr might have predicted, the sect that formed out of New Life Church was concerned to re-universalize the Christian message, albeit to the Guhu-Samane in particular. That is, both New Life and Reformed Gospel see themselves as heirs of the Holy Spirit revival of 1977, when the local language allowed God to become present in a way that was not possible with Lutheranism's "external" liturgical constraints. While one might expect Reformed Gospel to share quite a bit with New Life, its members work hard to distance themselves from what they tend to think of as New Life's cargo-cult forms, a process of complementary schismogenesis. As with the previous two churches discussed, these forms of embracing the universality of Christianity are importantly focused on the sounds produced in the Reformed Gospel. The character of voices and the language of songs come into focus here.

As part of their critique of New Life's over-localization of Christianity, Reformed Gospel gave up entirely on the use of drums in church services. Instruments in Reformed Gospel services include guitars, tambourines, and voices. Guitars in contemporary Papua New Guinea are the most common instruments of Pentecostal worship, and in using them, Reformed Gospel members place themselves within a Pentecostal mainstream that specifically avoids the local arguments about drumming. They do not sing songs that have traditional Guhu-Samane melodies, preferring instead to use songs that circulate through Papua New Guinea Pentecostal circles in Tok Pisin. But Reformed Gospel does not use Tok Pisin exclusively. Rather, they use local members to compose Guhu-Samane translations of the Tok Pisin lyrics, so that most songs will begin with Tok Pisin verses and choruses and then move into Guhu-Samane verses and choruses that repeat "the same thing" over again. In some cases, songs are trilingual, beginning in English, moving to Tok Pisin and then to Guhu-Samane. A song with only one verse might be sung for ten minutes at a time, as singers are led through multiple iterations of the verse in different languages. As I discussed in the previous chapter, Reformed Gospel cannot be characterized as anti-local in contrast to the localizing forms of either New Life or (in its nationally mediated form) the Lutherans. Instead, Reformed Gospel re-creates the local that will constitute their Christians in these compulsive retranslations within each song and many times over again within each sermon.

As I noted above, the strength of any church is generally evaluated by the nature of the singing throughout the service. This is particularly true for Reformed Gospel. Given the importance of singing to the church's spiritual health, it seems odd at first that songs are most loudly sung by informal choruses of little girls. Little girls are by far the least powerful of any category of Guhu-Samane people, made to become primary caregivers of small children while still small themselves and while their

FIGURE 11. Tambourine girls lead the music worship at the Body of Christ Crusade.

brothers are allowed to roam the forest with toy bows and arrows and few responsibilities. Church is the one place where little girls, otherwise entirely silenced by household distributions of power, seem to be most vocally present. Perhaps in recognition of this one instance of publicity, little girls are also the group most likely to sing church songs as they do chores around the village and in the nearby forest.[8]

In contrast to New Life's powerful male voices and masculine drums, Reformed Gospel's choruses of little girls are capable of producing a form of spirit that does not constitute the same kind of "noise" that has become so associated with New Life practice. The spirit is still transduced by sound, but only if that sound is produced by people who stand in opposition to the hot men of New Life's quasi-traditionalist men's house/church complex. Not even the Lutheran critique of New Life, which put drums in the hands of adult women, is enough of a contrast with traditional forms. If Reformed Gospel seems intent on re-localizing every aspect of Christianity in its practice of compulsive retranslation, little girls might be the only category of people who, in a sense, do not have to be retranslated in Christianity. Having always been at the furthest extreme from the centers of traditionality (and male dominance), little girls are already Christian in a way that even little boys cannot be. When coolness is declared a Christian virtue, it is something that little girls seem to have naturally, a product of their relative powerlessness in almost any other context. Girls' voices have become the sound of cool Christianity for Reformed Gospel.

However, little girls cannot on their own create real excitement in the church. This comes when the adult men, so uncomfortable with what has become a partly feminized form of worship, begin to dance and sing with the same alacrity as the girls themselves. Unlike New Life's masculine Christianity associated with the precision moves and drumbeats of men's house practices, Reformed Gospel men have a hard time bringing themselves into the spirit, which for Reformed Gospel is signaled by jumping and flailing around without order to the sound of upbeat, guitar-accompanied praise songs. On those infrequent days when the senior men of Titio village would hop around and sing in full voice, one knew that the church was really strong. When even the little girls do not sing, people know the church is in trouble.

Reformed Gospel men are not re-creating traditional drumbeats or dance moves, as they imagine New Life men are, but rather they have to embody a kind of spasmodic dance that has come index the presence of spirit within themselves. This, in a sense, is what all of Reformed Gospel's retranslations are after. Reformed Gospel men (and even adult women) are caught in the spirit only when they are brought through a history of mediating critiques of Christian forms, in particular Christian songs and soundscapes. When local leaders and big men finally get the spirit and overcome their ingrained bodily comportment, it is because of the difficult process of transformation that worship constitutes. That weekly process of being moved and being made to move in radically different ways is exactly the point. It may be a moment of immediacy, but it is one that carries with it a pedigree of critical mediations, transductions of men's house tradition and gender into a bodily experience of spasmodic vigor.

Patrick Eisenlohr (2009) has recently argued that religious forms of mediation have a tendency to lose their immediacy over time, to become symbols of rather than indexical links to God. And while this is one aspect of what is happening in the Waria Valley situation (drums and guitars have certainly becomes symbols of New Life and Reformed Gospel, respectively), it does not totally account for the Reformed Gospel brand of worship. Like Rutherford's Biak Christians (2006) who value Christianity only as an object of the foreign, Reformed Gospel members, especially male members, make indexical relations to God only through these practices of mediation—through the performative invocation of the history of critical discourse about sound and instruments that has been a central part of the denominational disputes for the past thirty years, the same critical history that makes it so unnatural for them to dance to guitar music in acceptable Reformed Gospel ways. The sounds of Christian worship in the Reformed Gospel case—the high-pitched voices of little girls accompanying Western guitars—are not valued for their capacity to produce immediacy, but for their capacity to produce the mediated sonic history of critique that I have sketched out here.

. . .

Niebuhr's story of the cyclic de-universalization of sects into the social and political particularities of churches was written in the shadow of Weber's specter of individualist secularization in modernity. As Keane has so cogently argued (2007), the semiotic ideologies of modernity seem to create both an individual and a bewildering number of pitfalls for the individual to stumble over. That is, as soon as the individual is ideologized as an autonomous entity, he or she is also therefore at great risk of losing the freedom of that autonomy in recognizing relationships to other people or objects. Niebuhr's model of denominationalism is an excellent example of this paradox: if the Christian individual should ever grasp onto any kind of identity, object, or instrument, the universalism of the relation between that individual and God is in great danger of being severely incapacitated. This, for Niebuhr, was politics.

It is also, on occasion, what seems to count as politics for Guhu-Samane Christians as well. In the often-heard complaints about the Garasa land claim, everyone was clear on exactly the ways in which New Life and Reformed Gospel were using local village groups as proxies for their own goals in their bids to control the buildings and land at the station. The land mediator's flawed ruling in favor of the Muniwa-based claims to Wakaia #2 and the adjoining Garasa land was, for many, just a sign of Mark's interference in the process. For everyone involved (and one gets the sense that this was true of both Mark and the land mediator as well), it was not a particularly Christian moment.

However, Niebuhr's model leaves us without much room to maneuver through the rest of the complex story of Guhu-Samane denominationalism. Is it politics all the way down? Is it Christian only in that first moment of sectarianism? The model of mediation gives us some purchase on the ways in which the critical history of denominational disputes are able to maintain indexical connections to the universalism of God that local people are after. These forms of mediation, constructed in a history of contestation, can be celebrated as the routes through which God is correctly hailed. These media do not have to produce a sense of the immediate but rather can produce a sense of the layers of critique that have brought a denomination into being. Mediation becomes its own form of immediacy, especially for a church like Reformed Gospel, whose sense of afterness is written into their very name. They have been *re-formed* (and are re-formed again every week) in God.

But note that what from the insider's perspective (say, Reformed Gospel members talking about their own musical practice) is a critique of past social forms that moves one into Niebuhr's universalism is just sociality from an outsider's perspective (say, a New Life member talking about Reformed Gospel as too devoted to nonlocal instruments like guitars). Thus it is crucial that one looks at both the forms through which critique happens and the form of critique (i.e., the particular qualities, senses, or mediations through which denominational disputes play out [see Harkness 2014], as well as the fact of denominationalism). These forms, from an insider's perspective, appear as a critique—on a universal(izing) basis—of parochial church forms. But from an outsider's perspective, these forms can appear as just another set of parochial church forms, which are themselves subject to critique using yet other forms, ad infinitum.

There are, then, two senses of politics that are pertinent. The first is the sense of politics as contestation or critique. In this sense, Protestant Christianity is fundamentally political, because critique is a fundamental part of the religious experience (as when Reformed Gospel members dance in particular ways). There is no neat distinction between the religious and the political in that sense. But note that this is basically the insider's perspective noted above. The second sense of politics—politics as part of this-worldly social life opposed to religious universalism and other-worldliness—is merely the outsider's perspective. However, as I've tried to show here, both are constitutive of denominationalism and Christian religious experience. The crucial point is an attention to form, which allows one and the same thing (e.g., soundscape—either considered as critique or as parochial sociocultural stuff) to operate in two different but simultaneous perspectives.

The first half of this chapter suggests that individualist Christianity is present at least in its remarked-upon absences during moments like the land dispute. The second half of this chapter suggests that Christianity can, in fact, be seen in terms of people's relations of interaction and incorporation with objects or media. The point throughout, though, has been to argue for both of these being moments of Christianity (Melanesian or otherwise), seen in terms of critique and in terms of the particular forms through which critique happens. While Christians might have to present the celebratory moments of mediation in terms of a history of critique—a renvoi to the moment of initial sectarianism—they work within a political world of religious critique.

Within this framing, the denominational disputes in the Waria Valley are best viewed as remnant churches. They can argue for a universality of Christianity even as they admit a sociohistorical particularity of the universal that emerges from critical, religious debate. The remnant church admits the importance of the Christian group as the earthly mirror of the church triumphant while also recognizing that the group's universality will always be partial and will always be the basis for the ongoing fight as the church militant. The remnant church is one that can argue, somewhat paradoxically, for a *new* basis for the universal, told in terms of particular formulations of sensory qualities, media, or, as in the previous chapter, intertextuality.

As I argued at the end of chapter 6, the historically particular arguments for universality that emerge from the denominationalist disputes of remnant churches have a way of collapsing into complementarily schismogenic identity categories: Reformed Gospel as the church that uses Tok Pisin and guitars in opposition to New Life as the church that uses Guhu-Samane and drums. Implicit in this movement toward a symmetrical attribution of characteristics is the de-historicization of the critical debate that led to a schism in the first place, a synchronic comparison in contrast to a diachronic process of critical evolution. This de-historicization is, however, a product of the remnant model itself. In creating a novel basis for the universal, a remnant church both admits and denies the sociohistorical realities of its emergence.

Rituals of historical memory, like the February 2 crusade speeches discussed in chapter 4, explicitly help to maintain the diachronic origin story of a particular church even as they objectify or entextualize the characteristics that allow for synchronic comparisons of denominational attributes. But even mundane practices like using drums or performing a thrashing, hopping dance to express one's cool Christian spirit, offer the same opportunities to reiterate histories of critique or lambast others for parochial differences. Indeed, it seems to suggest that more schisms and more remnant churches can be expected in the future. A new basis for universality—and a new way to constitute historical difference under the sign of God—is always available to the remnant.

CHAPTER 8

Kinship, Christianity, and Culture Critique

Learning to Be a Lost Tribe of Israel in Papua New Guinea

In the colonial world, Protestantism has had, at best, an ambivalent position with respect to European discourses of modernity and progress. Within Europe, religion was the premier antiprogressive force maintaining the status quo. Political liberalism defined the practice of critique as central to progress and defined religion as anti-critical, as keeping people from asking questions and using their rational faculties. J.S. Mill reserved pride of place for religion in discussing the "despotism of Custom" that kept geniuses (like himself) from flourishing (Mill [1859] 1978, 67). But at the same time that this secularist discourse was gaining ground in Europe, in the colonies, religion was essential to constructing the path of progress that Europe's colonial Others would have to take (Keane 2007, chap. 3). In other words, if religions of the book like Christianity were perfect examples of anti-progressive, anti-critical forces in Europe, then religions of the book were perfect vehicles for fostering progress among the so-called natives. According to missionaries, Christianity could be compared with a native's culture (then an emerging object of study itself), and the native could be taught to use Christianity to critically question his or her traditions. In the same way that a Pauline version of Christianity universalized the promises made originally only to the Jews, so missionaries would bring the colonial natives out of the stultifying particularities of their traditions into the universality—and the unity—of the European modern.

While most Euro-Americans today can easily scoff at the naïveté of the missionary project in such a history, the sense that critique is a pursuit done primarily in the secular public sphere is still a fundamental principle of liberal democracies, as the currently tense negotiations of church and state in the United States demonstrate. However, as Joel Robbins (2004b) and Birgit Meyer (1998, 1999) both discuss, Pentecostal Christianity, in particular, has become incredibly powerful in the global south precisely because it can so easily be adapted to provide a discursive position from which to critique one's local culture, a project that local communities enmeshed in global capital and projects of modernity want to participate in. Robbins and Meyer both focus on Pentecostalism because, in contrast to the stance of many of the mainline missions, which said local animist gods did not exist, Pentecostals accept the existence of these gods (as devils) and provide the ritual tools with which to fight them. As I have discussed over the past few chapters, this particular project of critique in Guhu-Samane Christian communities has centered on the men's house as both an example for and a competitor to proper, local, and transformative Christian practice.

In the sense of producing forms of cultural critique then, the missionary project has bourn significant fruit. But in addition to critique, missionaries also hoped to create a new basis of unity and universalism in which to enfold the "natives." And although Pentecostalism has been exceptionally powerful in producing critical stances on local cultural practices for people in the global south, Pentecostalism has also been exceptionally powerful in producing denomination after denomination, with each group creating its own critical perspective on the local. To take Melanesia as an example: in the early twentieth century, there were four mainline missions in the Papua and New Guinea territories—Catholics, Lutherans, Anglicans, and Methodists. Currently in the rapidly Pentecostalizing Papua New Guinean nation-state, there are countless denominations—not only international ones like Assemblies of God or Four Square and national ones like Christ for the Nation, but also thousands of local churches that respond to particular ethnic histories of critique in the more than eight hundred ethnic groups that are in the Papua New Guinean nation.

This book has focused only on three denominations: the Lutherans, the Pentecostalist New Life Church that broke from the Lutherans in the early days of the 1977 Holy Spirit revival, and the Pentecostalist Reformed Gospel Church that broke off from New Life in the mid-1990s. There are, however, many other denominations in the region.[1] And while each new church was started in the hopes of creating a unified Guhu-Samane ethnicity to match the seemingly unified and sacralized Guhu-Samane language developed in the New Testament translation, each church seemed to only create deeper divisions. New Life despises the Lutherans' mix of German, American, and local norms in their Christian practice; Reformed Gospel despises New Life's over-localization of Christianity; Lutherans despise Reformed Gospel's denial of all local traditions. Each denomination sees itself as having critiqued and expunged the bad aspects of culture and kept the good, and each denomination sees the others as having done just the opposite. And while it's possible to see in this nothing more than political maneuvering, there are often larger stakes involved: not only the future expression of local practices, but also the peaceful coexistence of denominationally divided communities. In the past, differences in things like instrumentation have led to violent confrontations.

In this chapter, I examine a particular instance of kinship-based denominationalist Christian critique and how the locally circulated theory that the Guhu-Samane are one of the Lost Tribes of Israel acts to overcome it and acts to overcome denominationalist strife in general. In the example I present, a Reformed Gospel preacher denounces his own genealogy and asks that all other Guhu-Samane do the same. This critical practice ends up creating a particular denominational social group—enacting Reformed Gospel as the critics of a cultural genealogy that has to be renounced in order for members to be "really Christian"—for them to be what Robbins talks about as the kind of ideological individuals that are central to Christianity.

However, Reformed Gospel members, as well as many other Guhu-Samane, also aim to overcome these divisions and produce a form of unity by creating an ethnic genealogy that positions the Guhu-Samane as the chosen people, like the ancient Israelites, and thus convertible, just as some of the Israelites converted to Christianity. Because as much as the Guhu-Samane are committed to their particular denominations, they are also aware that they are not living up to an idealized formation of Christian unity. The potentiality of the Lost Tribes hypothesis—the way in which an ancient Israelite connection seems to hold out the possibility of one day successfully replicating the transformation from Jew to early Christian—is what makes it attractive across these social divisions.

As people like Fenella Cannell (2005, 2006) discuss, Christianity is not just a religion of renunciation of the social. In addition to producing an ideological individualism, this dialectic movement between the creation, destruction, and re-creation of unity in the formation of denominations produces social forms that people celebrate as uniquely Christian. In this particular case, quite a few Guhu-Samane are able to both renounce ego-centric genealogies of sinfulness in an embrace of individualism and celebrate socio-centric (or ethnic) genealogies of potential transformation in an embrace of a Lost Tribes past. Being "lost" actually becomes a way to recognize others who are similarly engaged in a form of Christianity organized around cultural critique.

As I will discuss in the latter half of this chapter, Lost Tribes discourses are starting to be seen in a number of places across Papua New Guinea, and, moreover, are starting to be seen even in contexts of national electoral politics. Not simply a set of diverse and disparate groups each hitting upon this connection in ignorance of others, the Lost Tribes discourses in Papua New Guinea are starting to be seen as ways of recognizing others who are similarly engaged in a moral discourse of critique of the past and ways of turning toward new possibilities of unity for the future.

While this social formation would seem to share characteristics with the model of nationalism made popular by Benedict Anderson (1991), Lost Tribes discourses are, I argue, quite different. In Anderson's model, nationalism spread across the globe in the nineteenth and twentieth centuries because of its uniquely modular form. That is, nationalisms share a desire to manifest specific national pasts and traditions similar to but distinct from those that other nations have. A group demands its own nation-state because it has a particular history and set of traditions, just as other nations do.

But for groups that organize around Lost Tribes imaginaries, the goal is not to be unique, but to share a relationship to the Israelites that others could share as well. Lost Tribes discourses that work to guide moral transformations constitute a kind of future governed by a connection to the past that is specifically not modular in Anderson's sense of the term. Robbins (1998) argues that Papua New Guinea has what can be called a "negative nationalism," one that is predicated on a shared sense of inferiority. This negative nationalism can still be seen in Andersonian terms, even if it is not the celebratory sense of nationalism usually implied by the term. I am arguing here, however, that there is an emerging discourse of critique based on the image of the Lost Tribes that creates an open-ended invitation to addressees to celebrate the not-yet. Lost Tribes critiques hold out the possibility that there is a kind of moral reform of Papua New Guinea soon to be materialized. Placing oneself within that critical process is the crucial distinction, one that (hopefully—or ideally) trumps ethnic, linguistic, and denominational differences that have long been seen as problematic to forming a national consciousness.

Lost Tribes discourses, therefore, are at odds with the nationalisms that were particularly important in the post-independence eras of Pacific nations, when national politicians developed theories such as the "Melanesian Way," Bernard Narokobi's formulation of postcolonial Papua New Guinea, or the "Pacific Way," developed in Fiji (Lawson 2010). As I will discuss in more detail in the second half of this chapter, Lost Tribes discourses that specifically invoke and look to another nation-state—the contemporary state of Israel—subvert the particularities of specifically "Melanesian" national politics that dominated postindependence governance.

At the same time, this transformation in the basis of moral unity presents what are, by now, well-known problems for liberal democracies and modernization theories more generally (see Habermas 1991). Lost Tribes critiques are not based on the secular proceduralism of rational, critical debate. While Papua New Guinea's constitution states that it is a Christian nation, and while government meetings often begin with prayer, there has been a particularly strong move in recent years toward political discourses based upon Christian ethics, of which the Lost Tribes discourses are a part. Led in large part by Talal Asad's (2003) recent work, many scholars are rethinking the nature of secularism that has been assumed to be at the heart of liberal democracies across the world, particularly as religious discourses are more and more frequently becoming the basis for formations in the public sphere as well as counter-public formations (see Hirschkind 2006; Gifford 1998; Marshall 2009; Meyer and Moors 2006). The level of specifically Christian interventions in national Papua New Guinea politics are still relatively low, as Eves (2008) discusses. However, Christian and related discourses, like those employing Lost Tribes imagery, are becoming the basis on which people in Papua New Guinea are starting to recognize one another as having similar critical goals about their political and moral futures. A recent (2014) flare-up in Pentecostalite parliamentary politics that I briefly address at the end of this chapter suggests that this trend is on the rise.

KINSHIP VERSUS KINSHIP BEHAVIOR

Before talking about these Christian reformulations of kinds of related-ness and genealogical connections, I want to briefly discuss models of kinship in contemporary anthropology. For Asif Agha (2007, chap. 8), practitioners in the field of kinship studies made a fundamental error when they decided that the object of study would be abstract kinship systems. Instead, for Agha (2007, 340), "debates about 'concepts' of kinship are debates about reflexive models of kinship behavior." That is to say, the object at the center of any kinship investigation should not be some putative universal basis for kinship but rather the way each peo-ple's own models of relatedness are revealed through situated uses of kin terms and their use in discussing linguistic and non-linguistic behav-iors. Such a view allows us to understand how kin terms can then be swept up in projects of social transformation that seek to reformulate the bases of relatedness in society. For example, Agha discusses the ways in which Vietnamese kin terms were altered in the wake of Ho Chi Minh's rise to power. Where, previously, hierarchies in the social order were instantiated through the use of age-stratified and generationally stratified kin terms, after the Marxist revolution, the new model of social equality was instantiated in the now much reduced range of "fic-tive" kin terms used in address. Greatest deference was shown to Ho Chi Minh himself, but even there the world of social difference had been narrowed to such an extent that he was simply "senior uncle."

As Agha notes, it is rare and perhaps even unknown to find a com-munity in which only one model of relatedness is at work. Guhu-Samane speakers have several different models of genealogies, including tradi-tional ones and the Lost Tribes hypothesis, that establish different forms of relatedness. Guhu-Samane, to a large extent, engage in social action by deploying genealogical linkages, using them to claim land for houses, subsistence gardening, cash cropping, gold panning, and animal hus-bandry, as well as to claim trees and hunting grounds. Among Papua New Guinean groups, Guhu-Samane are somewhat unique in having extremely lengthy genealogies that are performatively argued for during land claims. Since the strongest claims to land are through clan connec-tions, and since clans are formed through matrilineal links, Guhu-Samane men engaged in land disputes can often recite genealogies of linking women and their mates through up to twelve generations. Genealogical knowledge is guarded carefully and often has to be purchased from a mother's brother. One does not really have genealogical connections unless one can skillfully and yet cryptically announce these sequential links. Patrilineal links are recognized in the inheritance of certain categories of goods (especially trees), but after two generations, it is hard to use a patriline to press a claim to land or other resources. There are, however, exceptions to the limits of using patrilineal links. Big men have genealogical models unique to their particular sociological circle, and claims to men's house leadership can occasionally go through more lengthy patrilineal genealogies. So even within the spheres of land claims and leadership, there are already multiple models of relatedness and rights that local people work with, and they are also reformulating these models in contemporary contexts where the state requires certain forms of legible links in proving ownership of pieces of land.

Now I want to discuss how people are in a process of reformulating reflexive models of relatedness in Christian contexts. To demonstrate that, I will first examine a segment of text that was taped during the 2005 Body of Christ crusade, a week-long event that occurs annually in the Waria Valley during the northern-hemisphere summer. In this segment, a pastor asks the primarily Reformed Gospel audience to renounce their ancestors, creating a denominationally specific critique of cultural genealogies. After that, I will discuss the question of Lost Tribe status of the Guhu-Samane, demonstrating the ways in which genealogies can also be reimagined as a unifying form of potential Christianity.

CHRISTIAN GENEALOGIES IN THE WARIA VALLEY

Like the New Life February 2 crusade discussed in chapter 4, Reformed Gospel crusades are multiday Christian gatherings during which many people recommit themselves or are baptized for the first time. The Reformed Gospel event is known locally (in English) as the "Body of Christ crusade," and it is an extraordinary break in the routine flow of events in Guhu-Samane village life. Every year, a Guhu-Samane man, here called Jordan, flies in from Lae to lead the crusade church services. Although it is supposed to be a nondenominational event, the influence of Reformed Gospel church is heavy. The crusade rotates among different communities, and the host community spends the year in preparation, planting enormous community gardens known as *dzoo gigi*s to provide food and building houses to provide shelter for the five hundred or so guests from across the Waria Valley.

An important element of this or any crusade is the baptism of new believers (depicted on the cover of this book), an event that has its own genealogical reordering. The sermon that preceded the baptisms at the 2005 Body of Christ crusade concentrated on why baptism was a kind of death in which one is immediately reborn into life and into new kinds of kinship relations (see also Jebens 2006). As Jordan said at another point in the crusade, every Christian becomes a child of God, so that Jordan's father called God "Father," Jordan calls God "Father," and Jordan's children call God "Father." This is a patriline that extends horizontally but does not extend vertically, that is, it is a patriline that encompasses all of the past and all of the future. The primarily matrilineal Guhu-Samane, who usually recognize patrilineal rights only in the first descending generation, are in a particularly good position to appreciate the miracle of immediacy in which God becomes everyone's father. That is to say, if God has no grandchildren, the links to God never diminish. At the same time, if God is everyone's father, then this is a way to unify people outside of the clan divisions that are strictly recorded in land claims and similar contexts.

This same baptismal reordering of genealogical connectedness—where the death of one's genealogy becomes the basis for one's life with Jesus—was the extraordinary emphasis of one of Jordan's most rousing sermons, where he publically denounced his genealogy and then asked everyone else to do the same. Jordan took his own family as an example, focusing on actions taken by his maternal grandmother and paternal grandfather over sixty years earlier. The section excerpted here is about halfway into the sermon.[2] Everything was spoken in Tok Pisin, except where noted.

In the first section below, Jordan recounts his mother's mother's elopement to a man from Papuan Waria region (1–8) and then asks for God's forgiveness (9–15).

1 Mi no sem long tok aut.
   I am not ashamed to say it.

2 Em tumbuna meri bilong mi, taim bilong wa
   My grandmother, [it was] the time of the [Second World] War

3 Na em ranawe i go long Papuan Waria
   and she ran away to Papuan Waria,

4 na dispela man bilong Papuan Waria i kolim Pena ia
   and this Papuan Waria man named Pena

5 em maritim tumbuna meri na i karim mama bilong mi. . . .
   married her, and she had my mother

6 Na mi wanpela kiau bin kamap long dispela hap.

And I am an egg that came from this area.

7 Na dispela em kiau nogut

It is a bad egg,

8 Em rabis kiau

a trash egg.

9 Na taim mi bin tanim bel, mi tok olsem

And when I converted, I said,

10 Papa God

Father God,

11   long nem bilong Jisas

   in the name of Jesus,

12   dispela kiau em mi les

   I am sick of this egg.

13   Mi katim dispela rop na mi pinis

   I cut the vine and I am done,

14   Mi pinis long dispela

   I am done with this.

15   Olsem na mi tok sori long dispela pasin pamuk i bin kamap long lain bilong mama bilong mi

   And so I say sorry for this promiscuity that occurred on my mother's line.

Parallel to this maternal history, Jordan then talks about the polygamous marriages of his father's father (16–21) and again tells how he asked God's forgiveness (22–26).

16 Na- ra- ra- long sait bilong papa bilong mi

And, ah- ah- on my father's side,

17 Em- tumbuna man bilong mi

my grandfather,

18 Kebare em dablim meri

Kebare doubled his wives [i.e., had two wives polygamously],

19 Em pamuk man!

he was a promiscuous man!

20 Kebare em pamuk man!
Kebare was a promiscuous man!

21 Em dablim mari
He doubled his wives,

22 Olsem na mi tu mi tok
and so I also said,

23 Mi les long dispela lain
I am sick of this line;

24 Mi katim long nem bilong Jisas
I cut it in the name of Jesus.

25 Mi nogat
[As for] me, no.

26 [In English:] I am going to create a righteous generation.

27 [Audience: Amen]

Jordan then talks about how hard it is for him and his audience to be good, God-fearing people, given these histories of sin (28–32). He repeats a version of the prayer of the renunciation of ancestors that he has already said twice above.

28 Sori.
Sorry.

29 Yumi laik kamapim ol manmeri i save pret long God
We [incl.] want to create people who are afraid of God,

30 Olsem na yumi mas marit stret.
and so we [incl.] must marry correctly.

31 Olsem na mi bihainim lain bilong mama i go na mi lukim em i go na paul
But I follow my mother's line, and I see that it goes amiss,

32 Na mi bihainim lain bilong papa i go em tu em go paul!
and I follow my father's line, and I see that it also goes amiss!

33 Olsem na mi tok
And so I say,

34 Mi tok
I say,

35 Papa God, em olsem
Father God, it is that,

36 long taim bilong tudak
during the time of darkness [i.e., before Christianity],

37 na ol i no save long tok bilong yu na lotuim
they did not know your word or to worship,

38 olsem na mi lusim sin bilong ol.
and so I forgive their sins.

39 Mi tok sori.
I say sorry.

Having modeled the kind of renunciation prayer that he is going to ask the audience to perform for themselves at the end of his sermon, Jordan goes back to his own family history to discuss what would happen if he neglected to atone for these ancestral sins.

40 Tasol Satan i laik kam long dispela rot bilong mama
But Satan likes to come along this road of my mother's

41 Na kisim pamuk spirit i kam insait long pikinini bilong mi na tumbuna
and bring this promiscuous spirit into my children and descendants.

42 Grace na Melissa bai i go na pamuk nabaut!
[My daughters] Grace and Melissa will go sleeping around!

43 [screaming:] NO!! NO!! NO!! NO!!!

44 Long nem bilong Jisas
In the name of Jesus,

45 mi katim dispela rop
I cut this vine,

46 Dispela beklain
this family past,

47 dispela haiwe
this highway.

48 Mi katim na mi rausim
I cut it and I get rid of it.

49 Na mi kamaut long nem bilong Jisas
And I come outside in the name of Jesus,

50 Na mi sanap long insait long Krais Jisas

and I stand beside [lit. inside of] Christ Jesus.

Without renouncing his ancestors, his two young daughters are in danger of repeating the kinds of sins his maternal grandmother committed (40–43). Satan uses these sins as paths (vines, roads, highways), which Jordan must ritually cut (44–45). He then repeats this for his father's side.

51 Na dispela rop bilong pamuk spirit i kam long Kebare na dablim meri nabaut ia

And this vine of the promiscuous spirit that comes from Kebare doubling his wives,

52 Long nem bilong Jisas mi katim dispela haiwe

in the name of Jesus, I cut this highway,

53 dispela rop

this vine,

54 dispela sem

this shame,

55 na mi tok

and I say,

56 mi kamaut

I come outside,

57 mi kamaut long dispela

I come out of this.

58 Mi laik statim nupela generesen insait long Krais Jisas

I want to start a new generation inside Christ Jesus.

In this excerpt, Jordan discusses the sins of his grandparents and models for his audience the kinds of prayers of renunciation he thinks they need to do as well. His maternal grandmother married many men (sequentially) and was thus *pamuk* (TP, sexually promiscuous). His paternal grandfather married two women (polygamously), and he too was *pamuk* for doing so. The point is not that these two grandparents should have known better (it was then the pre-mission era). It is rather that when people sin—in states of knowledge or ignorance—that sin creates a road, as Jordan says, on which Satan can travel, much as genealogical rights, privileges, and potentialities travel on roads in Guhu-

Samane kinship idioms (e.g., claiming land is to "follow in the footsteps of the ancestors," *bihainim lekmak bilong tumbuna*).[3]

As the grandchild of these two promiscuous *(pamuk)* people, Jordan himself is the "egg" of these sins that may one day "break open" and reveal in the light of day "the sins of the fathers." He must ask Jesus to destroy this road that connects Jordan to his relatives, which makes Jordan and his descendants recognizable to Satan. With the road to one's ancestors intact, Satan, in a sense, has directions to you; but once Jesus destroys that road and that genealogy through the creation of a new genealogy in which you are a child of God, Satan will be lost, unable to find you and your descendants (at least until you sin again and create a new road). And as shameful as it may seem, every person has these skeletons in the closet. Jordan asked that his audience members participate in an altar call—to come to the front of the stage to pray and be prayed over—in an effort to renounce their sinful genealogical roads.

As with genealogical imagery in land disputes, genealogies are potential roads on which recognition travels. But unlike genealogies in land disputes, one does not have to know one's genealogy in order for it to have an effect in one's life. All of our families are crooked, says Jordan in a later moment in the sermon (*em yumi olgeta famili bilong yumi i kam kruket na i stap,* TP), and all need to participate in this ritual and create a new genealogy that establishes individuals who can be seen as children of God rather than the descendants of sinners. So where the potentialities of genealogies are thought of positively in contexts of land tenure—every link seems to bring with it a possibility of claiming rights to a new piece of land—the potentialities of genealogies in Jordan's Christian reformulation are all negative. In Jordan's model of genealogical relatedness, life's possibilities are foreclosed, since genealogies only lead one to Satan. Almost everyone came up to the front of the stage for the altar call (fig. 12).

The extent to which the genealogies at play in this ritual are the same as the genealogies in land disputes was made clear by Jordan's comments that one cannot be ashamed of standing up and breaking these ties out of fear that others will then know you are a "bastard" child who could not be a true landholder. In local politics of land, the strongest claims are those that include genealogical links made solely through legitimate unions. But as Jordan says, let those who want to fight over the old earth do so; he and other Christians will wait for God's new heaven and new earth. (This is considerably easier for Jordan to say as a town-dweller who has essentially opted out of local land politics.)

FIGURE 12. An altar call to renounce the sins of one's ancestors at the Body of Christ Crusade.

Ancestors are not the only things that keep people from realizing their dreams of change and development. Stories of curses put on the region during the twentieth century circulate as reasons why the Waria Valley seems so undeveloped. Whether these are curses from World War II, when a Guhu-Samane soldier used a kind of magic that destroyed everything in the forest (particularly game), or curses from the early 1930s, when land owners of what is now the Garaina Station tried to keep development from encroaching upon their land, there are a whole host of forces that seem to be stacked up against local aspirations. Nobody knows who was responsible for the other curses, and thus nobody knows how to undo them. The sins of ancestors, which can be renounced in the altar call, are some of the only curses that can seemingly be removed by present-day Guhu-Samane. Renouncing one's ancestors is one of the only ways people feel they have to improve their chances in life.

This kind of renunciation is a relatively new phenomenon, although it is implicit in rituals like baptism. However, the effects of this turning away from kin ties are starting to be felt. People rarely make *dzoo gigi* gardens these days. As more and more people start to garden in small family plots, lateral kin are not invited as often as they once were to garden with extended families. Likewise, many marriages are today romantic matches, including ones that ignore moiety-based incest taboos. In certain villages, a large percentage of the younger couples are, from the perspective of their parents and grandparents, incestuously married. Whether or not these can be attributed to rituals like the altar call Jordan performed, it is clear that kin links are being attenuated in contemporary situations. The possibilities of renouncing one's ancestors, although in no sense evident in land claims, seems to be growing in Christian and other domains.

As I said before, *almost* everyone got up at the Body of Christ crusade to participate in this ritual renunciation of their genealogy. After taking a few photos of the audience assembled by the stage for the altar call, I happened to turn around and notice that all of the Lutherans who had come to the crusade were sitting off to the side, pointedly not participating in the events. From the Reformed Gospel perspective, the Body of Christ crusade was an opportunity to critique sinful marriage practices of the Guhu-Samane past. From the Lutheran perspective, however, this was a denominational event, characterized by a particular view of Guhu-Samane culture that was being critiqued. Even as a unity of being children of God was posited through Reformed Gospel practice, a denominational division was exacerbated. From the Lutheran perspective, God may be everyone's Father, but God doesn't have to replace all of the other fathers (or even mother's brothers) that one has.

For a particular strand of thought in the anthropology of Christianity, this kind of ideological individualization through the renunciation of one's past is standard practice in Protestantism. But for Guhu-Samane communities, this is only half of the story. While genealogies are renounced in a process that unwittingly produces denominational divisions, genealogies can also be used to try to overcome these divisions. This is where discourses of the Lost Tribes of Israel come in. Before getting to the Guhu-Samane versions of them, I want to briefly discuss the origins and circulation of Lost Tribes ideas in other contexts.

GENEALOGICAL THINKING IN CHRISTIAN
COMMUNITIES: THE LOST TRIBES

Christianity is historically and geographically rooted in the Middle East of two thousand years ago at the same time that it is argued to be a universal religion by most if not all of its adherents. In the first moments of New World missionization, church leaders anxiously debated the historical particularity of the inception and spread of Christianity through the then-known world. Were the Indians of the New World kept from the historical spread of Christianity because of historical accident or because they were not human? Was the universality of Jesus's redemptive work applicable to those who had never heard of it before?

As discussed by Tzvetan Todorov, quite a few early church leaders answered these questions by creating a genealogically based middle road. Noting many similarities in ritual and in language, Bartolomé de las Casas and fellow Spanish missionaries compared the others of Europe, the Jews, to the recently discovered others of the New World, the Indians (Todorov 1996). Could the Indians actually be Jews, the original convert society? Working off of Biblical clues that had been honed through long-standing interest among Europeans, the Indians became descendants of the Lost Tribes of Israel. Positing a Jewish origin for New World Indians established a genealogical and historical link to the Old World that put Indians squarely within the realm of the human, while the fact that they were "lost" accounted for why they had not heard of Jesus. The Lost Tribes hypothesis created a unity for humanity that nevertheless depended upon a sense of geographical and genealogical distance.[4]

The Lost Tribes hypothesis about the New World Indians was based on resemblances that the missionaries saw between Indians and Jews, although the sense of resemblance between the two populations needs to be qualified. Missionaries working in the Americas consistently found the rituals of cleanliness (such as separating women during menstruation), the guttural sounds of indigenous languages, and the dark skin and large noses of the populations to be indicators of Jewish descent (see Parfitt 2002; Eilberg-Schwartz 1990). These resemblances were signs in search of a causal linkage, which would position Indians firmly in the "capable of conversion" category. At the same time, proof against the Lost Tribes hypothesis could take the same form as proof for it. Parfitt (2002, 76) summarizes a portion of an argument against the Lost Tribes hypothesis as follows: "In addition there were many things the Indians did that the Jews patently did not: no Jew for instance would eat unclean meat, whereas the Indians would eat anything; no Jew would marry a whore but all Indian women were whores." Damned if you do, damned if you don't.

This semiotic hunting and pecking for evidence of Israelite-ness occurred across the globe as Europeans came in contact with new peoples, and Lost Tribes hypotheses existed for Asia, Africa, North America, South America, and Oceania. Moreover, these discourses were often taken up by local populations themselves, as is the case in Papua New Guinea.

THE LOST TRIBES HYPOTHESIS IN THE WARIA VALLEY

As I have discussed throughout this book, Guhu-Samane Christians have highly elaborate sets of criteria with which to distinguish different denominations. Musical instruments, languages used in services, dance styles, and the loudness with which one shouts amen can all be used to distinguish one church from another. From this field of finely constituted differences, the Lost Tribes hypothesis is one area of overlap among all the denominations. I call this a hypothesis since Guhu-Samane claims of Semitic origin are often expressed as questions to ponder, not answers to proclaim. Features of the local landscape and of the language—Hebrew writing identified on rocks or local language names that people see as cognate with names from the Bible—are often discussed as signs of Hebrew roots, material traces of a past that connects contemporary Guhu-Samane with the Israelites of old. While people seem to be in no rush to answer these questions, the hypothesis frames Guhu-Samane Christianity, making its mark on everyday religious practice. From the connection with the Ancient Israelites comes a connection to the contemporary state of Israel: a man with the Star of David tattooed onto his arm, or a baseball cap that offers "Greetings from Israel."

As I discussed in the introduction, a Jew for Jesus named Gabriel visited Guhu-Samane Christians in 2004 and made a large impact on local denominational debates. He suggested that they needed to maintain a link to their own culture in order to be authentic Christians, just as he did by maintaining his Jewish heritage while professing salvation in Jesus. He prays to Jesus with his kippah on his head, just as Guhu-Samane Christians should pray to Jesus with drums in their hands. Given the long debates about things like drums in Christian worship, Gabriel's sermons touched a nerve for many of his audience members.

By asserting a genealogical link to Jesus, Gabriel created for the Guhu-Samane a slippage between Jews of today and the "ancient Israelites"—as they are often referred to in Christian literature—of the Old and New Testaments. As a Jew, Gabriel seemed to the Guhu-Samane to inhabit multiple historical times at the same moment, living in (or having a connection to) the past as well as the present. This slippage between ancient and contemporary must also be looked at in terms of Gabriel's racial categorizations. Able to say "we, the white people," Gabriel presented the Guhu-Samane with something that they had probably experienced rarely, if ever, before: a white man of means and stature who nevertheless seemed to have a "tradition," some funny clothes, and a meaningful relationship to his ancestors. Here was a model of conversion that was alluded to in missions literature: a way to be both "traditional" and "modern"; part of an old culture (Jewish) at the same time as part of a new religion (being "for Jesus"). So while he specifically told people not to try to imitate him or "his people's traditions," the people who related this story to me all reflected on the correctness of his synthesis of traditions and Christianity. That is, the idea of being properly modern seemed to hinge on getting this synthesis right.

As is common across Papua New Guinea (see Knauft 2002a, 2002b), many Guhu-Samane sharply feel that they are living in a modern world only in the most defective sense of the term. The constant lament about a lack of development is one expression of that feeling. The local aspirations for development and questions about what is known in Tok Pisin as *kastom* (custom) reveal a sense that, at best, they are living within the letter of modernity, but not its spirit. Not so Jews for Jesus. For the Guhu-Samane, Jewish people seem to have a culture that at least at one point had the sanction of God (they are the "chosen people," as most Guhu-Samane know). The Jewish context was the one out of which Jesus came to spread the Good News. And, at least for someone like Gabriel, Jews are able to recognize God's later revelation and thereby be recognized by God as well. Having accepted Jesus, Jews for Jesus enter into universality, but do so authentically, with tefillin and kippot firmly attached. The challenge thrown down by this visit, quite overtly, was whether the Guhu-Samane could do the same, with drums and local musical styles in the place of leather boxes and skull caps.

Several of my interlocutors, however, saw the challenge differently. For them, they hope that their culture is sufficiently "like" the ancient Jewish form that they can eventually become "good Christians" like some of the Jews did, "good Christians" being people who do not fight or have social divisions like denominations. This is not a celebratory reformulation of specifically Guhu-Samane traditions that could be thought of as a micro-nationalist movement (see Worsley 1957; May 1982). The Guhu-Samane are, instead, trying to constitute themselves in terms of another culture. More specifically, they are trying to constitute themselves in terms of another culture that promises a future transformation into a different group altogether: from Guhu-Samane to ancient Israelite to modern Christian.

I want to take one last look at the crusade in this context. On entering the main crusade grounds in 2005, the first thing that one noticed was the series of flagpoles that stood in front of the raised stage. On the left and right sides were flagpoles flying the Morobe provincial flag and the Papua New Guinea national flag. In the middle, however, flying higher than the others, was the Israeli flag (see fig. 13). Jordan received the flag when he donated money to a group that helps Israel defend itself. As Jordan said, all Christians have a duty to defend Israel. Jordan was not interested in making claims that the Guhu-Samane were one of the Lost Tribes, at least not in the meetings I had with him or in the sermons he delivered at the crusade. However, he was interested in proclaiming a kind of spiritual brotherhood with—and a relation of debt to—the Jews in Israel. Thus, even though no specific genealogical relation to the ancient Jews was argued here, connections to Israel were standard, unspoken facets of local Christianity. As with many Christians in the United States and around the world, a general feeling of sympathy for and spiritual relation to the Jews is felt by the Guhu-Samane Christian community.

However, some Guhu-Samane take this relation a bit farther than just a spiritual brotherhood, suggesting a specific likeness to the ancient Israelites. For them, the Guhu-Samane people "have" culture in the same way that the ancient Jews "had" culture—taboos, rites, odd decorations—and do so in a way that distinguishes them from the colonial Australians (or anthropological Americans) who seemed to not have such things. Missionaries across Papua New Guinea ratify this sensibility, and some even publish booklets in local languages that ask people to draw comparisons between their own Papua New Guinean cultures and ancient Jewish cultures. Do you have the levirate? How are menstruating women treated? This kind of comparison really took off after Gabriel's visit.

Some other Guhu-Samane take this relation to its logical limit, positing a direct line of descent or transmission from the ancient Jews to the Guhu-Samane. The first introduction I had to this form of the Lost Tribes hypothesis was when Mark, head of the Old Testament translation project and leader in the Reformed Gospel church, explained why an interior, land-based group would have words for canoe, paddle, or various species of fish. He told me that the exact origins of the Guhu-Samane are unknown, but that he had narrowed them down to some probable locations across the sea. At first he thought that the Guhu-Samane would have come from Africa, since their skin is black like

FIGURE 13. The Body of Christ Crusade with Israeli, Papua New Guinean, and Morobe Provincial flags.

Africans. However, he had heard that Africans used to worship fetishes, and he said that the Guhu-Samane had never done so. Instead, he suggested India, Palestine, or Egypt.

Moreover, there were some lexical correspondences that he found intriguing. One of the lineages within the Basi clan is called Pita Basi, and one man in the village where I was living had "Pita" as his given name. "Pita" is also the spelling used in the Tok Pisin Bible for the apostle Peter. Mark could also identify that "Peter" derives from "Petros," and he suggested that "Pita" did as well (the dual Greek-Hebrew connection will be discussion more below). This seemed to him to be positive proof of a Jewish origin, rather than Indian. Over the next year or so, this story was repeated to me on many occasions as an important sign of a link to the Jews of the Bible. Later, Mark told me the myth in which a ship travels up the river valley, and that the remains of the boat could still be seen when he was a child. "Perhaps this was Noah's boat?" he asked.

A while later, I was visited by one of Mark's affines, a man who lives several days' walk away. He had made the trip up to the Middle Waria to conduct some business, but he had specifically gone out of his way to come to my house and ask me to visit him in his village at some point. He was anxious to have me come, because he said there were some rocks on the mountains above it that I would be interested in seeing, as an anthropologist. These rocks had some kind of writing on them, and he wanted me to bring my camera to take a photo. He could identify that the writing was not Roman script. It was Greek or Hebrew or perhaps Egyptian hieroglyphics; he wasn't sure. He insisted on my visit and felt that this would be essential for any anthropological investigation that would detail the origin and history of the Guhu-Samane, since it would point to biblical origins in the Middle East.

Later in my stay, I was visiting some villages near Garaina and was told of a myth in which the characters crossed the length of the entire valley, and the mythic action ended up close to the present-day town of Wau. This myth was unique for several reasons, including the fact that it involved a cow, an animal introduced to Papua New Guinea during the colonial era. The action ended with one of the main characters dying and being entombed in a rocky cave in the Chapman mountain range. The large rocks that formed the entrance to the tomb were covered in Hebrew writing. People shook their heads in awe and amazement at this, while one of the storytellers suggested Hebrew origins for this cultural hero.

The specific pieces of evidence for the Lost Tribes hypothesis did not add up to very much, and it would be easy to discount them, if it were not for the fact that people seemed so engrossed by the stories and circulated them widely. The evidence forms a series of potential iconic similarities, which people are trying to order into an indexical chain of relation. As with the Lost Tribes hypotheses in the New World, the corpus of evidence is a series of relations of likeness. If x looks like or sounds like *y*, then perhaps *x* is *y*. If "Pita" sounds like "Peter," perhaps that is because it is "Peter/Petros" and not a local name. To use terms from C.S. Peirce, people are engaged in a process of "abductive reasoning," or hypothesis making, where potential icons are placed in an indexical chain of causal meaning (see Lee 1997). Such moments of abductive reasoning and speculation have been discussed by a number of authors working across Papua New Guinea (e.g., Battaglia 1990, 8–11; Merlan and Rumsey 1991, 225; Munn 1990), although doing so in terms of traditional cultural forms rather than Christian ones.

LOST TRIBES IN PAPUA NEW GUINEA

Quite a few ethnic groups in Papua New Guinea claim an Israelite connection. In 2003, Tudor Parfitt, a geneticist from the School of Oriental and African Studies at the University of London, came to Papua New Guinea at the request of the Gogodala community and their Pentecostal Australian missionaries to conduct DNA testing on individuals (see Dundon 2012). Parfitt had made a big splash a few years earlier by demonstrating that an African group called the Lemba had genetic markers usually indicative of Jewish heritage. The hope was that similar markers could be found for the Gogodala. The missionaries first had the idea because of certain Gogodala phenotypic facial features (i.e., big noses), and after hearing about Parfitt's Lemba research, the missionaries thought that there might be an opportunity to concretize these surface similarities.

A few years later, a Papua New Guinean geoscientist named Samuel Were, who works in the mineral-resources industry but who has had divine visions of and revelations from God, wrote a book called *Bine Mene: Connecting the Hebrews,* which claims a connection between his ethnic group, the Bine, and ancient Israelites. Officially launched and effusively praised by the governor-general of Papua New Guinea, the book formalizes a set of connections similar to those that circulated orally among the Guhu-Samane. The connections that Were makes are primarily linguistic. Using three different reference Bibles that note the original Hebrew for a number of key terms, Were developed lists of what appear to be cognates. Hebrew *Torah* is related to Bine *Tora'a*. Less obviously, Were argues Hebrew *rabbi* (teacher) is related to Bine *Abiberajayame*. Moving beyond key terms to relatively random words, the Hebrew phrase *Ishi* (My husband is there) is given the Bine equivalent *Isi, Isine*. Were also lists a number of personal and place names in Bine that sound similar to Hebrew personal and place names.

Like the Guhu-Samane, Were also identifies a connection to Petros and adds a whole list of Greek-Bine and Hebrew-Bine similarities. What kind of connection is this, then, if it can include historical relations to two different languages from completely different language families? In an obvious sense, the strict genetic relation is unlikely, to say the least. But more importantly, what kinds of ancient Israelites are these different Papua New Guinean actors hoping to create connections to? The connection is not really to the Lost Tribes if that means the tribes who were lost in 700 BC. Rather the connection is to the Israelites who were living near the Eastern Mediterranean shore at the time that Jesus was alive; the Jews who would be a part of the trading world in which Koiné Greek was commonly spoken as a lingua franca; the Jews who would be converted to Christianity. It is a sacred ethnicity of future transformation: the Papua New Guinean sense of the Lost Tribes is that the connection makes one's group not only the chosen, but the chosen who can be changed through future processes of Christian critique.

The Lost Tribes discourses thus seem to share quite a bit with Pauline forms of evangelism that take it as axiomatic that critique of one's own culture is an important part of the transformation into Christianity. Mosaic Law has to be amended to accord with the new revelation, as Paul suggests when he argues that Gentile converts do not need to be circumcised (see Gal 3; 1 Cor 7). Among the Guhu-Samane, people likewise used Pauline arguments to critique traditional practices, arguing that, for example, pig sacrifice is no longer moral after Jesus's revelation and redemption of mankind as the "last sacrifice." At the same time, though, Paul himself was not always consistent in his missiological strategy. In 1 Corinthians 9:20, for example, Paul seems to suggest that critique cannot be so radical and that space must be left for traditional cultures to perdure, even if some changes must be made.[5] This ambiguity in Paul's statements about critique are mobilized today to support different denominational perspectives on Guhu-Samane tradition. But even with this ambiguity, the outcome seems to be the same. To the extent that local people can place themselves within this biblical history of Jewish/Christian cultural criticism (a primary focus of Acts 15, for example, when the Council of Jerusalem discusses the role of Mosaic Law for followers of Jesus), they can work to create a moral Christian future.

With this in mind, two aspects of the Lost Tribes hypothesis are important to the Guhu-Samane (and perhaps to other Papua New Guinean ethnic groups). First, if they are ancient Jews, then they are *a people*, a unity. Local traditions of myth-history vacillate between moments of unity and division in the Guhu-Samane past, but the Lost Tribes hypothesis would seem to offer a definitive, sacred statement of initial Judeo-Christian unity. Second, if they are a people with a culture like the ancient Jews—or even are descendants of the ancient Jews themselves—then through Christian culture critique, they can be Christians. In other words, if they critique their culture the way the apostle Paul seemed to critique his own Jewish culture, then they too might become "really" Christian. As with any of the kinship genealogies with which Guhu-Samane engage, relatedness offers a set of possibilities for recognition from others imagined in terms of roads that traverse different domains. In the present, when Guhu-Samane have each individually made their choices to belong to one church or another, the potentiality of Christian commitment gives way to a social reality of denominational division and antagonism. But within the temporal frame of the Lost Tribes hypothesis, Guhu-Samane figure themselves as united in their genealogically based *potential* to be Christian.

Anthropologists of Christianity have tended to focus on one or another moment of Christian social life. For Joel Robbins (2004a), the most important moment is the renunciation of social ties and the creation of moral individuals who cannot depend on others to, for example, get saved. For Mark Mosko (2010) or Fenella Cannell (2005, 2006), the most important moments are the formation of social ties through Christianity. But, as I suggest here, instead of arguing that Christianity is one or the other, one needs to examine the different moments of Christian sociality in the movements between critique, division, and the reconstitution of unity. And as I will argue in the next section, this approach can be used to understand Christian sociality at a number of different levels of social organization.

LOST TRIBES OF THE NATION

In addition to the Gogodala, Bine, and Guhu-Samane examples, Lost Tribes discourses have been noted for Engans (Jacka 2005), Mt. Hageners (Parfitt 2002, 175), Fijians (Kaplan 1990), Solomon Islanders (Burt 1994), and Biaks (Rutherford 2003), to name just a few nearby Melanesian groups. In fact, they are common across the world. But more than simply being a phenomenon comparable across ethnographic sites—for anthropologists to wonder how ten Lost Tribes became eight hundred

Papua New Guinean ethnic groups—the Lost Tribes discourse appears to be an incipient form of political organization in Papua New Guinean politics (compare Worsley's 1957 arguments about the proto-nationalist bent of cargo-cult activities). That is, taking up the mantle of being "lost" is a sign to others of being engaged in a process of critique that has not yet produced one's desired results. Being "lost" means living in a world of potential transformation that has not happened yet, of being divided by ethnic, cultural, and denominational schisms without having the unity of the ancient Jews or, even better, what many think of as the universal unity of Christianity. That is, the quest for modernity or development is itself understood in terms of this critical engagement with finding a moral relationship between Christianity and some form of tradition. Tribes discourses seem to be a way that Papua New Guineans are able to recognize others who are engaged in critical projects of their own. Even if these critical projects produce denominational differences at the local level, in their Lost Tribes form of critical hope (see Miyazaki 2006a, 2006b), they are able to produce a form of connection, and one that is visible across ethnic boundaries.

Lost Tribes discourses are thus an emerging basis for a kind of Christian public sphere in Papua New Guinea. Take, for example, the Mapai Levites Party, which first fielded candidates during the 2007 parliamentary elections. The name *Mapai* comes from an abbreviation of the original Israeli Labor Party formed by David Ben-Gurion, Mifleget Poalei Eretz Israel (Party of the Workers of the Land of Israel) and the Mapai Levites slogan is "Mapai Levites Party (PNG-Israeli Labour Party, Serving People)." The PNG Mapais also invoke the tribe of Levi in their party name and note that the Levites were priests who were set apart to fight religious battles.[6] As they say in their promotional material, "Historically, the Levites are known for being fierce, unyielding and ruthless in matters when relating to God's Covenant. They have no regards for anybody or anything. If the issue involved desecration of the holy things of God, [then] no amount of odds will deter them from exacting divine justice" (John Barker, personal communication) Here are political actors trying to rally together others in a determined critique and unification of Papua New Guinea society. Nevertheless, their political platform has a number of different foci that aim at both reform and restoration, in the same way that Guhu-Samane seem able to both deny and uphold genealogies in their spiritual lives. Thus, the Mapai Levites hope to institute a rural kibbutz system, develop an import substitution program, have mandatory Bible teaching in schools, and yet also preserve traditional wisdom.

The Mapai Party represents a new turn in Papua New Guinea politics, away from the postindependence projects of self-sufficiency through the celebration of what is generally called "the Melanesian Way." A term originally coined by Bernard Narokobi to describe the local form of governance to be practiced in postcolonial Papua New Guinea, Solomon Islands, Fiji, New Caledonia, and Vanuatu, "the Melanesian Way" would be based on the principles of consensus and local knowledge that were seen as part of regional traditional culture. "It is unnecessary for us to be perfect Englishmen or Americans if we know who we are" (Narokobi 1983, 9). Narokobi's vision was for a region that could find unity in tradition, a stance taken in opposition to the colonial gaze that saw only a democracy-denying variety of languages and cultures.

> We should spring from our cultural values to forge ahead in a world that is moving more and more towards a confused uniformity, monotony and insensitivity to the fine, subtle and sublime beauty of diversity. It is the simplistic imperialist who seeks uniformity as a technique to command obedience while portraying Papua New Guinea as a land of division, of disunity, of 700 languages and thousands of cultures. Some have even dared to call it a land of chaos. These are arguments of defeat and despair, betraying an inability to transcend one's cultural conditioning. (Narokobi 1983, 7)

In contrast to the colonizer's chaos of diversity or the globalizing trend of "confused uniformity," the Melanesian Way would be able to establish consensus in traditional "person to person" (Narokobi 1983, 6) forms of interaction, even if this would now take place at the level of the nation-state rather than the village.

As Lawson (2010) argues, this and cognate calls for a "Pacific Way" were anticolonial positions, but ones that have had the effect of entrenching a leadership elite that has established its own forms of hegemonic power. For many voters in recent elections, the Melanesian Way is starting to be synonymous with the failures of the contemporary Papua New Guinean nation-state, as Eves (2008) and others have noted. Instead of "Melanesian" leaders, much contemporary political discourse demands that politicians be "good Christians" first.

There has not been, however, a simple transfer of legitimating force from local tradition to Christian morality. There is still considerable disagreement about how to bring Christianity into the political sphere. In the 2007 elections, for example, many criticized the Electoral Commission for holding elections on a Saturday in provinces like Morobe and the Southern Highlands, which have a large population of Seventh-day Adventists (SDA). SDA members hold Saturday as the Sabbath, and they felt that it would be impossible for them to vote on the Sabbath. In letters to the editor in all the major newspapers, writers debated if polling should be moved to another day to accommodate SDA members. Likewise, while many churches encourage young men to stand for elected office in provincial or national governments, they also feel it is necessary to expel or otherwise demote those same men during the time that they are engaging in the world of electoral politics (see Eves 2008).

This suggests an unstable sense of the boundaries of secularism. Christian churches and missions have long been an important part of colonial and postcolonial politics in Papua New Guinea. In rural areas, colonial missions and contemporary churches have been or are the government, for all intents and purposes, providing many of the health and education services available to communities. But local people nevertheless see a difference between these activities and governance as such. For members of both mainline churches and their evangelical cousins, politics and religion remain somewhat separate domains of social life, and people are unsure how this boundary should be treated.

The Mapai Levites Party thus seems to represent a turn toward an integration of these two domains. Israelite perspectives provide the basis for a political platform in an unambiguous way. The leader of the party, Paul Kamakande, is an itinerant evangelical preacher who sees his political work to create a kibbutz system of moral labor as an extension of his spiritual work. But this movement toward the integration of religious discourse in electoral politics does more than just upset the categories of secular liberal democracy. They also disrupt the specifically Melanesian basis of postindependence politics that Narokobi and many others long championed. As one author in a letter to the editor of the *National* put it, "ISRAEL is now in PNG! I wonder if it sounds good to attach a name of another sovereign nation to a PNG political party. Basing your policies on platforms is OK with me but on a name? Don't tarnish PNG politics with this name" (*National,* December 6, 2007, emphasis in original). Not only has another sovereign nation become the moral center of the Mapai party, but in doing so, the Mapai Levites have also displaced Melanesia as a unifying force. Unity, for the Mapai Levites, comes from the different ways in which people work to create indexical connections to Israelites, contemporary or ancient, rather than from their local traditions. Or, in the forms used by the Guhu-Samane and other Papua New Guinean groups, local traditions become legitimate places for moral unification only when they are given a capacity to draw indexical connections to Israel. Critique within a political process is used to magnify and reify these indexical connections. Mapai Levites see the brutal force of Levite priests ("ruthless in matters when relating to God's Covenant") as the proper basis of political critique in a quest to create a moral Christian future.

One can see this conflict between the Israelite and Melanesian forms of political unity even in the logos used to identify political parties. In the Mapai Levites logo, there is a flag of Papua New Guinea amended to hold a menorah, the sign of Judaism, rather than the southern cross and bird of paradise, which are the official symbols of Papua New Guinea and its place in a political world dominated by Australia and New Zealand (which also have the southern cross on their flags). The Mapai Levites logo, following Zechariah 4—which is cited on the logo—depicts olive branches and a container of oil. It also includes a phrase about the origins of all actions: "Not by might nor by power, but by God's spirit" (Zec 4:6). In contrast to this, we can look to the Melanesian Alliance Party logo: a traditional Papua New Guinean with handheld drum, native body coverings and decorations, and a coconut tree near the sea shore. Here is the old model of adaptation, which asked that indigenous culture be used to look toward a new horizon of independence that would unify society. Surrounding this traditional character are slogans from the independence era, using the two colonial lingua francas originally imagined as the languages through which to unite an ethnically disparate people, Tok Pisin and Hiri Motu (although note they can't even decide on one lingua franca). In the two languages, it says "we ourselves" or "just us," meaning "we can do it on our own!" a message of self-empowerment. The Mapai Levites, in contrast, find in God a vengeful power with which to tear down the desecrations that postindependence society has brought. Rather than traditional culture being the warrant for authentic modernity, Lost Tribes discourses and Israelite models of critique are the warrant for future moral transformations.

. . .

In this chapter, I have tried to demonstrate how critique is used in a somewhat paradoxical way to foster unity. And indeed, critique does develop and exacerbate divisions, creating the need for more critical efforts at unification. This process of Christian schism includes not only Guhu-Samane denominationalism but also denominationalism in numerous other contexts, particularly of Pentecostal Christianity (Meyer 1999; Jebens 2006; Errington and Gewertz 1995; Wishlade 1965). Guhu-Samane have been able to find a multiplicity of models of unity in their engagements with Christianity. One important model for unity is the Pauline interpretation of Judaism, which was potentially redeemable if Jews could throw off their cultural rules, like circumcision. Indeed, not only is this a model, as I have shown, it is now a reality—Guhu-Samane and other Papua New Guinean groups are making themselves into the ancient Jews. The Lost Tribes model puts the possibility of unity into sacred discourse: even if unity isn't working out now, we can hope that it still might work out in the future. It is in this mode of the potential that unity seems achievable. Above and beyond denominational confrontations about the morality of traditional culture, Guhu-Samane people from all different denominations think about the possibilities of the Lost Tribes connection.

As Asif Agha has discussed, anthropologists of kinship misidentified their object of study when they tried to construct a universal basis for kinship. For Agha and others concerned with the recuperation of kinship as an anthropological topic, the real targets are the local models (in the plural) that people use to create connections of relatedness, and the ways that these models are transformed over time. Two innovative ways of constituting relatedness are being developed simultaneously in Guhu-Samane communities. First, people engaged in Reformed Gospel church discourses are starting to see ego-centric genealogies not as modes of potential access to land or other resources, but rather as a mode through which the potential access to the greatest resource—God—is denied. Ego-centric genealogies of ancestral sinfulness then have to be renounced. At the same time, a socio-centric or ethnic mode of connection—one with an entirely different set of technologies for proving relatedness—is being formed in order to salvage some sense of genealogies as modes of potential accretion of rights. Ethnic genealogies about the Lost Tribes are not formed through performances in which one names a series of specific ancestors, as in land claims or even in the renunciative rituals of the Body of Christ crusade. Ethnic Lost Tribes genealogies are formed through the identification of lexical and archeological connections. If ethnic connections can be made to a community that local people see as having gone through a successful conversion to Christianity, then not only can Guhu-Samane religious unity be established but genealogy can become yet again a mode of potential securing of rights and access—in this case to God and salvation. Where a number of other anthropologists of Christianity have focused on either the renunciation of the social or the celebration of it, I have presented here a model of a denominational dialectic that accounts for both of these moments.

Unfortunately for the Mapai Levites political party, none of the sixteen candidates that they fielded in the 2007 parliamentary elections won a seat. The Lost Tribes is, as I noted, an *emerging* discourse of political mobilization. Nevertheless, this project of Christian critique, which seems to create so many denominational divisions at the level of the ethnic group, produces a platform from which to organize with others at a supra-ethnic level. Christianity—with its denominational divisions—is not hindering the formation of a public and a way to organize, as it is so often depicted as doing in secularist Western discourses, but it is actually producing a way for people to recognize one another across ethnic, linguistic, and denominational boundaries: being lost is way to be found.

In 2014 the speaker of Parliament, Theo Zurenuoc, decided that the ornamental carvings on the Parliament building had been allowing demonic forces to guide members of Parliament toward corruption and other sins. The building, which is modeled on a Sepik River men's house, had a wooden lintel carved with the heads of anthropomorphic spirits. Zurenuoc had the lintel taken down, cut in half with a chain saw, and thrown in the trash behind Parliament. In its place he has proposed what he calls the Unity Pole, a Christianization of local totem poles, on which the word "unity" is inscribed in all of the over eight hundred languages of Papua New Guinea (for more on this controversy, see Schram 2014; Eves et al. 2014). For Zurenuoc and his supporters, purges of traditional cultural artifacts can recapitulate the spiritual work of covenant keeping that Jews engage in. Ethnicity, culture, and language are all the sites of transformation, the necessary mediations of difference that constitute the critical, remnant church.

Notes

INTRODUCTION

1. The organization Jews for Jesus performs outreach to Jews to have them recognize Jesus as the Messiah. Although it now works at an international level, it began in the early 1970s in San Francisco, CA, and was part of the counter-cultural movement that produced a number of new forms of religious practice. Despite the fact that many other Jews consider Jews for Jesus to be Christians, Jews for Jesus do not consider themselves Christians, nor do they consider themselves to have converted. At the same time, some work with Christian organizations.

2. Gabriel spoke in English, but other people involved in the event translated his comments. Guhu-Samane Christians speak the local vernacular, also called Guhu-Samane, and most speak Tok Pisin, the English-based creole lingua franca of Papua New Guinea. Some people with high school diplomas read English, and many people have English-language Bibles, regardless of their level of competence. I address the linguistic situation in more detail later in this introduction.

3. I should emphasize that this summary of Gabriel's sermon comes from several independent Guhu-Samane reports. Gabriel himself might characterize his comments in different terms.

4. On cargo cults more generally, see Burridge 1960; Lawrence 1964; Worsley 1957; for critiques of this category, see Jebens 2004; Kaplan 1995; Lattas 1998; Lindstrom 1993.

5. The sociology of religion might be the only social science subdiscipline that has an interest in Christians organized into groups; unfortunately, these scholars engage in a reductionism that sees religious groups as stand-ins for other demographic forms, as groups competing in a spiritual "market," or else as evolutionary survivals in the quest for solace at times of tragedy (see Finke

and Stark 2005; Bainbridge 1997 for good examples). In other words, Christianity as such does not survive the analysis.

6. H. Richard Niebuhr (1894–1962) is perhaps less well known than his older brother, Reinhold Niebuhr. H. Richard Niebuhr was a prominent member of what is known as the Yale School of "postliberal" theology.

7. Nevertheless, Augustine, in the end, supported acts of state violence against the Donatists (themselves prone to violence) in order to finally suppress this schismatic group.

8. These data come from the Ethnologue entry for Guhu-Samane (www.ethnologue.com/language/ghs).

1. SACRED SPEAKERS OR SACRED GROUPS

1. Mark Mosko's recent (2010) critique of the anthropology of Christianity can generously be understood as Papua New Guinea–inspired realizations that individuals are overly emphasized in much current scholarship. However, Mosko's response misses the mark by ignoring any individualist values in Papua New Guinean Christianity. I address Mosko's position in more detail in chapter 4.

2. There is a slightly different literature on the bodily aspects of Christian worship worth mentioning here (e.g., Lester 2005; Cannell 2005; see also Hirschkind 2006). Cutting the modernist world into a different dualism of mind v. body rather than group v. individualized subject, this literature works against the sacred speaking subject by focusing on the corporeal aspects of worship and belief. However, in the cases cited above, the body becomes the unstructured and unconstrained site of immediacy in contrast to the structured mediations of language, in the same way that the speaking subject is the asocial unit of salvation and belief in contrast to social groups in the literature discussed previously. This newer focus on the body also leaves little room for discussions of the sociality of Christian worship. So, for example, when Pickstock (2010) argues for thinking about performance of the liturgy in bodily terms, she also moves her attention from structured "congregations" to unstructured "masses" and "crowds."

3. The mainline missions mostly abided by gentlemen's agreements about mission territories. The Lutherans controlled most of the territory from Madang east to the British/Australian Papuan border, while the Catholic Society of the Divide Word worked from Madang west to the border with (then Dutch-controlled) West Papua. There was something of a free-for-all scramble when the interior areas started to open up after WWI.

4. Wilhelm Flierl (a son of the original Lutheran missionary, Johannes Flierl) appears to have been the only missionary on staff when the memorandum was written who was both born in New Guinea and old enough to be considered a "senior missionary" (see the list of missionaries at end of Frerichs 1959). The fact that the memorandum includes anecdotes and facts mostly about Kâte also points toward Wilhelm Flierl's authorship, since he was one of the primary missionaries who developed Kâte-language materials (Reitz 1975, 32).

5. It is clear that the first term in each of the examples is reduplicated (*ju-ju, go-go, kep-kep, ande-ande,* etc.). In the Guhu-Samane and Yopno cases the reduplicated forms are variants of the existential verb *to be.* I would assume that this morpho-syntactic uniformity comes from Lutheran imposition, as a calque of the Kâte form, but it is possible that these forms predate Lutheran intervention.

6. That is, the Evangelical Lutheran Church of New Guinea, the institutional heir of the Lutheran Mission New Guinea that was formed in 1956 to develop an autonomous and independent church.

7. I discuss Donald McGavran and the Church Growth movement in more detail in the next chapter.

8. SIL publications describe members' work specifically in terms of providing a sense of "linguistic self-esteem" for minority language speakers. See, for example, Kenneth Pike's remembrance of his own work in these terms (www.sil.org /about/klp/publications/my-pilgrimage-mission/formal-study-of-linguistics).

2. LINGUISTIC LOCALITY AND THE ANTI-INSTITUTIONALISM OF EVANGELICAL CHRISTIANITY

1. In terms of the twentieth-century political and religious landscape of the United States, the missionaries and theologians I discuss in this chapter would largely be considered conservative (although see Aldridge 2012 and below for a discussion of SIL as one of the least conservative of the major evangelical groups in the twentieth century). Unless otherwise indicated, when I use the term *liberal* in this chapter I refer to the commitment to engage in noncoercive critical debates that (ideally) end in conversion, rather than to a specific place on a liberal/conservative spectrum.

2. "Translation," from an undated document, "Introduction to the Basic Principles of Wycliffe Bible Translators, Inc." in the SIL PNG archives. (The biblical references are: "milk of the word," 1 Pt 2:2; "sword of the spirit . . ." Eph 6:17; "word of God which liveth and abideth forever," 1 Pt 1:23, all from the King James Version.)

3. Eugene Nida (United Bible Society), R. Daniel Shaw (Fuller Seminary), and Sherwood Lingenfelter (Fuller Seminary) all spent time working with or as members of SIL. Tom Headland (SIL) has spent time at Fuller, where McGavran's School of World Missions is located (now known as the School for Intercultural Studies). Aldridge (2012, 95) argues that SIL's summer camps, in fact, helped to pave the way for more academic approaches to missions, and indeed helped pave the way for the School of World Missions. Every SIL member has to have a BA from a secular or Bible college, and quite a few have degrees from Fuller, although I have no statistics on this. There are other, less formal, ways in which demonstrate the ongoing influence of Fuller thinkers. For example, while I was visiting SIL headquarters in Papua New Guinea, I was at a well-attended event where the audience listened to a tape of a lecture by Fuller's Daniel Shaw and had a lively debate about it afterward.

4. John Kelly (2003) outlines a very similar stance among American foreign-policy makers in this era. Arguing against calling the United States an "empire,"

Kelly says that Americans never had imperial ambitions in the sense of actually colonizing major swatches of the world. Instead, they wanted to create "open-door" policies that would allow the United States economic and political access to other countries. In the case of the church growth movement, one could say that "culture" became the route to opening religious doors.

5. Although there is some similarity here to the language of Darwinian evolution, the missionary sense of human cultural adaptation to local contexts is not evolutionary in a strict sense. Humans are united (and unchanging) in having a particular set of universal features, like a propensity for sin and a capacity for salvation, which other organisms do not have. A more likely reference point for this kind of environmental determinism would be Montesquieu (1989), who argued that different systems of government could be traced in part to the effects of local climate.

6. "Pioneers," from an undated document, "Introduction to the Basic Principles of Wycliffe Bible Translators, Inc." in the SIL PNG archives. On the relationship between Wycliffe and SIL, see below.

7. These statistics are from SIL International's Information Sheet, www .sil.org/sites/default/files/sil-intl-info-english-letter.pdf.

8. SIL does occasionally work in areas where Christian missionization is not allowed. In these cases, work is limited to literacy training and linguistics, and Bible translation is not part of the job.

9. Entry for Friday, 6 July in "Daily Report of Activities of Dick Pittman, Bill Oates and Jim Dean since Leaving Melbourne on Monday 23 June, 1956" found in SIL PNG archives. A similar agnosticism about the future life of languages is present in Pike's (1959) discussion of SIL policy to readers of *The Bible Translator*.

10. "Notes on answers given by Dr. J. Dean to questions asked about the SIL program," Lutheran Conference Minutes 1960, 59. Material between quotation marks are, I assume, direct quotes from Dean's talk, while material outside the quotation marks are summaries by the person taking minutes. Note that members of SIL are identified in this document as "Wycliffe Bible Translators of the Summer Institute of Linguistics."

11. As Aldridge notes, many other evangelical missionaries also do not consider SIL translators proper missionaries either, seeing them as spending too much time trying to maintain scientific credentials. With professional linguists often renouncing SIL members as poor linguists and evangelical missionaries often renouncing SIL members as poor missionaries, SIL can often seem to have a confused identity—neither fish nor fowl.

12. Just as linguistics has moved away from anthropology toward cognitive science, SIL translation theories have moved away from Nida's dynamic equivalence model toward what are known as "relevance" models (Gutt 1991) that are based on cognitive and psychological principles (Sperber and Wilson 1986). In that sense, this is a discussion specifically about SIL in the middle and late twentieth century.

13. After Nida and his protégé William Wonderly left SIL for the United Bible Society, SIL developed a faith statement that allowed for three different opinions on literalism. Rather than answer the problem in a single, united way,

the SIL organization allows members a good deal of latitude, and in doing so, allows for these tensions to remain (Aldridge 2012, 115).

14. SIL's sense that literacy is a neutral technology is contradicted in B. Schieffelin's work (1996, 2000, see also citations there).

3. TRANSLATING LOCALITY

1. The boundary splitting the eastern half of New Guinea island was determined by the Anglo-German compromise of 1885 and was drawn on paper to give Britain and Germany equal territory. The actual boundary remained mysterious for several decades, and the 1909 Mixed Boundary Commission was one of the first attempts to mark the boundary on the ground (van der Veur 1966, 126–27).

2. A chart in MOROBE report 4 of 50/51 shows the locations of all men working outside the area from this patrol area. 51 percent of Lower Waria and 85 percent of Upper Waria men absent were in Wau and Lae, but only 37 percent of Middle Waria labor absentees were in Wau or Lae, and the other 63 percent were scattered widely across the Territories.

3. Letter dated 19 August 1957, Haviland to Murphy, MOROBE report 4 of 56/57.

4. "The History and Growth of SIL in New Guinea," undated, unpaginated, in the SIL archives in PNG.

5. Soon after this, other SIL teams were allocated in the Waria region, with Maurice and Helen Boxwell working with the Weri (Upper Waria) language group; Alan Pence, Doris Bjorkman, and Elaine Geary working with the Gadzili (Bubu/Kunimaipan) language group; and Raymond and Marjorie Dubert working with the Biangai language group (a Kunimaipan group living close to Wau town, but still within the original boundaries of the Lutheran Zaka Circuit).

6. The model of the married SIL team at that time was that the man was the main translator while the woman was primary caregiver to the couple's children. Marjorie Richert, known as Margarita to the Guhu-Samane people, took a back seat to her larger-than-life husband, although she learned the Guhu-Samane language and later taught sewing, hygiene, and home economics classes for the wives of Ernie's translation helpers in the academy that Ernie started. Note that SIL allows for teams of unmarried, childless women in addition to married couple teams. In fact, the third and fourth allocations to Eastern Highlands communities, just before the Richerts, were two teams of single women. In the contemporary cases I am familiar with, one woman will tend to focus on translation, and the other will focus on literacy programs.

7. I do not have access to Richert's papers, if any still exist. SIL does not archive the personal papers of their translators. This sketch of Richert's activities comes from interviews with Guhu-Samane people and some SIL members who knew him, as well as from an examination of his published works.

8. See, for example, GARAINA 1 of 72/73 for a list of Papuan Waria villages with SIL literacy classes.

9. I will discuss this connection between peace and Christianity more in chapter 5.

10. Zaka Bericht ueber das erste Hallbjahr 1924, Rev. Karl Mailander, in the archives at the Ampo Lutheran Center, Lae, PNG.

11. Burce (1983, chap. 10) discusses the ways in which the revivalists used their Academy Morse code training to interact with Jesus. For them, the Academy's selection of courses was not nearly as contingent as it may have been for Richert.

12. Lutheran Mission Annual Conference Minutes 1960, 5.

13. I base this list on the examples provided by Richert in his 1965a article on translation. Mark was the first gospel Richert translated. The order of the epistles is less clear, but he probably would have started with James's epistle rather than any of the ones by Paul.

14. The only other SIL New Guinea member who published in the SIL International series *Notes on Translation* during the 1960s was Ellis W. Deibler, who worked in the Eastern Highlands on Gahuku (see Deibler 1966, 1967). Richert does not appear to have had much of a leadership role in linguistics (as opposed to his translation work), nor does he appear to have spent much time on his linguistic work (for example, his linguistics papers were not published until after a good deal of the translation work was done, see Richert 1975, Richert and Richert 1972). Ken McElhanon, Karl Franklin, Alan Healey, Alan Pence, and Bruce Hooley were the guiding lights of SIL New Guinea linguistics, and all had prominent roles in academic research on non-Austronesian languages.

15. Lutheran Mission, Zaka Circuit, Annual Report, 1958.

16. J.B. Phillips was an Anglican minister who produced a translation of Paul's letters (1947) that was aimed at younger British speakers in the post-WWII period. It is written in colloquial British English, since Phillips felt that the King James Bible was not able to "speak" to these Christians or potential Christians. Phillips's translation into contemporary language has continued to be a model for domesticating Bible translators. Contemporary Bibles aimed at American children that are formatted to look and read like teen magazines owe their existence to Phillips's original *Letters to Young Churches*.

17. Like Inoue's (2006) discussion of "women's speech" in Japan, it is possible to quote something that, in fact, did not exist prior to the moment of quotation; that is, to bring the source text into existence in quoting from it.

18. Remember that dynamic equivalence translation theory suggests that source-text sentences have to be deconstructed to make verbal arguments (agents, patients, etc.) overt or to put sentences in logical or sequential order. This gets the translator to the underlying message of the source text, which is, as Richert put it, "occasioned by" the actual source text. In the example below, I provide the Guhu-Samane New Testament receptor text with interlinear glosses and English back-translation, an English text (the NIV) with which to compare the Guhu-Samane translation, and Richert's account of "the underlying message" of the source text (or my best reconstruction of what Richert was using as that "underlying message." Note that Richert's source text would have been Koiné Greek, used in consultation with English and Kâte translations.

Abbreviations used in interlinear glosses are: 1, 2, 3—number; AUX—auxiliary verb; ADJ—adjective; COMP—complementizer; DEM—demonstrative; DS—different subject; EMPH—emphatic; FUT—future; GEN—genitive;

IMP—imperative; INCL—inclusive; INF—infinitive; IRREAL—irrealis; LOC—ocative; NEG—negation; OBJ—object; PAST—past tense; PL—plural; PRES—present tense; PROG—progressive; QUOT—quotative; SER—serial verb; SG—singular; SS—same subject; SUB—subject. In the Guhu-Samane orthography, doubled vowels indicate length, 'q' is used for a glottal stop, and 'tt' is used for a voiceless dental stop.

4. REVIVAL VILLAGES

1. Because these are stories that are used in land claims and are circulated only very carefully, I do not provide full transcripts or summaries of clan migration histories.

2. Almost comically short versions of these post-death events are held for relatively unimportant men. Not long after Bernard's death, another man in the village died one morning while he was bathing in the nearby river. Unlike Bernard, this man was considered a *rabisman* (TP, "man without standing"), and his funeral services reflected that. Between roughly 10 a.m., when his body was found at the river, and 6:30 p.m., when he was buried, people rushed through the important steps, starting with a brief moment of ritual wailing from women of the clan he married into, a small distribution of cooked food to his clan, a quick sermon and Christian blessing over his body, and a final sprint to the hastily prepared grave in the nearby cemetery.

3. *Crusade* is a local term roughly equivalent to *tent revival*. I keep the local terminology to avoid confusion with the 1977 revival.

4. As I discuss in later chapters, New Life members distinguish themselves as truly inspired by the Holy Spirit by refusing to recognize Bible college credentials from the religious institutions in urban Papua New Guinea. Ulysses prides himself on not being an educated man, but simply a religiously devoted one. Part of this pride in the locality and sacrality of the Guhu-Samane language and institutions might have also made him reluctant to speak in Tok Pisin in front of a crowd.

5. Throughout the chapter, I look at different segments of this very long speech. Each segment is numbered individually, although the segments are presented here mostly in the order in which they appeared. Lines are broken by breath groups; square brackets provide necessary contextual information; false starts are indicated by a dash; the audience backchannel of *dzoobe* (GS, thank you) is in parenthesis. In this text, all instances of *we* or *us* are INCLUSIVE unless otherwise noted. Portions of the speech delivered in Tok Pisin are unmarked, while lines in Guhu-Samane are underlined.

5. THE SURPRISE OF SPEECH

1. But see http://peterbergen.com/the-madrassa-scapegoat, which reports that, contrary to the claim that madrasa-based rote learning leads to violence, perpetrators of the most violent terrorist attacks against US targets have been on average more highly educated than the general American public and have usually been educated in European or American institutions of higher learning.

2. As I discuss in chapter 4, stereotypical clan imagery is a clan on the road, either in terms of clan stories about migratory pathways, in fondly remembered images of long lines of clanspeople walking on a path wearing identically

painted clan insignia on their bark-cloth capes, or in genealogical knowledge that details the movements of generations of women.

3. Noting the similarities to biblical stories, Jesus as Lamb of God is sometimes referred to as the *Hoo Dzoba*, "the [sacrificial] Roast Pig" of God.

4. Indeed, Richert's power extended to being able to change the valley itself. On several occasions, people spoke of forest spirits that had not been seen since Richert arrived in the 1950s.

5. Undoubtedly people could make similar accusations against me, since I (following my own cultural script) ran to get Tylenol and Neosporin in a rather lame attempt to help the young woman myself.

6. Land ownership is a complex issue deserving more space than I can give it here. Briefly, Guhu-Samane recognize several levels of ownership. As nineteenth-century migrants from the coast, nobody (with one clan as an exception) is autochthonous; however, there are clans that are recognized as having come first to an area, as well as clans that married into the original clan. The original clan, which has the greatest rights over the land, is called the *ee gotta* (GS, tree trunk), while the later clans are called *bidzaga* (GS, parasites—as in the mushrooms that bloom on top of a felled tree trunk). People recognize up to three or four mushroom clans for a given piece of ground. In this dispute, Isaac was claiming that his matri-clan, not the matri-clan of the garden-builders, was the tree-trunk owner of the land.

7. Men who had been to translators training courses at SIL talked about spending an entire night debating against the rest of the (Highlands) students about lineality: should people be matrilineal (*bihainim mama,* TP) or patrilineal (*bihainim papa,* TP)? They reported that they were able to convince the patrilineal highlanders that matrilineality is not only better, it is the only right way to do things, since, of course, you can actually see a woman who is pregnant and who then gives birth, while paternity can always be fudged.

8. As of 2014, Sean has started to organize committees to get going on some of this dialect translation work.

9. This prayer was conducted mostly in Tok Pisin, largely for the benefit of my husband and me (as in Robbins's 2001 analysis, we were "ratified overhearers"). On the relationship between Guhu-Samane, Tok Pisin, and English as sacred languages, see chapter 6.

6. EVENTS OF TRANSLATION

1. "Text" here refers to both published works ("text artifacts") as well as segments of speech in interaction.

2. Pituro was ordained as a nondenominational evangelical reverend when Ernest Richert sponsored his studies in the United States in the early 1980s.

3. Reverend Pituro's ordination is a special case, since it was organized by the translator Richert and thus still part of the process of localization created through the translation.

4. I will analyze one of these gatherings in chapter 8.

5. In this transcript, Tok Pisin is unmarked, Guhu-Samane is single-underlined, and English is double-underlined. Bible quotations and voicings thereof are indented.

6. I omitted several lines of text in which Pastor Bosepo hesitates before reading the Bible verse.

7. Popular choices include the Christian Leaders' Training College in Banz, Western Highlands Province, and the Lighthouse Bible College in Madang, Madang Province.

8. Given this emphasis in Christian practice on the roles of foreignness and locality, my own attendance in church services and at other events was frequently commented upon, but in ways that should be very familiar at this point. I was a white person coming into the local situation, following in the footsteps of the Richerts and other (post)colonial whites for New Life members; I was, as one Reformed Gospel pastor suggested, a visitor and "not from here," just like Christians are also visitors to "this land" and really from heaven.

7. MEDIATING DENOMINATIONAL DISPUTES

1. Niebuhr is by no means the only author to have such a generationally focused sense of religious renewal. Donald McGavran, the founder of the highly influential church growth movement in American evangelical missiology (discussed in chapter 2), suggests that in convert societies, generational revivals would be the only way to ensure a spirit-guided, proper Christianity (i.e., one that did not descend into syncretism or cultism). See McGavran 1970. It might also be worth mentioning here that in the realm of secular liberalism, a generational renewal model also exists. Thomas Paine believed that proper democracies would have to throw out all laws every thirty years so that government could keep pace with the will of the people.

2. This is where it is hard to conjoin the state-sponsored version of Garasa's origins with Ulysses's version. One the one hand, the local Council boasted of his allocation of funds to constituents. With such a visible sign of external authority for this project, why would people laugh at the New Life members building the airstrip? But, on the other hand, given what was then forty years of unfulfilled state promises for a road, local skepticism about this project's completion might be understandable.

3. It is not uncommon for SIL teams to become frustrated with SIL's hands-off, translation-only model of Christian evangelism, and there are a number of groups, like PIM, that are composed of ex-SIL workers interested in different kinds of missionary methods.

4. "Tribe" and its Tok Pisin calque, *traib,* do not have any well-established equivalents in Guhu-Samane. Some of this importation of anthropological terms seems to be coming from state-mediated land claims, where terms like *tribe, clan,* and *sub-clan* are in circulation. Both *tribe* and *sub-clan* have been given local Guhu-Samane definitions that are quite distinct from standard anthropological uses (if any exist).

5. Richert did include one of his own Guhu-Samane language compositions in the booklet, to be sung to the tune of "Row, Row, Row Your Boat."

6. Many of Robbins's comments (2004a, 266–67) about the rituals of hand-shaking hold for Guhu-Samane as well. Among Yopno speakers living on the Morobe/Madang border, where I also spent time, handshaking has become so

integrated with (Lutheran) Christianity that people generally shake hands with three separate pumps, "for Father, Son, and Holy Spirit."

7. This man was also a *maripa* and thus was structurally well placed to take on this "cool" religion.

8. The only time I heard boys singing Christian songs was when I invited a group of girls over to help me record and transcribe lyrics to the Guhu-Samane verses of the songs sung in church. The boys stood outside the house, belting out verses. But this might have had as much to do with the excitement of hanging out with the anthropologist and drinking lots of tea as with wanting to sing.

8. KINSHIP, CHRISTIANITY, AND CULTURE CRITIQUE

1. These include Lutheran Reformed, Lutheran Renewal, Assemblies of God, Church of Christ, Associated Local Church, Four Square, and Seventh-Day Adventist.

2. In the transcript below, each line break is a pause or change in intonation. Quoted speech is indented once. Statements said in a louder voice have an exclamation point at the end; statements that are said in a very loud voice are in all-caps. Information or context necessary for my translation from Jordan's Tok Pisin text is in square brackets.

3. Note that Satan has a cognatic model of sinful connection.

4. The story of the lost tribes as discussed in the Bible can be summarized as follows: The twelve tribes of Israel were divided into a northern kingdom of ten tribes and a southern kingdom of two. When Assyrian kings invaded the northern kingdom around 700 BC (in 732 and 721 BC) they carried these ten tribes into exile (2 Kings 17). These are the ten "lost" tribes, which later became important in the prophetic books (e.g., Isaiah and Jeremiah) in which the reunion with the lost tribes would be a harbinger of the final redemption of Israel. References to them are scarce in the Bible, although these sources were later augmented with various "sightings" of and correspondence with the lost tribes in early European history (Parfitt 2002).

5. "To the Jews I became like a Jew, to win the Jews. To those under the law I became like one under the law (though I myself am not under the law), so as to win those under the law." (1 Cor 9:20, New International Version)

6. Ben-Gurion's Mapai Party was a specifically secular one. The pairing of the Mapai name with that of Jewish priests is thus a particular innovation of on the part of these Papua New Guinean actors.

References

ARCHIVAL SOURCES

Archives at the Ampo Lutheran Center, Lae, PNG

Zaka Bericht ueber das erste Hallbjahr 1924, Rev. Karl Mailander.

Archives at the Martin Luther Seminary, Lae, PNG

1953 Annual Report, Zaka Circuit, Missionary Schuster
1957 Annual Report, Zaka Circuit, Missionary Schuster
1958 Annual Report, Zaka Circuit, Missionary Schuster
1958 Annual Report, Zaka Circuit, Missionary Horndasch
1960 Annual Report, Zaka Circuit, Missionary Horndasch
1961 Annual Report, Zaka Circuit, Missionary Horndasch
1962 Annual Report, Zaka Circuit, Missionary Horndasch
1964 Annual Report, Zaka Circuit, Missionary Horndasch
1964 Annual Report, Zaka-Garaina Circuit, Missionary Dahinten
1948 Minutes of the Lutheran Mission New Guinea Annual Conference
1959 Minutes of the Lutheran Mission New Guinea Annual Conference
1960 Minutes of the Lutheran Mission New Guinea Annual Conference
1961 Minutes of the Lutheran Mission New Guinea Annual Conference
1961 Minutes of the Lutheran Mission New Guinea Annual Conference

Archives at the Summer Institute of Linguistics, Papua New Guinea,
Ukarumpa, Eastern Highlands Province

Daily Report of Activities of Dick Pittman, Bill Oates and Jim Dean since Leaving Melbourne on Monday 23 June, 1956.

Introduction to the Basic Principles of Wycliffe Bible Translators, Inc. n.d. History and Growth of SIL in New Guinea, undated, unpaginated.

Guhu-Samane Literacy Primers, E. Richert, Ukarumpa: SIL

n.d. Ana Hiire 1. [I Say]. 34 pp.
n.d. Noma ma Naka [Little Brother and We Two]. Unpaginated.
1963. Sama Korakora Noo [Health and Hygiene]. 19 pp.
1964. Isaisa Dzooma 1 [Birth reader]. 32 pp.
1964. Isaisa Ttittidzoma 2 [Crawling reader]. 36 pp.
1965. Isaisa Tarama 3 [First-steps reader]. 40 pp.
1965. Isaisa Qooba 4 [Walking reader]. 52 pp.
1965. Isaisa Qeema 5 [Moving reader]. 40 pp.
1965. Isaisa Torouma 6 [Running reader]. 32 pp.
1965. Tunaho Noo [Eagle Talk]. 51 pp.

Papua New Guinea National Archives, Patrol Reports

MOROBE report 3 of 50/51
MOROBE report 4 of 50/51
MOROBE report 5 of 51/52
MOROBE report 2 of 53/54
MOROBE report 1 of 54/55
MOROBE report 1 of 56/57
MOROBE report 4 of 56/57
MOROBE report 2 of 62/63
MOROBE report 3 of 62/63
GARAINA report 5 of 66/67
GARAINA report 1 of 72/73
GARAINA report 2 of 72/73

Paul Kuder Collection, Archives of the Evangelical Lutheran Church of America, Chicago, IL

Kuder Brief to Administration, 1959

SECONDARY SOURCES

Agamben, Giorgio. 2005. *The Time That Remains: A Commentary on the Letter to the Romans*. Stanford, CA: Stanford University Press.
Agha, Asif. 2007. *Language and Social Relations*. Cambridge: Cambridge University Press.
Aldridge, Fredrick. 2012. *The Development of the Wycliffe Bible Translators and the Summer Institute of Linguistics, 1934–1982*. PhD diss., University of Stirling.
Allen, Roland. 1912. *Missionary Methods: St. Paul's or Ours?* Grand Rapids, MI: Eerdmans.
Anderson, Benedict. 1991. *Imagined Communities: Reflections on the Origin and Spread of Nationalism*. London: Verso.

Anonymous. 1966. *Marekoho Isere Qidza ma Dzakopoho Dzaira Pepa. The Gospel of Mark and Epistle of James.* Sydney: British and Foreign Bible Society in Australia.

———. 1974. *Poro Tongo Usaqe. The New Testament in Guhu-Samane.* Lae: The Bible Society of Papua New Guinea.

———. 1978. *New International Version Bible.* Grand Rapids, MI: Zondervan.

———. 1989. *Buk Baibel. The Bible in Tok Pisin.* Port Moresby: The Bible Society of Papua New Guinea.

———. 1999. *Genesis ma Eksodas. Genesis and Exodus in Guhu-Samane.* South Holland, IL: The Bible League.

Asad, Talal. 1986. "The Concept of Translation in British Social Anthropology." In *Writing Culture: The Poetics and Politics of Ethnography,* edited by James Clifford and George E. Marcus, 141–64. Berkeley: University of California Press.

———. 1993. *Genealogies of Religion.* Baltimore, MD: Johns Hopkins University Press.

———. 2003. *Formations of the Secular: Christianity, Islam, Modernity.* Stanford, CA: Stanford University Press.

———. 2013. "Free Speech, Blasphemy, and Secular Criticism." In *Is Critique Secular? Blasphemy, Injury, and Free Speech,* edited by T. Asad, W. Brown, J. Butler, and S. Mahmood, 14–57. New York: Fordham University Press.

Bainbridge, William. 1997. *The Sociology of Religious Movements.* New York: Routledge.

Bakhtin, M.M. 1981. *Dialogic Imagination.* Translated by Caryl Emerson and Michael Holquist. Austin: University of Texas Press.

Barker, John. 1990. "Mission Station and Village: Religious Practice and Representations in Maisin Society." In *Christianity in Oceania,* edited by J. Barker, 173–96. ASAO Monographs. Lanham, MD: University Press of America.

———. 1993. "'We Are Ekelesia': Conversion in Uiaku, Papua New Guinea." In *Conversion to Christianity,* edited by R. Hefner, 199–230. Berkeley: University of California Press.

———. 1996. "Village Inventions." *Oceania* 66 (3): 211–29.

Bateson, Gregory. 1958. *Naven.* Stanford, CA: Stanford University Press.

Battaglia, Debbora. 1990. *On the Bones of the Serpent: Person, Memory, and Mortality in Sabarl Island.* Chicago: University of Chicago Press.

Bauman, Richard, and Charles Briggs. 1990. "Poetics and Performance As Critical Perspectives on Language and Social Life." *Annual Review of Anthropology* 19: 59–88.

Benge, Janet, and Geoff Benge. 2000. *Cameron Townsend: Good News in Every Language.* Seattle: YWAM Publishing.

Benjamin, Walter. 1968a. "The Task of the Translator." In *Illuminations,* edited by Hannah Arendt, 69–82. New York: Schocken Books.

———. 1968b. "Theses on the Philosophy of History." In *Illuminations,* edited by Hannah Arendt, 253–64. New York: Schocken Books.

Besnier, Niko. 1995. *Literacy, Emotion, and Authority: Reading and Writing on a Polynesian Atoll.* Cambridge: Cambridge University Press.

Bialecki, Jon. 2010. "Angels and Grass: Church, Revival, and the Neo-Pauline Turn." *South Atlantic Quarterly* 109 (4): 695–717.

———. 2012. "Virtual Christianity in an Age of Nominalist Anthropology." *Anthropological Theory* 12 (3): 295–319.

Biehl, João. 2005. *Vita: Life in a Zone of Social Abandonment.* Berkeley: University of California Press.

Biehl, João, and Peter Locke. 2010. "Deleuze and the Anthropology of Becoming." *Current Anthropology* 51 (3): 317–51.

Biehl, João, and Amy Moran-Thomas. 2009. "Symptom: Subjectivities, Social Ills, Technologies." *Annual Review of Anthropology* 38: 267–88.

Bielo, James. 2009. *Words upon the Word: An Ethnography of Evangelical Group Bible Study.* New York: New York University Press.

Blommaert, Jan, and Jef Verschueren. 1998. "Nationalist Ideologies." In *Language Ideologies: Practie and Theory,* edited by B. Schieffelin, K. Woolard, and P. Kroskrity, 189–210. Oxford: Oxford University Press.

Bolter, J. David, and Richard Grusin. 2000. *Remediation: Understanding New Media.* Cambridge, MA: MIT Press.

Briggs, Charles, and Richard Bauman. 1992. "Genre, Intertextuality, and Social Power." *Journal of Linguistic Anthropology* 2 (2): 131–72.

Browden, Paul. 2003. "Pentecostalism in Translation: Religion and the Production of Community in the Haitian Diaspora." *American Ethnologist* 30 (1): 85–101.

Brunton, Ron. 1980. "Misconstrued Order in Melanesian Religion." *Man* n.s., 15 (1): 112–28.

BTA Handbook. 1995. Compiled and edited by Bill Martin. Ukarumpa: SIL PNG.

Burce, Amy. 1983. *Knowledge and Work: Ideology, Inequality, and Social Process in the Waria Valley, Papua New Guinea.* PhD diss., Stanford University.

Burrdige, Kennelm. 1960. *Mambu: A Melanesian Millennium.* London: Methuen.

Burt, Ben. 1994. *Tradition and Christianity: The Colonial Transformation of a Solomon Islands Society.* Chur, Switzerland: Harwood Academic Publishers.

Cannell, Fenella. 2005. "The Christianity of Anthropology." *Journal of the Royal Anthropological Institute* 1 (2): 335–56.

———. 2006. "The Anthropology of Christianity." In *The Anthropology of Christianity,* edited by F. Cannell, 1–50. Durham, NC: Duke University Press.

Chakrabarty, Dipesh. 2000. *Provincializing Europe: Postcolonial Thought and Historical Difference.* Princeton, NJ: Princeton University Press.

Chomsky, Noam. 1965. *Aspects of the Theory of Syntax.* Cambridge, MA: MIT Press.

Cohn, Bernard. 1990. "The Command of Language and the Language of Command." In *An Anthropologist among the Historians and Other Essays.* Oxford: Oxford University Press.

Coleman, Simon. 2006. "Words and Gifts in the Construction of Charismatic Pentecostal Identity." In *The Anthropology of Christianity,* edited by F. Cannell, 163–84. Durham, NC: Duke University Press.

Comaroff, Jean, and John Comaroff. 1991. *Of Revelation and Revolution.* Volume 1. Chicago: University of Chicago Press.

Comaroff, John. 2010. "The End of Anthropology, Again: On the Future of an In/Discipline." *American Anthropologist* 112 (4): 524–38.

Cowan, George. 1979. *The Word That Kindles*. Chappaqua, NY: Christian Herald Books.

Crapanzano, Vincent. 1999. *Serving the Word: Literalism in America from the Pulpit to the Bench*. New York: New Press.

Dawkins, Richard. 2008. *The God Delusion*. New York: Houghton Mifflin Harcourt.

Deibler, Ellis. 1966. "Comparative Constructions in Translation." *Notes on Translation* 22: 4–10.

———. 1967. "Back-Translation Helps on James." *Notes on Translation* 25: 5–16.

De Vries, Hent. 2001. "In Media Res." In *Religion and Media,* edited by Hent de Vries and S. Weber, 3–42. Stanford, CA: Stanford University Press.

Dumont, Louis. 1986. *Essays on Individualism: Modern Ideology in Anthropological Perspective*. Chicago: University of Chicago Press.

Dundon, Alison. 2012. "The Gateway to the Fly: Christianity, Continuity, and Spaces of Conversion in Papua New Guinea." In *Flows of Faith: Religious Reach and Community in Asia and the Pacific,* edited by L. Manderson, W. Smith, and M. Tomlinson, 143–59. Dordrecht, Netherlands: Springer.

Durston, Alan. 2004. *Pastoral Quechua: The History of Christian Translation in Colonial Peru, 1550–1650*. South Bend, IN: University of Notre Dame Press.

Eilberg-Schwartz, Howard. 1990. *The Savage in Judaism*. Bloomington: Indiana University Press.

Eisenlohr, Patrick. 2006. *Little India: Time, Diaspora, and Ethnolinguistic Belonging in Hindu Mauritius*. Berkeley: University of California Press.

———. 2009. "Technologies of the Spirit: Devotional Islam, Sound Reproduction and the Dialectics of Mediation and Immediacy in Mauritius." *Anthropological Theory* 9: 273–96.

Elisha, Omri. 2011. *Moral Ambition: Mobilization and Social Outreach in Evangelical Megachurches*. Berkeley: University of California Press.

Engelke, Matthew. 2007. *The Problem of Presence: Beyond Scripture in an African Church*. Berkeley: University of California Press.

Errington, Frederick, and Deborah Gewertz. 1995. *Articulating Change in the "Last Unknown."* Boulder, CO: Westview Press.

Errington, J.J. 2001. "Colonial Linguistics." *Annual Review of Anthropology* 30: 19–39.

Eves, Richard. 2008. *Cultivating Christian Civil Society: Fundamentalist Christianity, Politics and Governance in PNG*. Australian National University: State, Society and Governance in Melanesia.

Eves, Richard, N. Haley, R.J. May, J. Cox, P. Gibbs, F. Merlan, and A. Rumsey. 2014. *Purging Parliament: A New Christian Politics in Papua New Guinea?* Australian National University: State, Society and Governance in Melanesia. Working Paper 2014/1.

Fader, Ayala. 2009. *Mitzvah Girls: Bringing Up the Next Generation of Hasidic Jews in Brooklyn*. Princeton, NJ: Princeton University Press.

Feld, Steven. 1990. *Sound and Sentiment: Birds, Weeping, Poetics, and Song in Kaluli Expression*. Philadelphia: University of Pennsylvania Press.

———. 1991. "Waterfalls of Song: An Accoustemology of Place Resounding in Bosavi, Papua New Guinea." In *Senses of Place,* edited by S. Feld and K. Basso, 91–136. Santa Fe, NM: School of American Research.

Finke, Roger, and Rodney Stark. 2005. *The Churching of America, 1776–1990: Winners and Losers in Our Religious Economy.* New Brunswick, NJ: Rutgers University Press.

Firth, Stewart. 1982. *New Guinea under the Germans.* Carlton, VIC: Melbourne University Press.

Flannery, Wendy. 1983. "Bilip Grup." *Religious Movements in Melanesia Today,* no. 2., edited by W. Flannery and G. Bays, 155–93. Goroka, PNG: Melanesian Institute.

Foster, Robert. 1990. "Nurture and Force-Feeding: Mortuary Feasting and the Construction of Collective Individuals in a New Ireland Society." *American Ethnologist* 17 (3): 431–48.

Foster, Stephen. 1991. *The Long Argument: English Puritanism and the Shaping of New England Culture.* Chapel Hill: University of North Carolina Press.

Foucault, Michel. 1997. "What Is Critique?" In *The Politics of Truth,* edited by S. Lotringer, 41–81. Los Angeles: Semiotexte.

Frerichs, Albert C. 1959. *Anutu Conquers in New Guinea.* Columbus, OH: Wartburg Press.

Gal, Susan. 2003. "Movements of Feminism: The Circulation of Discourses about Women." In *Recognition Struggles and Social Movements,* edited by Barbara Hobson, 93–118. Cambridge: Cambridge University Press.

Gaustad, Edwin, and Leigh Eric Schmidt. 2002. *The Religious History of America.* New York: Harper Collins.

Geertz, Clifford. 1973. *The Interpretation of Cultures.* New York: Basic Books.

Gell, Alfred. 1995. "The Language of the Forest: Landscape and Phonological Iconism in Umeda." In *The Anthropology of Landscape,* edited by E. Hirsch and M. O'Hanlon, 232–54. Oxford: Clarendon Press.

Gifford, Paul. 1998. *African Christianity: Its Public Role.* Bloomington: Indiana University Press.

———. 2004. *Ghana's New Christianity: Pentecostalism in a Globalising African Economy.* Bloomington: Indiana University Press.

Godelier, Maurice. 1986. *The Making of Great Men: Male Domination and Power among the New Guinea Baruya.* Cambridge: Cambridge University Press.

Goffman, Erving. 1981. *Forms of Talk.* Philadelphia: University of Pennsylvania Press.

Gow, Peter. 2006. "Forgetting Conversion: The Summer Institute of Linguistics Mission in the Piro Lived World." In *The Anthropology of Christianity,* edited by F. Cannell, 211–39. Durham, NC: Duke University Press.

Gutt, Ernst-August. 1991. *Translation and Relevance: Cognition and Context.* Oxford: Basil Blackwell.

Habermas, Jurgen. 1991. *The Structural Transformation of the Public Sphere.* Cambridge, MA: MIT Press.

Hallpike, C.R. 1977. *Bloodshed and Vengeance in the Papuan Mountains: The Generation of Conflict in Tauade Society.* Oxford: Clarendon Press.

Halvaksz, Jamon. 2005. *Re-Imagining Biangai Environments: Mining and Conservation in the Wau Bulolo Valley, Papua New Guinea*. PhD diss., University of Minnesota.

———. 2006. Becoming "Local Tourists": Travel, Landscapes and Identity in Papua New Guinea. *Tourist Studies* 6 (2): 99–117.

Handman, Courtney. 2007. "Access to the Soul." In *Consequences of Contact*, edited by M. Makihara and B. Schieffelin, 166–88. Oxford: Oxford University Press.

———. 2010a. "Events of Translation: Intertextuality and Christian Ethno-Theologies of Change among Guhu-Samane, Papua New Guinea." *American Anthropologist* 112 (4): 576–88.

———. 2010b. *Schism and Christianity*. PhD diss., University of Chicago.

Hann, Chris. 2007. "The Anthropology of Christianity per se." *European Journal of Sociology* 48 (3): 383–410.

Hann, Chris, and Hermann Goltz. 2010. "Introduction: The Other Christianity?" In *Eastern Christianities in Anthropological Perspective*, edited by C. Hann and H. Goltz, 1–29. Berkeley: University of California Press.

Harding, Susan. 2000. *The Book of Jerry Falwell: Fundamentalist Language and Politics*. Princeton, NJ: Princeton University Press.

Harkness, Nicholas. 2014. *Songs of Seoul: An Ethnography of Voice and Voicing in Christian South Korea*. Berkeley: University of California Press.

Harries, Patrick. 1987. "The Roots of Ethnicity: Discourse and the Politics of Language Construction in South-East Africa." *African Affairs* 346: 25–52.

Harrison, J. Daniel. 1978. "Community Education among the Guhu-Samanes." *Notes on Literacy* 23: 1–5.

Harrison, Simon. 1985. "Concepts of the Person in Avatip Religious Thought." *Man*, n.s., 20 (1): 115–30.

———. 1993. "The Commerce of Cultures in Melanesia." *Man*, n.s. 28 (1): 139–58.

Haynes, Naomi. 2013. "Egalitarianism and Hierarchy in Copperbelt Religious Practice: On the Social Work of Pentecostal Ritual." Paper presented in the department of social anthropology, University of Bergen.

Healey, Alan. 1968. "English Idioms." *Kivung* 1: 71–108.

Helmreich, Stephen. 2007. "An Anthropologist Underwater: Immersive Soundscapes, Submarine Cyborgs, and Transductive Ethnography." *American Ethnologist* 34 (4): 621–41.

Herder, Johann G. 1966. *Essay on the Origin of Language*. Translated by J. Moran and A. Gode. New York: F. Ungar.

Hill, Jane. 1998. "'Today There Is No Respect': Nostalgia, 'Respect,' and Oppositional Discourse in Mexicano (Nahuatl) Language Ideology." In *Language Ideologies: Practice and Theory*, edited by B. Schieffelin, K. Woolard, and P. Kroskrity, 68–86. Oxford: Oxford University Press.

Hirschkind, Charles. 2006. *The Ethical Soundscape: Cassette Sermons and Islamic Counterpublics*. New York: Columbia University Press.

Inoue, Miyako. 2006. *Vicarious Language: Gender and Linguistic Modernity in Japan*. Berkeley: University of California Press.

Irvine, Judith T., and Susan Gal. 2000. "Language Ideology and Linguistic Differentiation." In *Regimes of Language,* edited by P. Kroskrity, 35–84. Santa Fe, NM: School of American Research.

Jacka, Jerry. 2005. "Emplacement and Millennial Expectations in an Era of Development and Globalization: Heaven and the Appeal of Christianity for the Ipili." *American Anthropologist* 107 (4): 643–53.

Jebens, Holger, ed. 2004. *Cargo, Cult, and Culture Critique.* Honolulu: University of Hawaii Press.

———. 2006. *Pathways to Heaven: Contesting Mainline and Fundamentalist Christianity in Papua New Guinea.* New York: Berghahn Books.

Johnson, Benton. 1963. "On Church and Sect." *American Sociological Review* 28 (4): 539–49.

Jorgensen, Dan. 2005. "Third Wave Evangelism and the Politics of the Global in Papua New Guinea: Spiritual Warfare and the Recreation of Place in Telefolmin." *Oceania* 75 (4): 444–61.

Kant, Immanuel. (1784) 1970. "An Answer to the Question: 'What Is Enlightenment?' *Political Writings,* edited by H.S. Reiss, 54–60. Cambridge: Cambridge University Press.

Kaplan, Martha. 1990. "Meaning, Agency, and Colonial History: Navosavakadua and the 'Tuka' Movement in Fiji." *American Ethnologist* 17 (1): 3–22.

———. 1995. *Neither Cargo Nor Cult: Ritual Politics and the Colonial Imagination in Fiji.* Durham, NC: Duke University Press.

Keane, Webb. 1997. "From Fetishism to Sincerity: Agency, the Speaking Subject, and Their Historicity in the Context of Religious Conversion." *Comparative Studies in Society and History* 39 (4): 674–93.

———. 2007. *Christian Moderns: Freedom and Fetish in the Mission Encounter.* Berkeley: University of California Press.

Kelly, John. 2003. "US Power, After 9/11 and Before It." *Public Culture* 15 (2): 347–69.

Kipp, Rita. 1995. "Conversion By Affiliation: The History of the Karo Batak Protestant Church." *American Ethnologist* 22 (4): 868–82.

Knauft, Bruce. 2002a. *Exchanging the Past: A Rainforest World of Before and After.* Chicago: University of Chicago Press.

———. 2002b. "Trials of the Oxymodern: Public Practice at Nomad Station." In *Critically Modern,* edited B. Knauft, 105–43. Bloomington: Indiana University Press.

Koschade, A. 1967. *New Branches on the Vine.* Minneapolis, MN: Augsburg.

Kraft, Charles. 1979. *Christianity in Culture.* Maryknoll, NY: Orbis Books.

Kulick, Don. 1992. *Language Shift and Cultural Reproduction: Socialization, Self, and Syncretism in a Papua New Guinean Village.* Cambridge: Cambridge University Press.

Latour, Bruno. 1987. *Science in Action.* Translated by C. Porter. Cambridge, MA: Harvard University Press.

———. 1993. *We Have Never Been Modern.* Translated by C. Porter. Cambridge, MA: Harvard University Press.

———. 1999. "The Slight Surprise of Action." In *Pandora's Hope: Essays on the Reality of Science Studies.* Cambridge, MA: Harvard University Press.

Lattas, Andrew. 1998. *Cultures of Secrecy: Reinventing Race in Bush Kaliai Cargo Cults.* Madison: University of Wisconsin Press.

Lawrence, Peter. 1956. "Lutheran Mission Influence on Madang Societies." *Oceania* 27 (2): 73–89.

———. 1964. *Road Belong Cargo: A Study of the Cargo Movement in the Southern Madang District.* Manchester, UK: University of Manchester Press.

Lawson, Stephanie. 2010. "Post-Colonialism, Neo-Colonialism and the 'Pacific Way': A Critique of (Un)Critical Approaches." *State, Society, and Governance in Melanesia* discussion paper 2010 no. 4.

Lee, Benjamin. 1997. *Talking Heads: Language, Metalanguage, and the Semiotics of Subjectivity.* Durham, NC: Duke University Press.

Lehner, Stephen. (1911) 1935. "The Balum Cult of the Bukaua of Huon Gulf, New Guinea." Translated by C. Wedgewood. *Oceania* 5 (3): 338–45.

Lester, Rebecca. 2005. *Jesus in Our Wombs: Embodying Modernity in a Mexican Convent.* Berkeley: University of California Press.

Levi-Strauss, Claude. 1955. *Tristes Tropiques.* Paris: Plon.

Lindstrom, Lamont. 1993. *Cargo Cult: Strange Stories of Desire from Melanesia and Beyond.* Honolulu: University of Hawaii Press.

Locke, John. 1979. *An Essay Concerning Human Understanding.* Edited by P.H. Niddich. Oxford: Clarendon.

———. (1690) 1980. *Second Treatise on Government.* Edited by C.B. Macpherson. Indianapolis: Hackett.

Luhrmann, Tanya. 2001. "Metakinesis: How God Becomes Intimate." *American Anthropologist* 106 (3): 518–28.

———. 2012. *When God Talks Back: Understanding the American Evangelical Relationship with God.* New York: Alfred Knopf.

Mahmoud, Saba. 2001. "Feminist Theory, Embodiment, and the Docile Agent." *Cultural Anthropology* 6 (2): 202–36.

Marsden, George. 1980. *Fundamentalism and American Culture.* Oxford: Oxford University Press.

———. 1987. *Reforming Fundamentalism: Fuller Seminary and the New Evangelicalism.* Grand Rapids, MI: Eerdmans.

Marshall, Ruth. 2009. *Political Spiritualities: The Pentecostal Revolution in Nigeria.* Chicago: University of Chicago Press.

Mauss, Marcel. 1954. *The Gift: Forms and Functions of Exchange in Archaic Societies.* Translated by W.D. Halls. Glencoe, IL: Free Press.

May, R.J., ed. 1982. *Micronationalist Movements in Papua New Guinea.* Canberra: Research School of Pacific Studies, Australian National University.

McArthur, Margaret. 1971. "Men and Spirits in the Kunimaipa Valley." In *Anthropology in Oceania,* edited by L.R. Hiatt and C.J. Jayawardena. Sydney: Angus and Robertson.

———. 2000. *The Curbing of Anarchy in Kunimaipa Society.* Sydney: University of Sydney.

McGavran, Donald. 1955. *The Bridges of God.* New York: Friendship Press.

———. 1963. *Church Growth in Mexico.* Grand Rapids, MI: Eerdmans.

———. 1970. *Understanding Church Growth.* Grand Rapids, MI: Eerdmans.

Merlan, Francesca, and Alan Rumsey. 1991. *Ku Waru: Language and Segmentary Politics in the Western Nebilyer Valley.* Cambridge: Cambridge University Press.

Merry, Sally Engle. 2006. *Human Rights and Gender Violence: Translating International Law into Local Justice.* Chicago: University of Chicago Press.

Meyer, Birgit. 1998. "Make a Complete Break with the Past: Memory and Post-Colonial Modernity in Ghanaian Pentecostal Discourse." *Journal of Religion in Africa* 28 (3): 316–49.

———. 1999. *Translating the Devil: Religion and Modernity among the Ewe in Ghana.* Trenton, NJ: Africa World Press.

———. 2006. "Religious Revelation, Secrecy and the Limits of Visual Representation." *Anthropological Theory* 6 (4): 431–53.

———. 2011. "Mediation and Immediacy: Sensational Forms, Semiotic Ideologies, and the Question of the Medium." *Social Anthropology* 19 (1): 23–39.

Meyer, Birgit, and Annelies Moors, eds. 2006. *Religion, Media, and the Public Sphere.* Bloomington: Indiana University Press.

Mill, J.S. (1859) 1978. *On Liberty.* Indianapolis, IN: Hackett.

Miyazaki, Hirokazu. 2006a. "Economy of Dreams: Hope in Global Capitalism and Its Critiques." *Cultural Anthropology* 21 (2): 147–72.

———. 2006b. *The Method of Hope.* Stanford, CA: Stanford University Press.

Montesquieu, Charles de Secondat. 1989. *The Spirit of the Laws.* Edited by Anne Cohler, Basia Miller, and Harold Stone. Cambridge: Cambridge University Press.

Mosko. Mark. 1983. "Conception, De-Conception, and Social Structure in Bush Mekeo Culture." *The Australian Journal of Anthropology* 14 (1): 24–32.

———. 2010. "Partible Penitents: Dividual Personhood and Christian Practice in Melanesia and the West." *Journal of the Royal Anthropological Institute* 16 (2): 215–40.

Munn, Nancy. 1990. "Constructing Regional Worlds in Experience: Kula Exchange, Witchcraft and Gawan Local Events." *Man* n.s. 25 (1): 1–17.

Narokobi, B. 1983. *The Melanesian Way.* Boroko, PNG: Institute of Papua New Guinea Studies.

Nida, Eugene. 1947. *Bible Translating: An Analysis of Principles and Procedures with Special Reference to Aboriginal Languages.* New York: American Bible Society.

———. 1954. *Customs and Cultures: Anthropology for Christian Missions.* New York: Harper.

———. 1968. *Toward a Science of Translating, with Special Reference to Principles and Procedures Involved in Bible Translating.* Leiden: E.J. Brill.

Niebuhr, H. Richard. 1929. *The Social Sources of Denominationalism.* New York: H. Holt.

Noo Supu [Triglot Dictionary: Guhu-Samane, English, Tok Pisin]. 2002. Ukarumpa, PNG: SIL PNG.

Oates, Lynette Frances. 1992. *Hidden People: How a Remote New Guinea Culture Was Brought Back from the Brink of Extinction.* Claremont, CA: Albatross Books.

O'Neill, Kevin. 2010. *City of God: Christian Citizenship in Postwar Guatemala.* Berkeley: University of California Press.

Ogden, C.K., and I.A. Richards. 1923. *The Meaning of Meaning: A Study of the Influence of Language upon Thought and the Science of Symbolism.* New York: Harcourt, Brace.

Parfitt, Tudor. 2002. *The Lost Tribes of Israel: The History of a Myth.* London: Weidenfeld and Nicolson.

Peirce, C.S. 1998. "What Is a Sign?" In *The Essential Peirce: Selected Philosophical Writings,* edited by the Peirce Edition Project, 4–10. Bloomington: Indiana University Press.

Pence, Alan. 1962. "The Summer Institute of Linguistics in New Guinea." *Oceanic Linguistics* 1: 42–56.

Peters, John Durham. 1999. *Speaking into the Air: A History of the Idea of Communication.* Chicago: University of Chicago Press.

Phillips, J.B. 1947. *Letters to Young Churches: A Translation of the New Testament Epistles.* New York: Macmillan.

Pickstock, C.J.C. 2010. "Liturgy and the Senses." *South Atlantic Quarterly* 109 (4): 719–39.

Pietz, William. 1985. "The Problem of the Fetish, I." *Res: Anthropology and Aesthetics* 9 (Spring): 5–17.

———. 1987. "The Problem of the Fetish, II: The Origin of the Fetish." *Res: Anthropology and Aesthetics* 13 (Spring): 23–45.

———. 1988. "The Problem of the Fetish, IIIa: Bosman's Guinea and the Enlightenment Theory of Fetishism." *Res: Anthropology and Aesthetics* 16 (Autumn): 105–24.

Pike, Kenneth. 1947. *Phonemics: A Technique for Reducing Languages to Writing.* Ann Arbor: University of Michigan Press.

———. 1959. "Our Own Tongue Wherein We Were Born." *The Bible Translator* 10 (2): 3–16.

———. 1967. *Language in Relation to a Unified Theory of the Structure of Human Behavior.* The Hague: Mouton.

Povinelli, Elizabeth. 2002. *The Cunning of Recognition.* Durham, NC: Duke University Press.

Rafael, Vicente. 1993. *Contracting Colonialism: Translation and Christian Conversion in Tagalog Society under Early Spanish Rule.* Durham, NC: Duke University Press.

Reitz, Gerhard. 1975. *The Contributions of the Evangelical Lutheran Church of Papua New Guinea to Papua New Guinea.* Lae, PNG: ELCPNG.

Richert, Ernest. 1963a. "Native Reaction as a Guide to Meaningful Translation." *Notes on Translation* 1(8): 4–7.

———. 1963b. "Suggested New Testament Commentaries." *Notes on Translation* 1 (7): 1–4.

———. 1963c. "Suggested Old Testament Commentaries." *Notes on Translation* 1 (7): 5–6.

———. 1964. "Is Right Always Right?" *Notes on Translation* 1(10): 10–11.

———. 1965a. "How the Guhu-Samane Cult of 'Poro' Affects Translation." *The Bible Translator* 16: 81–87.

————. 1965b. "Multiple Meanings and Concordance." *Notes on Translation* 1(16): 3.

————. 1975. "Sentence Structure of Guhu-Samane." In *Studies in Languages of Central and South-East Papua,* edited by T. E. Dutton, 771–815. Pacific Linguistics C, 29. Canberra: Australian National University.

————. 1977. *Freedom Dynamics: A Unique Rendering of Romans.* Big Bear Lake, CA: The Thinker.

————. n.d. An Introduction to Mid-Waria Grammar. www-01.sil.org/pacific/png/pubs/48970/Guhu-Samane_Mid-Waria_Grammar.pdf.

Richert, Ernest, and Marjorie Richert. 1972. "Phonology of Guhu-Samane." *Te Reo* 15: 45–51.

Richter, Gerhard. 2011. *Afterness: Figures of Following in Modern Thought and Aesthetics.* New York: Columbia University Press.

Robbins, Joel. 1998. "On Reading 'World News': Apocalyptic Narrative, Negative Nationalism and Transnational Christianity in a Papua New Guinea Society." *Social Analysis* 42 (2): 103–30.

————. 2001. "God Is Nothing but Talk: Modernity, Language and Prayer in a Papua New Guinea Society." *American Anthropologist* 103 (4): 901–12.

————. 2003. "What Is a Christian? Notes Toward an Anthropology of Christianity." *Religion* 33 (3): 191–99.

————. 2004a. *Becoming Sinners: Christianity and Moral Torment in a Papua New Guinea Society.* Berkeley: University of California Press.

————. 2004b. "The Globalization of Pentecostal and Charismatic Christianity." *Annual Review of Anthropology* 33: 117–43.

————. 2004c. "On the Critique in Cargo and the Cargo in Critique: Towards a Comparative Anthropology of Critical Practice." In *Cargo, Cult and Culture Critique,* edited by H. Jebens, 243–59. Honolulu: University of Hawaii Press.

————. 2007. "Continuity Thinking and the Problem of Christian Culture: Belief, Times and the Anthropology of Christianity." *Current Anthropology* 48 (1): 5–38.

————. 2012. "Why Is There No Political Theology among the Urapmin?" In *Christian Politics in Oceania,* edited by M. Tomlinson and D. McDougal, 198–210. New York: Berghahn.

Robbins, Joel, and Alan Rumsey. 2008. "Introduction: Cultural and Linguistic Anthropology and the Opacity of Other Minds." *Anthropological Quarterly* 81 (2): 407–20.

Roberts, E. Mei-Li. 2006. *Translating Identities: "Being a Missionary" in Papua New Guinea.* PhD diss., St. Andrews University.

Rosaldo, Michelle Z. 1982. The Things We Do with Words: Ilongot Speech and Speech Act Theory in Philosophy. *Language and Society* 11 (2): 203–37.

Rutherford, Danilyn. 2003. *Raiding the Land of the Foreigners: The Limits of the Nation on an Indonesian Frontier.* Princeton, NJ: Princeton University Press.

————. 2006. The Bible Meets the Idol: Writing and Conversion in Biak, Irian Jaya, Indonesia. In *The Anthropology of Christianity,* edited by F. Cannell, 240–72. Durham, NC: Duke University Press.

Sahlins, Marshall. 1963. "Poor Man, Rich Man, Big-Man, Chief: Political Types in Melanesia and Polynesia." *Comparative Studies in Society and History* 5 (3): 285–303.

———. 1985. *Islands of History.* Chicago: University of Chicago Press.

———. 1991. "The Return of the Event, Again." In *Clio in Oceania: Toward a Historical Anthropology,* edited by Aletta Biersack, 37–100. Washington, DC: Smithsonian Institution Press.

———. 2004. "Culture and Agency in History." In *Apologies to Thucydides: Understanding History as Culture and Vice Versa,* 125–94. Chicago: University of Chicago Press.

Sanneh, Lamin. 1989. *Translating the Message: The Missionary Impact on Culture.* Maryknoll, NY: Orbis Books.

Schieffelin, Bambi. 1996. "Creating Evidence: Making Sense of Written Words in Bosavi." In *Interaction and Grammar,* edited by E. Ochs, E. Schegloff, and S. Thompson, 435–60. Cambridge: Cambridge University Press.

———. 2000. "Introducing Kaluli Literacy." In *Regimes of Language,* edited by P. Kroskrity, 293–327. Santa Fe, NM: School for American Research Press.

———. 2002. "Marking Time: The Dichotomizing Discourse of Multiple Temporalities." *Current Anthropology* 43 (s4): S5–S17.

———. 2007. "Found in Translating: Reflexive Language across Time and Texts in Bosavi, Papua New Guinea." In *Consequences of Contact,* edited by M. Makihara and B. Schieffelin, 140–65. Oxford: Oxford University Press.

———. 2008. "Speaking Only Your Own Mind: Reflections on Talk, Gossip, and Intentionality in Bosavi, PNG." *Anthropological Quarterly* 81 (2): 431–41.

———. Forthcoming. "Language Ideologies and Chronotopes in Christian Contexts." *Current Anthropology* 55 (s10).

Schieffelin, Edward. 1991. *Like People You See in a Dream: First Contact in Six Papuan Communities.* Stanford, CA: Stanford University Press.

Schram, Ryan. 2014. "A New Government Breaks with the Past in the Papua New Guinea Parliament's 'Haus Tambaran.'" www.materialworldblog .com/2014/02/a-new-government-breaks-with-the-past-in-the-papua-new-guinea-parliaments-haus-tambaran.

Scott, James. 1998. *Seeing Like a State: How Certain Schemes to Improve the Human Condition Have Failed.* New Haven, CT: Yale University Press.

Scott, M. 2007. *The Severed Snake: Matrilineages, Making Place, and a Melanesian Christianity in Southeast Solomon Islands.* Durham, NC: Carolina Academic Press.

Shoaps, R. 2002. "'Pray Earnestly': The Textual Construction of Personal Involvement in Pentecostal Prayer and Song." *Journal of Linguistic Anthropology* 12 (1): 34–71.

Silverstein, Michael. 2000. "Whorfianism and the Linguistic Imagination of Nationality." In *Regimes of Language,* edited by P. Kroskrity, 85–138. Santa Fe, NM: School of American Research Press.

———. 2003. "Translation, Transduction, Transformation: Skating 'Glossando' on Thin Semiotic Ice." In *Translating Cultures,* edited by P. Rubel and A. Rosman, 75–105. New York: Berg.

Silverstein, Michael, and Greg Urban. 1996. "The Natural History of Discourse." In *Natural Histories of Discourse,* edited by M. Silverstein and G. Urban, 1–17. Chicago: University of Chicago Press.

Smith, Anthony D. 1991. *National Identity.* London: Penguin.

Spadola, Emilio. 2014. *The Calls of Islam: Sufis, Islamists, and Mass Mediation in Urban Morocco.* Bloomington: Indiana University Press.

Sperber, Dan, and Deborah Wilson. 1986. *Relevance: Communication and Cognition.* New York: Wiley.

Stasch, Rupert. 2009. *Society of Others: Kinship and Mourning in a West Papuan Place.* Berkeley: University of California Press.

———. 2010. "The Category 'Village' in Melanesian Social Worlds: Some Theoretical and Methodological Possibilities." *Paideuma, Mitteilungen zur Kulturkunde* 56: 41–62.

———. 2013. "The Poetics of Village Space When Villages Are New: Settlement Form as History-Making in West Papua." *American Ethnologist* 40 (3): 555–70.

Steiner, George. 1975. *After Babel: Aspects of Language and Translation.* Oxford: Oxford University Press.

Stoll, David. 1982. *Fishers of Men or Founders of Empire? The Wycliffe Bible Translators in Latin America.* London: Zed Press.

Strathern, Marilyn. 1988. *The Gender of the Gift: Problems with Women and Problems with Society in Melanesia.* Berkeley: University of California Press.

Svelmoe, William. 2008. *A New Vision for Missions: William Cameron Townsend, the Wycliffe Bible translators, and the Culture of Early Evangelical Faith Missions, 1896–1945.* Tuscaloosa: University of Alabama Press.

Swatos, William. 1998. "Church-Sect Theory." *Encyclopedia of Religion and Society.* Walnut Creek, CA: Altamira Press. Also available online at http://hirr.hartsem.edu/ency/cstheory.htm.

Tippet, Alan. 1967. *Solomon Islands Christianity: A Study of Growth and Obstruction.* London: Lutterworth Press.

———. 1970. *Church Growth and the Word of God: The Biblical Basis of the Church Growth Viewpoint.* Grand Rapids, MI: Eerdmans Press.

Todorov, Tzvetan. 1996. *The Conquest of America: The Question of the Other.* New York: Harper and Row.

Tomasetti, Friedegard. 1998. "Traditional Religion: Some Perceptions by Lutheran Missionaries in German New Guinea." *Journal of Religious History* 22 (2): 183–99.

Tönnies, Ferdinand. 2011. *Community and Association.* London: Routledge and Kegan Paul.

Troeltsch, Ernst. 1912. *Protestantism and Progress.* Boston: Beacon Press.

———. 1931. *The Social Teaching of the Christian Churches.* Translated by O. Wyon. New York: Macmillan.

Turner, Victor. 1957. *Schism and Continuity in an African Society: A Study of Ndembu Village Life.* Manchester, UK: University of Manchester Press.

UNESCO. 1951. "Statement by Experts on Problems of Race." *American Anthropologist* 53: 142–45.

———. 1953. *The Use of Vernacular Languages in Education*. Monographs on Fundamental Education. Paris: UNESCO.

Van der Veur, Paul. 1966. *Search for New Guinea's Boundaries: From Torres Strait to the Pacific*. Canberra: Australian National University.

Venuti, Lawrence. 1995. *The Translator's Invisibility: A History of Translation*. London: Routledge.

———. 1998. *The Scandals of Translation: Toward an Ethics of Difference*. London: Routledge.

Voloshinov, V.N. 1986. *Marxism and the Philosophy of Language*. Translated by L. Matejka and I.R. Titunik. Cambridge, MA: Harvard University Press.

Wagner, Herwig, and Hermann Reiner, eds. 1986. *Lutheran Church in Papua New Guinea: The First Hundred Years, 1886–1986*. Adelaide, Australia: Lutheran Publishing House.

Wagner, Roy. 1974. "Are There Social Groups in the New Guinea Highlands?" In *Frontiers of Anthropology*, edited by M.J. Leaf, 95–122. New York: Van Nostrand.

———. 1975. *The Invention of Culture*. Chicago: University of Chicago Press.

———. 1977. "Analogic Kinship: A Daribi Example." *American Ethnologist* 4 (4): 623–42.

Wallis, Ethyl, and Mary Bennett. 1959. *Two Thousand Tongues to Go: The Story of the Wycliffe Bible Translators*. New York: Harper.

Watson-Gegeo, Karin, and David Gegeo. 1991. "The Impact of Church Affiliation on Language Use in Kwara'ae (Solomon Islands)." *Language in Society* 20 (4): 533–55.

Weber, Max. 1957. *The Protestant Ethic and the Spirit of Capitalism*. Edited by T. Parsons. New York: Charles Scribner.

———. 1978. *Economy and Society*. Berkeley: University of California Press.

Weiner, Annette. 1985. "Inalienable Wealth." *American Ethnologist* 12 (2): 210–27.

Weinreich, Uriel, William Labov, and Marvin Herzog. 1968. "Empirical Foundations for a Theory of Language Change." In *Directions for Historical Linguistics: A Symposium*, edited by W. Lehmann and Y. Malkiel, 95–195. Austin: University of Texas Press.

Werbner, Richard. 2011. *Holy Hustlers, Schism, and Prophecy: Apostolic Reformation in Botswana*. Berkeley: University of California Press.

Were, Samuel. 2006. *Bine Mene: Connecting the Hebrews*. Port Moresby: Voice of the Tora'a Mene Ministry.

Whorf, Benjamin Lee. 1956. *Language, Thought, and Reality: Selected Writings*. Edited by J.B. Carroll. Cambridge, MA: MIT Press.

Willis, G. 1950. *Saint Augustine and the Donatist Controversy*. London: SPCK.

Wishlade, R.L. 1965. *Sectarianism in Southern Nyasaland*. London: Published for the International African Institute by the Oxford University Press.

Woolard, Kathryn. 1989. *Double Talk: Bilingualism and the Politics of Ethnicity in Catalonia*. Cambridge: Cambridge University Press.

Worsley, Peter. 1957. *The Trumpet Shall Sound: A Study of "Cargo" Cults in Melanesia*. London: MacGibbon and Kee.

Yelle, Robert. 2013. *The Language of Disenchantment: Protestant Literalism and Colonial Discourse in British India.* Oxford: Oxford University Press.

Zahn, Heinrich. 1996. *Music and Mission: Jabêm Traditional Music and the Development of Lutheran Hymnody.* Translated by P. Holzknecht. Edited by D. Niles. Boroko: Institute of Papua New Guinea Studies.

Index

www.ingramcontent.com/pod-product-compliance
Ingram Content Group UK Ltd.
Pitfield, Milton Keynes, MK11 3LW, UK
UKHW041422250125
454191UK00004B/154